Agamben and Colonialism

Critical Connections

A series of edited collections forging new connections between contemporary critical theorists and a wide range of research areas, such as critical and cultural theory, gender studies, film, literature, music, philosophy and politics.

Series Editors
Ian Buchanan, University of Wollongong
James Williams, University of Dundee

Editorial Advisory Board

Nick Hewlett
Gregg Lambert
Todd May
John Mullarkey
Paul Patton
Marc Rölli
Alison Ross
Kathrin Thiele
Frédéric Worms

Agamben and Colonialism edited by Marcelo Svirsky and Simone Bignall
Badiou and Philosophy edited by Sean Bowden and Simon Duffy
Laruelle and Non-Philosophy edited by John Mullarkey and Anthony Paul Smith

Forthcoming titles in the series

Rancière and Film edited by Paul Bowman
Virilio and Visual Culture edited by John Armitage and Ryan Bishop

Visit the Critical Connections website at
www.euppublishing.com/series/crcs

Agamben and Colonialism

Edited by Marcelo Svirsky and Simone Bignall

EDINBURGH
University Press

© editorial matter and organisation Marcelo Svirsky and Simone Bignall, 2012
© in the individual contributions is retained by the authors

Edinburgh University Press Ltd
22 George Square, Edinburgh

www.euppublishing.com

Typeset in 11/13 Adobe Sabon
by Servis Filmsetting Ltd, Stockport, Cheshire, and
printed and bound in Great Britain by
CPI Group (UK) Ltd, Croydon, CR0 4YY

A CIP record for this book is available from the British Library

ISBN 978 0 7486 4394 3 (hardback)
ISBN 978 0 7486 4393 6 (paperback)
ISBN 978 0 7486 4395 0 (webready PDF)
ISBN 978 0 7486 4926 6 (epub)
ISBN 978 0 7486 4925 9 (Amazon)

Contents

Acknowledgements

Like all collections, this work has in many ways been a group effort and we are grateful to the people who have offered assistance and advice along the way. From the start, Ian Buchanan and James Williams were enthusiastic supporters of the project, which has immeasurably benefited from their early input. We also give our thanks to those individuals working within the fields related to our subject matter, who so generously gave their advice or help at many points along the way: Peter Fitzpatrick, Paul Patton, Daniel McLoughlin, Stewart Motha, Paul Muldoon, Yoni Molad, Andrew Schaap, Ewa Ziarek, Alex Murray and Steven DeCaroli. We offer our very special appreciation to David Atkinson for stepping into the void at short notice. Especially in the final stages of production, we were privileged to receive the assistance of Eliza Wright, Carol MacDonald and the editorial team at Edinburgh University Press.

A version of the chapter by Mark Rifkin first appeared in *Cultural Critique*, 73(Fall) 2009: 88–124, Copyright © 2009 Regents of the University of Minnesota. We thank the author and the University of Minnesota Press for allowing us to reprint this article in the current collection.

The chapter by Ariella Azoulay and Adi Ophir is a revised version of material first published in Hebrew in 2008 by Resling Press. A previous version of Yehouda Shenhav's chapter first appeared in Hebrew in *Theory and Criticism*, 29(Fall) 2006: 205–18 and is reproduced with permission of the Van Leer Jerusalem Institute. We are grateful to the authors and their publishers that we have been able to include English translations of these articles, which appear here as significantly revised versions of the originals.

Simone would especially like to thank Greg Dayman and Katija Daly. She also thanks Marcelo Svirsky for inviting her participation in the project. Marcelo would like to thank Simone Bignall for her partnership. Finally, we have been blessed to work with the contributing authors, who have been unfailingly generous and responsive to our efforts to shape the collection to its final form: we extend our appreciation and thanks to each.

Introduction: Agamben and Colonialism

Simone Bignall and Marcelo Svirsky

Although Giorgio Agamben is concerned with the origins and development of Western political and legal thought and the ways in which it supports exclusionary structures of sovereign power and governance, he does not explore the ways in which the geopolitical entity of 'the West' emerged as such through its imperial domination of others. And while he carefully explicates erudite aspects of the determining political thought of the Greeks, with the formal separation of *bios* and *zoē* defining the capacity of some subjects to live as citizens, he does not dwell on how this was predicated on the fact of slavery as a condition for the realisation and operation of the *polis*. Agamben's references to slavery are made merely in passing – chiefly in the context of his analysis of messianic time and *klēsis* in his discussion of Paul's *Letter to the Romans* – and they do not reflect upon its material conditions or imperial causes (for example, Agamben 2005b: 12–14, 19ff.; 2004: 37). Likewise, he makes only swift and oblique reference to colonisation and to colonial prison camps (Agamben 1998: 166). His essay *Metropolis* (2006) describes Agamben's most focused engagement with tropes of colonial and postcolonial analysis, but here, too, he is not overtly concerned with concrete histories of colonisation and the material legacy of colonial violence on colonised peoples. Italy's own colonial history, which in the 1930s involved the internment and genocide of the Cyrenaican nomads according to a particular colonial logic of political and legal exception that characterised Italian rule in Libya, is nowhere acknowledged or interrogated in the work of this Italian philosopher.

Nor does he engage with the broad field of enquiry defining postcolonial criticism, or with the thinkers and writers of the postcolony. Agamben's intellectual lineage begins with Aristotle and is drawn almost exclusively from the scholarship of luminary thinkers working (often critically) within the Western tradition, such as Walter Benjamin, Martin Heidegger and Hannah Arendt. Somewhat scandalously, Agamben's thinking on the sovereign exception takes inspiration from the work of Carl Schmitt, the chief juror of the Third Reich. He also is heavily indebted to the work of Michel Foucault, whose historical account of the emergence of biopolitics he claims to 'correct' or 'complete' (Agamben 1998: 9; cf. Fitzpatrick 2005: 56–8; Patton 2007; Derrida 2009: 315–34); his later books pay close attention to the series of lectures on the topics of power, biopolitics and sovereignty, given by Foucault at the Collège de France during the 1970s (Foucault 2003; 2008).

While the influence of Hannah Arendt's *The Origins of Totalitarianism* is palpable at many points in his work, Agamben's interests fall more to the paradigmatic analysis of the exclusions internal to European society and which he sees as underlying totalitarian tendencies within Western political society, rather than to investigating the imperial origins and influences that Arendt points to (Arendt 1966: 185–221). Accordingly, although he is often concerned with the status and treatment of Europe's oppressed others and the legal anomalies and forms of state-sanctioned violence that make such oppression possible, this concern is largely focused in his discussion of the internment and attempted extermination of the European Jewry in concentration camps during the Second World War. Similarly, although he claims that his work is directed towards finding an answer to the question: 'What does it mean to act politically?' (Agamben 2005a: 2), the biopolitical themes he investigates are not considered outside of the circumscribed arena of 'Western' politics, as if the 'West' can be thought of as sealed off from its defining globalising processes. When Agamben suggests that the camp is the 'fundamental biopolitical paradigm of the West' and we must therefore 'rethink the political space of the West' (Agamben 1998: 188), this project is conceived without reference to colonialism and so also outside of the critical interventions that have already been made by colonised peoples engaged in revolutionary retaliation against their oppression by a properly imperial logic of control based upon racial exclusions.

This in turn occludes analysis of the important ways in which the very 'Western' processes that Agamben is concerned with – the capture of 'life itself' within the political realm by way of an 'inclusive exclusion', originating with the ancient political separation of *bios* and *zoē* and continuing through their convergence with the modern invention of human rights – are themselves influenced in the modern epoch by ideas of *universal* entitlement to *human* liberty and equality. These are ideas shaped not only by the West's own citizen subjects (and particularly by the thinkers of the Enlightenment), but also by (and sometimes for) Europe's 'external' but 'internalised' others: the peoples it had subjected to its imperial rule in the colonies, and who often vociferously contested their contradictory civil status as Europe's included-excluded political subjects.

It is one of the contentions of this book that a renewed attention to Agamben's core concepts such as 'the camp' and '*homo sacer*', considered in terms of the colonial context and with respect to rich histories of colonial rebellion and resistance, can enable a more nuanced understanding of the forms of agency available to individuals and peoples that have been rendered *homo sacer* by a politics of 'inclusive exclusion' (see also Fitzpatrick 2008; Fitzpatrick and Tuitt 2004: xii). As one author says of the scholarship influenced by Agamben's writing on *homo sacer*, these accounts feature 'subjects to whom all manner of things are done, often in arbitrary and violent ways, but [who are] rarely agents in their own right' (Walters 2008: 188). Attending to the struggles waged by colonised peoples in response to imperially orchestrated 'states of exception' makes visible an active subjectivity that can operate as an alternative to the abandoned and hopeless figure of the Muselmann, that most extreme embodiment of the form of (de)subjectivation defined by Agamben as *homo sacer*. For example, Ronit Lentin's reinvestment of 'the Palestinian subject with the potentiality of the "insurrection of subjugated knowledges", which includes, inter alia, violent resistance to colonial oppression as a means of re-assuming subjecthood' is an attempt to relocate the relation between bare life, victimisation and resistance (Lentin 2008: 14).

Agamben maintains a relative silence about colonialism and appears disinclined to engage with those anti-colonial and post-colonial writers and activists whose experiences of exclusion and abandonment as *homo sacer* have not rendered them utterly debilitated and, indeed, whose work articulates a range of critical subject positions defined in active response to imperial Europe's exclusionary politics. And yet, his concepts, frameworks and methods of philosophical analysis undoubtedly offer important and valuable resources for thinking critically about the political exclusions and abandonments characteristic of colonial situations. In particular, his writing on 'homo sacer' and the 'state of exception' has been mined (and at times contested) to support critical analyses of colonial processes and the social, political and legal structures they both produce and rely upon. For example, drawing upon Agamben's theorisation of homo sacer in his philosophical reflection on 'necropolitics', Achille Mbembe notes that

> it is notably in the colony and under the apartheid regime that there comes into being a peculiar terror formation [. . .] The most original feature of this terror formation is its concatenation of biopower, the state of exception and the state of seige. (Mbembe 2003: 22)

Accordingly, he concludes, 'in modern philosophical thought and European political practice and imaginary, the colony represents the site where sovereignty consists fundamentally in the exercise of a power outside the law' (Mbembe 2003: 23). Similarly, Robert Eaglestone (2002) suggests that 'the colony' might provide a more apt paradigm for modernity than does 'the camp'. However, in considering 'to what extent we are to read the colonial as an iteration of the modern', Nasser Hussain references with approval Agamben's 'astute precision' in conceptualising the 'relation of exception [. . .] by which something is included solely through its exclusion' (Hussain 2003: 7, 20–1; Agamben 1998: 18). This thinking helps Hussain to theorise 'the colonial concept of law', here argued to be predicated upon a 'jurisprudence of emergency'. Similarly thinking about the formative and recursive relationships between law, modernity and imperialism, Peter Fitzpatrick (2001) references Agamben's writing on exclusion, abandonment and the sacred. Other scholars working in the field of critical legal scholarship, including Stewart Motha (2002), Paul Muldoon (2008) and Mark Rifkin (2009), employ Agamben's notion of the 'inclusive exclusion' to explore the complicated relationship at law between an imposed colonial sovereignty and the indigenous forms of governance or 'Aboriginal sovereignty' that were denied and replaced with the event of the sovereign imposition.

Agamben's work also has been taken up by cultural and political theorists thinking about social processes and engagements inflected by colonisation. Writing in the Australian context, Deirdre Tedmanson (2008) employs Agamben's concepts of the 'camp', 'exception' and '*homo sacer*', linking these with analysis of a colonial legacy which includes ongoing experiences of settler racism and sovereign-state violence, vividly illustrated by Aboriginal deaths in custody. Other theorists have responded critically to Agamben's concepts and developed them in work more overtly aimed at evaluating and enabling the transformation of colonial structures and relations. For example, writing on the reasons for assuming responsibility in processes of postcolonial reconciliation, Andrew Schaap (2004) engages critically with Agamben when the latter insists that the concept of responsibility is 'contaminated by law' and must be reconceived in ethical terms (Agamben 1999: 20). Arguing that this finally results in Agamben pressing for 'a responsibility that is unassumable because conceived in terms of an ethics that is uncontaminated by worldly institutions', Schaap instead asserts that it is necessary to understand subjective and collective responsibility for righting historical wrongs in terms that are primarily political, rather than legal or ethical (Schaap 2004: para. 27; see also 2005). Ronit Lentin's *Thinking Palestine* (2008) offers a non-conclusive response to the question of the general applicability of the notion of the 'state of exception' with respect to the state of Israel. In *The Power of Inclusive Exclusion* (Ophir et al. 2009), the authors demonstrate that 'the suspension of the law and the forsaking of life do not completely overlap' (23). In fact, as the chapters in this collection show, it is the production of dynamic sets of regulations and procedures, replacing the law, that enables and perpetuates abandonment in the occupied Palestinian territories. They also evidence the problematic nature of humanitarianism, pointed to by Agamben, in the 'significant role humanitarian considerations have come to play as an integral part of the machinery of the occupying power itself' (24).

While such scholarship evidences a growing interest in understanding the connections between Agamben and colonialism, the positive scope for transformation suggested by certain of Agamben's concepts and concerns is far less often explored in the context of colonial and postcolonial analysis. In part, this might be explained by the tendency of writers to dwell on his later, better-known works – *Homo Sacer* and *State of Exception* – rather than his early work on ontology, philology and history, or his more recent writing on temporality and method. As Leland de la Durantaye (2009) emphasises, the long trajectory of Agamben's thought is characterised by a continuity of concern with the resistant or transformative force of concepts such as 'potentiality', 'inoperativity' and 'decreation'. Perhaps also because postcolonial theory remains largely defined by a critical mode directed at colonial legacies, rather than attending specifically to the constructive conditions required for creating genuinely *post*colonial order, these rich resources are yet to be taken up by writers in their attempts to theorise the postcolonial.

This book acknowledges the importance of the 'Agamben effect' (Ross 2008) in contemporary thinking about sovereignty, the 'state of exception' and biopolitics. It affirms the ways in which Agamben's critical theory allows us to reflect on the difficult relations between legal and political bodies and their subjects, revealing how these bodies are shaped by hierarchical selections that reify two interconnected spheres of existence, *zoē* and *bios*. These selections define a paradigm that has been important for thinking about modern democracies as reliance on bare life and on abandonment, rather than on more visible claims to equality. However, in order to extend the critical evaluation of this effect in the analysis of modern or contemporary life, the collection addresses Agamben's work in specific postcolonial contexts and in explicit relation to postcolonial modes of analysis and thought. This focus permits the authors to respond to the frequently made criticism that Agamben's work arises out of a disregard for the specific histories and concrete social circumstances of present states of exception, of relations of abandonment in colonial frameworks, and of colonial and imperial relations.

In seeking to answer this criticism, this collection leads to a better understanding of the cultural, legal and political phenomena of exception and abandonment in Western and non-Western polities, as constituted by colonial or imperial projects. These projects have determined modernity in its historical and geographical dimensions. This book demonstrates the wider relevance of Agamben's thought once postcolonial frameworks of interpretation have been taken into account. Accordingly, the contributions deal with theoretical aspects of the connection between Agamben, colonialism and post-colonialism – with the post-colonial understood as 'the critical attention to the continuing legacy of colonisation in national life' (Bignall 2011: 3) – as well as offering explorations of the connection in different spaces and societies constituted by colonial relations in America, Russia, the Middle East, Africa and Australia. They demonstrate that, independent of its final validity as a claim about biopolitics, Agamben's thought provides us with an essential set of concepts for critical debates around colonialism and colonial states of exception. Our critical task is to identify the 'colonial encounter' as a formative dimension of Western political paradigms. Furthermore, by attending to Agamben's methodological approach, which seeks to access an open potentiality within the entrenched political structures that characterise the contemporary world, this collection not only offers an illustration of the ways colonial relations have permeated the formation of political subjects, but also opens perspectives of escape from subjection and of collective renewal.

The essays comprising this collection thereby provide a critical bridge connecting two previously unrelated fields of exploration: Agamben's theorisation of the paradigmatic phenomena of the 'state of exception' and 'biopolitics' in Western liberal regimes is here situated in explicit relation to the historical and actual existence of these phenomena in the context of colonial relations. Accordingly, the essays gathered here examine the complex and puzzling relationship between Agamben and colonialism by engaging two general lines of questioning. The first asks whether colonisation constitutes a concealed or veiled ground for the phenomena that Agamben takes as his direct critical focus: To what extent are Agamben's conceptualisations of 'Western' political processes, its modes of subjectivation and its organising structures, indebted to an original imperial event? The second line of query investigates the ways in which Agamben's paradigms, including 'the camp', *homo sacer* and 'the state of exception', can be employed fruitfully in the critical analysis of concrete colonial situations and legacies in the contemporary world. Extending this critical endeavour, some contributors additionally ask a related question, one more specifically aimed at the reconstructive aspects of postcolonialism: in what ways might the concepts of 'potentiality', 'the coming community', 'the open', 'form-of-life', 'whatever being', and so forth, invite new postcolonial thinking? In responding to these questions, the essays gathered here contribute new dimensions to historically grounded analyses of colonialism and colonisation in specific locations, as well as opening up new directions for postcolonial theory and for Agamben scholarship.

The collection is comprised of four sections, organised thematically. The first section considers colonial renditions of the 'state of exception'. The first essay in the collection is by Yehouda Shenhav.

He considers Agamben's interpretation of Walter Benjamin's *Critique of Violence* (1921), read here in light of Frantz Fanon's *The Wretched of the Earth* (1967). Shenhav criticises Agamben for ignoring the role of European imperialism in conceptualising European sovereignty. This first chapter paves the way for positioning Agamben's work within the realm of the 'colonial'.

The second chapter, by Sergei Prozorov, considers Agamben's writing on exception and abandonment through the lens of postcommunist Russia and in terms of the Russian concept of *bespedel* that emerged in the early 1990s to designate the postcommunist condition. For Prozorov, the application of Agamben's political theory to the postcommunist condition yields both theoretical and empirical benefits. On the one hand, Agamben's claims are empirically substantiated through analysis of the anomic character of postcommunist Russia following the dissolution of the Soviet empire. On the other, Agamben's approach provides a theoretical framework adequate for grasping the Russian state of exception other than in the merely negative sense of 'disorder', 'instability' or 'illegality'.

The third chapter, written by Marcelo Svirsky, focuses on the notion of exceptionality in Agamben's *oeuvre*, expanding this from its limited treatment in relation to 'states of exception' in order to provide a cultural analysis of colonial relations in Israel-Palestine. His chapter expands Agamben's conceptual apparatus by appealing to two sources: one is Esposito's 'immunitarian' paradigm and the other is Deleuze and Guattari's politics of desire. In the first case, Esposito helps relocate exception in terms of the immunitarian isolation of particular ways of existence; in the second case, Deleuze and Guattari offer a framework for theorising the active foundation of the masses as a source of legal and political exception.

The second section of the book focuses more intently upon issues relevant to the 'state of exception' that resides at the heart of colonial sovereignty. In Chapter 4, Mark Rifkin argues that 'sovereignty' functions as a placeholder that has no determinate content. In fact, this topos functions as a part of a fundamentally circular and self-validating performance that grounds the legitimacy of settler-state rule on nothing more than the axiomatic negation of Native peoples' authority to determine or adjudicate for themselves the normative principles by which they will be governed. Through Agamben's theory of the 'exception', the essay explores how the supposedly underlying sovereignty of the US state is a retrospective projection generated by, and dependent on, the 'peculiar'-isation of Native peoples.

In Chapter 5, Stephen Morton argues that Agamben's analysis of the 'state of exception' fails to consider how colonial sovereignty was experienced as a permanent state of emergency from the standpoint of the colonised. His chapter considers how the state of emergency in Kenya from 1952–60 has been codified in the literary and legal rhetoric of British colonialism, and criticised by postcolonial African writers and intellectuals as a sign of the inherent violence of European colonial rule.

In the sixth chapter of the book, Stewart Motha focuses on the proliferation of 'forms of life' in philosophical discourses that tackle contemporary political and legal problems. He argues that sovereignty and its relationship to the political is a key progenitor of why various theorists have found it necessary to attend to ethical, political and juridical problems through a 'form of life'. After establishing the connection between sovereignty, the political and political discourses about a 'form of life' with particular reference to South Africa, Motha's analysis shifts in genre to literature by discussing the post-apartheid novel *Agaat*, written by Marlene van Niekerk. Motha explains how this novel presents the possibility of attending to the singularity of being, and is a site for imagining life not within the constraints of juridical and political forms which might be relatively closed or open, but for attending to everyday existence. *Agaat* illustrates the liminal existences of post-apartheid beings as 'forms of life' that exceed the factual and engage with the imagination of new orders.

At this point, the collection again shifts focus, this time to consider questions of 'bare life' and biopolitics in colonial situations. David Atkinson explains how Agamben's conceptual frames can clarify the nature of Italian colonisation in Libya as the reduction of local populations to bare life amidst a wider state of exception. This was, some argue, an authentic genocide; it also demonstrates Agamben's bleak theories of state sovereignty *in extremis*. However, Atkinson also notes here that while Agamben's thinking is rooted in Italy and its intellectual traditions of Classical and Renaissance learning, the wider elision of the Italian colonial record in Italian society also echoes through his work, thus representing a missed opportunity for being 'contemporary', in Agamben's particular sense of this word.

In the eighth chapter, Ariella Azoulay and Adi Ophir conceptualise abandonment in Gaza. They analyse the nature of Israeli rule in the Gaza Strip since June 1967. While the Israeli occupation of the Palestinian Territories has developed into a *sui generis* regime, the occupation in Gaza is a special case within this system, which vividly illustrates the abandonment of Palestinians as non-citizens within this regime. The chapter shows how the retreat of the legal and other administrative apparatuses from the Strip has exposed the civilian population in Gaza to various types of state terror, but has also been coordinated with (and compensated by) the humanitarian management of the ongoing situation of crisis. In this construction, the Israeli Supreme Court plays a key role in delineating the threshold of the catastrophe which Israeli state apparatuses should avoid crossing.

Silvia Grinberg discusses the results of research into biopolitical processes and mechanisms of control, as experienced in contexts of extreme urban poverty in the Buenos Aires metropolitan area. The project was carried out in areas that, in the sixteenth century, constituted the limit of the territory that colonial authority could enter; now, these same areas serve as a boundary between shantytowns and the outside world. Grinberg discusses the inhabitants of these spaces as figures of *homo sacer*, subjects left to their own devices in abject territories. To survive, they must take responsibility for living in a state of exception that has become a political norm.

The contributions in the final section of the collection draw mainly from Agamben's writing on method and history; on temporality and potentiality. Chapter 10 by Leland de la Durantaye gives special attention to Agamben's reflections on colonisation in his lecture 'Metropolis' (2006). He begins by noting that, for Agamben, there is no line of thought which is not strategic and that philosophy always and everywhere has a political potential. He then turns to consider the strategic dimensions of Agamben's lecture on 'Metropolis', explaining that from the etymology of this term he will develop a *paradigm* of colonialism. Agamben is thus not concerned with colonialism per se, but with the paradigm it provides for understanding a more general set of problems. *Metropolis* comes to mean, for Agamben, a 'dislocated and dishomogenous' space – one that can be traced in every city of the Western world. As de la Durantaye explains, the strategic element of Agamben's thought inheres in the 'historical' element of his methodology: his paradigms are aimed less at understanding the past than at understanding the present situation, for in coming to understand the constitution of the present we may also come to understand its potential for development.

Jessica Whyte interrogates Agamben's account of rights through the lens of Haiti. For Agamben, the discourse of human rights is a biopolitical one, which erases the border between life and politics and enmeshes a life reduced to survival in the order of sovereign power. In tracing the development of biopolitics, he traces lines of continuity to reveal the hidden connections that link our present to the remote past. In contrast to the argument of *Homo Sacer*, according to which rights develop according to a linear logic of historically increasing biopolitical management, Whyte attends to Haiti's colonial history and to the struggles for liberty waged by the slaves in San Domingue in order to retrieve the historical impact of their uprising and to 'trace the imprint that their struggle has left on the present'. She accordingly argues that the question of rights can best be understood in terms of what Agamben elsewhere terms the 'messianic modality', exigency, which disrupts linear time and historical progress to enable a redemptive orientation to the past (Agamben 2005b: 39).

The final chapter, by Simone Bignall, is future-oriented and critically directed towards philosophical issues of postcolonial temporality. Her discussion is framed around the Australian government's recent policy of intervention in indigenous communities in the Northern Territory. While noting the intervention describes an obvious operation of a colonial style 'state of exception', Bignall discusses the event primarily in terms of the treatment of the 'sacred life' of the indigenous peoples concerned. She then draws from Agamben's recent writing on method and temporality and his relatively early work on the 'coming community', to engage with trenchant debates internal to the field of postcolonial theory and to raise questions about 'the time of the postcolonial', considered here in relation to the politics of intervention.

Taken together, the chapters in this collection demonstrate how aspects of Agamben's work can assist the critical analysis of colonialism in its past and current modes of operation. They also suggest that, when positioned in relation to colonial history and with attention to local and specific contexts, some of Agamben's concepts can be used in the service of a strategic postcolonial politics of transformation that is mindful of colonial legacies and histories of resistance. Such a strategic orientation seeks to address critically colonial vestiges in the conditions of the present, and yet also strives to access from within these post-colonial conditions of the contemporary present, an open potentiality which can enable the emergence of new styles of non-imperial community, new modes of subjectivity and new uses of law. Agamben has remarked that 'the genuinely philosophical element in any work, be it a work of art, one of science, or one of thought, is its capacity for elaboration' (Agamben 2009: 8). In their various ways, the essays in this collection each seek to identify this capacity in Agamben's own work, and to develop this capacity in relation to ideas of colonialism and the postcolonial.

References

Agamben, G. (1998), *Homo Sacer: Sovereign Power and Bare Life*, trans. D. Heller-Roazen. Stanford: Stanford University Press.
—(1999), *Remnants of Auschwitz: the Witness and the Archive*, trans. D. Heller-Roazen. New York: Zone Books.
—(2004), *The Open: Man and Animal*, trans. K. Attell. Stanford: Stanford University Press.
—(2005a), *State of Exception*, trans. K. Attell. Chicago: University of Chicago Press.
—(2005b), *The Time That Remains: A Commentary on the Letter to the Romans*, trans. P. Dailey. Stanford: Stanford University Press.
—(2006), 'Metropolis', Seminar given at the Nomad University in November, trans. A. Bove. *Generation-Online*, available at http://www.generation-online.org/p/fpagamben4.htm, accessed 23 September 2011. Audio file available at http://www.globalproject.info/imG/mp3/giorgio_agamben.mp3, accessed 23 September 2011.
—(2009), *The Signature of All Things: On Method*, trans. L. D'Isanto with K. Attell. New York: Zone Books.
Arendt, H. (1966), *The Origins of Totalitarianism*. New York: Harvest.
Benjamin, W. (1921), *Critique of Violence*, trans. E. Jephcott. New York: Schocken Books.
Bignall, S. (2011), *Postcolonial Agency: Critique and Constructivism*. Edinburgh: Edinburgh University Press.
de la Durantaye, L. (2009), *Giorgio Agamben: A Critical Introduction*. Stanford: Stanford University Press.
Derrida, J. (2009), *Beast and Sovereign*, trans. G. Bennington. Chicago: University of Chicago Press.

Eaglestone, R. (2002), 'On Giorgio Agamben's Holocaust', *Paragraph: Journal of Modern Critical Theory*, 25(2): 52–67.

Fanon, F. (1967), *The Wretched of the Earth*, trans. C. Farrington. London: Penguin Books.

Fitzpatrick, P. (2001), *Modernism and the Grounds of Law*. Cambridge: Cambridge University Press.

—(2005), 'Bare Sovereignty: *Homo Sacer* and the Insistence of Law', in A. Norris (ed.), *Politics, Metaphysics, and Death: Essays on Giorgio Agamben's* Homo Sacer. Durham: Duke University Press, 49–73.

—(2008), *Law as Resistance*. Farnham: Ashgate.

Fitzpatrick, P. and P. Tuitt (eds) (2004), *Critical Beings: Law, Nation and the Global Subject*. Farnham: Ashgate.

Foucault, M. (2003), *Society Must be Defended: Lectures at the Collège de France, 1975–1976*, trans. D. Macey. New York: Picador.

—(2008), *The Birth of Biopolitics: Lectures at the Collège de France 1978–1979*, trans. G. Burchell. New York: Palgrave Macmillan.

Hussain, N. (2003), *The Jurisprudence of Emergency: Colonialism and the Rule of Law*. Ann Arbor: University of Michigan Press.

Lentin, R. (ed.) (2008), *Thinking Palestine*. London and New York: Zed Books.

Mbembe, A. (2003), 'Necropolitics', trans. Libby Meintjes, *Public Culture*, 15(1): 11–40.

Motha, S. (2002), 'The Sovereign Event in a Nation's Law', *Law and Critique*, 13: 311–38.

Muldoon, P. (2008), 'The Sovereign Exceptions: Colonization and the Foundation of Society', *Social and Legal Studies*, 17(1): 59–74.

Ophir, A., M. Givoni and S. Hanafi (eds) (2009), *The Power of Inclusive Exclusion: Anatomy of Israeli Rule in the Occupied Palestinian Territories*. New York: Zone Books.

Patton, P. (2007), 'Agamben and Foucault on Biopower and Biopolitics', in M. Calarco and S. DeCaroli (eds), *Giorgio Agamben: Sovereignty and Life*. Stanford: Stanford University Press, 203–18.

Rifkin, M. (2009), 'Indigenising Agamben: Rethinking Sovereignty in Light of the "Peculiar" Status of Native Peoples', *Cultural Critique*, 73(Fall): 88–124. (Reprinted as Chapter 4 in this volume.)

Ross, A. (ed.) (2008), *The Agamben Effect: Special Issue of The South Atlantic Quarterly*, 107(1). Durham: Duke University Press.

Schaap, A. (2004), 'Assuming Responsibility in the Hope of Reconciliation', *borderlands*, 3(1), available at http://www.borderlands.net.au/vol3no1_2004/schaap_hope.htm, accessed 15 September 2011.

—(2005), *Political Reconciliation*. London and New York: Routledge.

Tedmanson, D. (2008), 'Isle of Exception: Sovereign Power and Palm Island', *Critical Perspectives in International Business*, 4(2/3): 142–65.

Walters, W. (2008), 'Acts of Demonstration: Mapping the Territory of (Non-) Citizenship', in E. Isin and G. Nielsen (eds), *Acts of Citizenship*. London: Zed Books.

I. Colonial States of Exception

Imperialism, Exceptionalism and the Contemporary World

Yehouda Shenhav

I acquired Giorgio Agamben's *State of Exception* in London on 7 July 2005, rather coincidentally on the very same day in which four bombs went off in its public transportation system. Upon returning to my hotel next to the underground stop at Russell Square, I found that the area had been sealed off and declared a 'sterile zone'. In order to get into the hotel I had to identify myself at a checkpoint, submit to a thorough body search, and be escorted by the police force. At the same time, the British government set out to fight terrorism, employing new decrees and detaining (mainly Muslim) suspects in the Belmarsh Prison without a charge or a trial, under the provisions of the Anti-terrorism, Crime and Security Act 2001. London was under a state of exception.

Similarly in 2001, the American government had issued the 'Patriot Act', under which it likewise strove to control and dissuade terrorism.[1] Under the authority of the 'Patriot Act', the United States put hundreds of administrative detainees in Guantánamo Bay without trial. Amnesty International reported that these detainees were constantly at risk of being tortured: some were drowned in cold water, they received electrical shocks and their religious beliefs were ridiculed (Judt 2005). The *Washington Post* reported that the US also incarcerated tens of detainees in secret prisons – known as 'legal black holes' – spread throughout Eastern Europe (Priest 2005). To use Agamben's terminology, these detainees were turned from lives 'worthy of living' into 'bare lives'. They never stood trial, they did not enjoy basic human rights, and their biopolitical management was often outsourced to the hands of private corporations. The existence of the extrajudicial regime in Guantánamo allows for the emergence of 'sovereignty gaps' which allow the deployment of violence outside or beyond the rule of law. The anomalous nature of the law and the anomalous nature of those territories ('sterile zones', 'black holes', 'Guantánamo') existing within sovereign space were thus revealed. Despite a ruling of the Supreme Court, the American government claimed that constitutional protection does not apply to these 'extra-territorial zones' of illegality.

Recent evidence about the management of the Abu Ghraib prison in Iraq reveals similar features of legal and administrative anomalies. In the absence of a clear law regulating correct procedures towards those interred in the prison, the operation of Abu Ghraib was based on the 'production of secret memoranda' and 'extraordinary emergency' (Gourevitch and Morris 2009: 29). American bureaucrats who managed the prison claimed legal improvisations that allowed them 'to implement sweeping institutional changes with a speed and autonomy', in a process that 'appeared increasingly arbitrary'. They further described how the directions 'seemed as deliberately vague as the identities of the men who gave them'. As one of the bureaucrats testified, 'It was all just word of mouth' and 'deception'. Or, as another testified, 'the absence of a code was the code in Abu Ghraib' (21, 24, 94–5, 171, 92).

As an Israeli, experiences of 'state of exception' and 'emergency ruling' are not foreign to me. The Israeli state was founded on emergency legislation, reviving and thickening the legacy of the British imperial rule in Palestine. These regulations continue to be used in various forms to control the Palestinian population within, and outside, its international borders. From its inception in 1948 almost until the 1967 war, Israel controlled its Palestinian citizens[2] under a military regime which was founded on the state of exception. Since 1967, Israel has exercised a military rule over 4.5 million Palestinians in the West Bank and Gaza. These people are devoid of citizenship rights and have no recourse to civil protection while their towns and villages are surrounded or sealed off. While Israel attempts to describe its military regime as 'legitimate self-defence' in the face of anti-Israeli terrorist attacks, the history of the occupation reveals that it is a result of a long-term project of governmentality, which includes territorial expansion, settlement and continuous ethnic cleansing.[3] These are all made possible by the 'miraculous' nature of the 'exception', to use Schmitt's terminology.

Agamben's *State of Exception* provides a theoretical framework that is helpful in assisting thinking about these issues. He examines how the 'exception' has become a permanent working paradigm of Western democracies. He explores the European genealogy of 'exception', articulates the relationships between exception and the law, and provides a fulcrum from which practices of state violence can be read afresh. Yet, Agamben's book ignores a critical thread rooted in the history of exception: colonialism and imperialism. Whereas it is crucial to show that state of exception has a long European history and is in fact embedded within its modern theory of the state, it was imperialism that provided the main arena in which the state of exception was practised most vigorously, systematically and violently. Recognition of this point is crucial to remind us that the 'exception' not only has become a dominant theoretical paradigm following the bombing attacks on the Twin Towers in New York, or the bombings in London, but was in fact a key condition of colonial rule, making possible the passage of imperial history in the European colonies.

The Intellectual Roots of Agamben's Thesis

In 1921, Walter Benjamin published his *Critique of Violence*, in which he examined the dialectical relationships between violence and the rule of law. He distinguishes in particular between the violence that constitutes the law, and the violence that preserves and verifies the rule of law. In contrast to these sources of violence, he positions 'pure violence' (or 'revolutionary violence') which resides outside of the rule of law. Benjamin formulates 'pure violence' in religious-theological redemptive parole which is aligned with the tradition of the oppressed. When Schmitt published his infamous *Political Theology* in the 1920s, he implicitly addressed this theological basis of the political.[4] He suggested that all significant concepts of modern theory of the state are secularised theological concepts, and that the omnipotence of the modern lawgiver is derived from theology. Schmitt pointed an accusing finger towards liberal political theory that allegedly incapacitated the sovereign who is forced to rely on, and is restricted by, the rule of law. He criticised liberal law and democratic parliamentary institutions for their lack of 'decisionism' and for their neglect of the 'exception', namely how the legal system suspends itself in time of political threats, in order to preserve its power of jurisdiction (Schmitt 1988: 14). Instead of the legal rule of law, he suggested that 'Sovereign is he who decides on the exception' (5), and that the exception in jurisprudence is analogous to the miracle in theology (36). The state of exception is encapsulated in the figure of the sovereign and is necessary for the survival of the state, making it a normative condition of sovereign power.[5]

Agamben accepts the tenets of political theology as outlined by Benjamin and Schmitt, among others, and develops the logic of exception, which he argues provides a necessary supplement to Foucault's (2004) concept of governmentality. In his *Homo Sacer*, Agamben invokes a particular model of the subject of 'exception' which he draws from the Roman codex. The exemplary subject of exception is that of the 'sacred man', who is a person whom people have judged on account of crime: 'It is not permitted to sacrifice this man, yet he who kills him will not be condemned for homicide' (Agamben 1998: 71). Agamben also describes how in the so-called 'camp' (be it the concentration camp, Guantánamo Bay, or the Abu Ghraib prison), life becomes 'bare': the legal 'person of rights' is purged, thus erasing the biography and subjectivity of inmates. The camp is a space in which the rule of law is suspended under the cover of the law. While, for Agamben, life is the deployment and the manifestation of power, he defines sovereignty as the capacity to manage death and mortality.

Agamben offers a partial genealogy of the 'state of exception' as a paradigm for contemporary democratic governance. He describes its origin in Roman law, in revolutionary and modern France, in Weimar Republic and the Nazi regime, in Switzerland, Italy, England and the United States. One of the typical historical examples of scholarly thinking in this tradition is provided by Benjamin Constant, who already at the beginning of the nineteenth century recognised the menace associated with exceptions to the law, which he identified as more dangerous than overt despotism (see Fontana 1988: 143). Whereas in traditional political theology, the exception was defined in relation to temporality, in theorising the camp as the exemplary site of exception Agamben added a spatial dimension to the phenomenon. Yet, Agamben's frame of reference is Europe, accepting its naturalised presence in time and space as given. As Kalyvas has rightly noted: '[u]nfortunately, *Homo Sacer* returns to a representation of time – the time of sovereignty – as uniform, one-directional and rectilinear' (Kalyvas 2005: 111). Accordingly, Agamben's work remains firmly situated 'within the horizons of the Occidental political tradition, the political destiny of the West' (114).[6]

What is conspicuously absent in this genealogy is sustained analysis of the role of the 'exception' in the history of imperialism.[7] This is unfortunate, if only because at the beginning of the twentieth century Western colonies occupied some 85 per cent of the world's territory (Fieldhouse 1967), creating political spaces in which imperial powers used alternative models of rule, and thus providing a rich arena in which to study sovereignty. As Hussain puts it: 'Colonialism is the best historical example for any theoretical study of norm and exception, rule of law and emergency' (Hussain 2003: 31). Emergency in the colonies was used as an elastic category, stretching over political disturbances such as riots and insurgencies, as well as to allow for imperial capitalism.

Agamben owes some of his insights not only to Schmitt, Benjamin and Foucault, but also to Hannah Arendt;[8] however, he fails to take seriously her perspective on imperialism. In *Origins of Totalitarianism* (1951), Arendt turned her gaze to the increasing gap between the political centres in Europe and the colonies, which she described as the inevitable result of an insatiable imperial appetite for new lands. Arendt suggested that when imperial conquerors disengaged their actions of conquest from the European state and its democratic laws, they replaced democratic culture with despotism and coercive rule over the 'subject races'. As the locus of her political enquiry, she points to the initial gap between the legal status of citizens in the home country and the 'subject races' in the colonies, which were never permitted to exist as fully fledged citizens. She argues that this gap partially explains the rise of totalitarianism, when the colonisers arrived back to the European societies. Arendt usefully described the exceptions and violence that emerge through this political structure, although she failed to extend her analysis to the operation of exception to European political theory itself.[9]

Frantz Fanon: Responding to the Imperial State of Exception

Walter Benjamin prophetically described the philosophy of history from the standpoint of the oppressed: 'The tradition of the oppressed teaches us that the "state of emergency" in which we live is not the exception but the rule. We must attain to a conception of history that is in keeping with this insight' (Benjamin 1978: 257). Whereas Benjamin formulated his thesis in the context of the holocaust, it was Frantz Fanon who painfully described how the exception became the rule in the imperial context. To him, as a colonial subject whose life was forced into bare existence, the contours of the colonially imposed 'state of emergency' overlapped with racialised distinctions shaping different modes of subjectivity. Fanon left the colony (Martinique) for France; in fact, he ran away intending not to come back. In Paris he discovered with great dismay that the black subject could not escape his blackness, and so he left once more for Lyon. Fanon's *Black Skin, White Masks* (1967a) (*Peau noire, masques blancs*, 1952) was one of the first books born of this tormented intellectual and chronic transgressor of boundaries. Fanon provides an assertive depiction of the ways in which the cultural melting pot of colonial encounters is at best an illusion of lives shared, portraying the splits, attractions and rejections that characterise every colonial subject. Fanon was drafted into the French occupation forces in Algiers, only to resign and join the FLN anti-colonial forces. His biography traces his movement from a post-colonial subject who aspired to integrate into the French Republic, to an anti-colonial fighter who strove to see it disintegrated. In 1961, when he was dying of leukaemia at the age of thirty-six, he put together his *The Wretched of the Earth* (1967b) (*Les damnés de la terre*, 1961), a book that emerged out of the heart of darkness. *The Wretched of the Earth* became a quintessential anti-imperialist text; it was translated into twenty-five languages and sold more than a million copies in the English language alone.[10] During the sixties in the United States Hannah Arendt condemned this text, arguing that it infused black politics of liberation with a penchant for violence (Arendt 1970).

As an anti-colonial thinker, Fanon explained in this book why revolutionary violence ('pure violence' in Benjamin's terminology) is essential if the oppressed are to successfully fight imperial violence: 'colonialism is not a thinking machine, nor a body endowed with reasoning faculties. It is violence in its natural state, and it will only yield when confronted with greater violence' (Fanon 1967: 61; see also Macey 2000). As a psychiatrist in the French army, he witnessed the atrocities of imperial power and saw how 'Western democracy' suspends the law and employs a 'state of exception' to advance its imperial expansionism. Fanon therefore resolved to use the master's tools against the master: '[t]he violence which has ruled over the ordering of the colonial world, which has ceaselessly drummed by the rhythm for the destruction of native social forms [. . .] that same violence will be claimed and taken over by the native' (40).

If the sovereign power abandoned the rule of law in order to facilitate colonisation, so should do the 'subject races' to facilitate liberation. Thus, for Fanon, anti-colonial violence should become the mirror image of imperial violence: '[t]he violence of the colonial regime and the counter-violence of the native balance each other and respond to each other in an extraordinary reciprocal homogeneity' (Fanon 1967: 88). Frantz Fanon personified the 'partisan' in Schmitt's terminology, employing 'pure violence' in Benjamin's terminology.[11] His manifesto, *The Wretched of the Earth*, testifies to the distinction between 'legitimate violence' and 'illegitimate violence,' which characterises the architecture of the modern European state, and shows how it becomes blurred in the imperial context. It also clearly suggests that in the colonial context, the 'state of exception' has become the rule rather than the anomaly.

Colonial and Post-colonial Zones of Exception

It suffices to browse through anti-colonial manifestos of resistance in order to realise that legal exceptions, state of emergency, closure, administrative detainees, and assassinations authorised by the state were the norm rather than the exception during times of colonial rule. Imperial bureaucrats, such as Warren Hastings and Lord Curzon in India, Lord Cromer in Egypt, Lord Charles Somerset at the Cape, Sir Harry Smith in South Africa, Sir George Grey in New Zealand, or Lord Lytton in Afghanistan, among others (Burroughs 1999), have created a new political nomos that produced anomalous and partial models of sovereignty in which ruling was based on legal patchwork and ad hoc arrangements or exceptions, rather than on a single liberal rule of law. Evidently, they had no handbook about which forms of the law were best to institute in colonial settings; rather, they treated European legal traditions as a 'useful collection from which they might draw selectively in crafting colonial legal systems' (Benton 2002: 261). The colonisers relied 'on the blueprint of metropolitan law for distinguishing among categories of legal actors, and they looked for analogous distinctions in indigenous law', sometimes reinventing what they labelled as indigenous 'customary law' (18). As a result, the colonies 'tend not to be organized under a single, vertically-integrated sovereignty sustained by a highly centralized state [. . .] rather they consist in a horizontally woven tapestry of partial sovereignties' (Comaroff and Comaroff 2006: 61).

This resulted in endless negotiations and disagreements which Johnston (1973) has coined 'jurisdictional imperialism', and Benton (2002) has defined as 'jurisdictional politics', 'jurisdictional flexibility' and 'jurisdictional jockeying'. These 'anomalous models' have resulted in sites of lawlessness under the auspices of the law: foreign jurisdiction, exterritorial jurisdiction, administrative decrees, partial annexations, combat zones, martial law and states of emergency (see, for example, Mitchell 1991; Hussain 2003). Ann Stoler has used the concept of 'imperial formations' to describe these features:

> Critical features of imperial formations include harbouring and building on territorial ambiguity, redefining legal categories of belonging and quasi-membership, and shifting the geographic and demographic zones of partially suspended rights [. . .] The legal and political fuzziness of dependencies, trusteeships, protectorates, and unincorporated territories were all part of the deep grammar of partially restricted rights in the nineteenth and twentieth century imperial world [. . .] Imperial states by definition operate as states of exception that vigilantly produce exceptions to their principles and exceptions to their laws. (Stoler 2006: 2, 8, 10)

Egypt is a case in point. As Timothy Mitchell has demonstrated, the British established there a system of control which was tantamount to the introduction of legal exceptions (Mitchell 1991: 97).[12] The system was based on the so-called 'Brigandage Commissions' and was composed of abrupt military raids, secret police, local informants, massive imprisonments and the systematic use of torture. A decade after they were introduced, these commissions were replaced by a more disciplined and consolidated bureaucratic system. It included selective use of the law, endless decrees, and an abruptly changing set of rules and regulations about movement in the region (Mitchell 2002: 96). Similar methods of supervision and governance were applied for capitalist production in Egypt. This is not surprising, since methods of population control that were initially used for combating insurgencies became institutionalised methods of exercising biopower through population control in general. Mitchell describes the process by which these methods were used to prevent labour desertion from colonial lands in which crops were grown. In order to coerce villagers to cultivate export corps and deliver them to government warehouses, they used methods such as the regulation of population census, taxation penalties and usurpation of land. Furthermore, when crop monopoly was met by resistance when villagers deserted their lands guarded by the military, and moved to agricultural lands beyond government control, a permit regime was introduced whereby military-issued permits were required for travel outside of the village locality (Mitchell 2002: 60–1; Mitchell 1991: 34, 40–3). The land laws and decrees that were issued represented attempts to compel individuals to remain on their lands, and to confirm the seizure of lands from those who fled.

As revolts occurred, the political reasoning shifted again: from pure economic justification concerned with preventing desertion, into prescriptions of control over those posing a 'security threat'. Villagers were required to round up 'depraved and malicious persons and suspicious characters' (Mitchell 1991: 97) in their locality, who were then sent to labour or to the army. If, after the assigned period, the 'suspicious characters' were found in the districts, the headmen would be punished. Imperial governance also placed gangs under continuous police control to oversee a system of 'tickets' that were handed out to workers in their villages before they travelled to their work sites, 'but only to those men whom the local police deemed not to be troublemakers' (97). Besides the organisation of the police force, a system of English inspection was set up within the Ministry of the Interior; 'the interior of Egyptian village life was thus to be under continuous supervision' (Mitchell 1998: 98). Thus, this intervention in capitalist production was based on population control and impediments on movement, which was created under the autonomous political nomos of imperial governance. In this form, the notion of sovereignty and the notion of governmentality became enmeshed and practically indistinguishable.

The British founded their rule on the theological percept of divine providence bestowing 'law and order' and good governance upon its racialised subjects. The sovereign – both *de facto* and *de jure* – viewed the colony as a feudal state, with the Queen as the natural sovereign ruling under God (Cohn 2004: 216). Indeed, the church was a legal authority that profoundly influenced the functioning of colonial law (Benton 2002: 13). As Cohn firmly puts it, in the context of India: 'The British Monarch rules under God and divine providence. The Viceroy then becomes the physical representative of the divine order and the monarchy' (Cohn 2004: 219). Thus, British imperialism was anchored in the Christian moral code: it allowed for judicial intervention (the analogue of the divine miracle) to manufacture uncertainty for its racialised subjects; it was based on personal and traditional domination rather than on formal written documents; and it manufactured capricious administrative decrees rather than the predictable nature of the rule of law.

Racially Based Exceptions as Acts of Sovereignty

In colonial locations, the political-theological form of the state of exception was used to differentiate between different political communities, based on the racial distinction between Europeans and 'natives', between indigenous groups and their rulers in settlers' societies, or between Jews and Palestinians in the context of Palestinian territories (see also Lentin 2008; 2011; Goldberg 2008). In the economics of the biopolitical, racial hierarchies became the definers of life and death as well as their justification. As Hussain (2003: 113) has suggested, 'it is race that undermines the legal identity between metropole and colony'. As a mechanism differentiating between 'subjects' who are European citizens and 'subject races' who are not, the bureaucracy was central to the foundation of the political order. To be sure, race is sometimes camouflaged and justified by alternative regimes of justifications: a national struggle, a security paradigm, a distinction between a friend and a foe, and various other definitions (such as class), all can mask racial hierarchies.[13]

Yet, the relationships between Europe and its 'subject races' have changed since the era of decolonisation. Whereas in the past the 'subject races' were to be found mainly across the ocean, today they are present *en masse* in the metropole. As Allan Buena, a spokesperson for the French right wing, stated already in 1946, Europe has become the colony of all colonies (Spektorowski 2000). Some features of the imperial rule and its mixed methods of perpetrating the 'state of exception' are to be found now at the very centre of these Western postcolonial societies.

The core distinctions are no longer confined to the binary of metropole versus colonies. Whereas the two were formerly geographically and culturally distinct, they now often constitute a heterogeneous centre in which a simple distinction between 'friend' and 'foe' may not be easily discerned. It is 'race' that became a signifier for the distinction. Imperialism has shifted locus from the colonies, back to Europe. The imperial diasporas brought with them masses of 'subject races' who now struggle for equal rights in the capitals of Europe. Some argue that this internal division is a bigger threat to Europe than conflicts with external powers. In 2002, the head of Interpol argued that resources should be transferred slowly and gradually from the NATO forces to homeland security (see also Agamben 2000). Immigrants from the 'Third World' blend the traditional party lines and threaten 'security' at the European metropoles. For example, during the unrest of immigrants of North African descent in Paris in September 2005, the government used the same emergency measures that were legislated to control the unrest in Algiers in 1955. We have come full circle. The emergency rules which guide the war on terrorism and the management of these societies today painfully resemble those of the imperial age.

Despite his neglect of imperial history, Agamben's book reminds us that we need to look at 'exceptions' as acts of state sovereignty. One prominent example for this position is the unfounded claim that Israel withdrew from Gaza in 2005. As imperial history has taught us, occupation can also be administrated from a distance, without permanent military presence and without settlers. Israel is still enacting an occupation regime in Gaza, as it denies the latter's elected government, controls its economy, holds the border crossings, prevents access from the sea and air, and wages an ongoing war against the leaders of the struggle. Each week Israel's Ministry of Defence decides how many calories its subjects in Gaza will consume and which products will enter the Strip. The apparent ending of occupation in Gaza, and the disengagement which accompanied it, only mark the continued colonisation by other means. The fact that Israel did not apply its political sovereignty in Gaza (or in the West Bank) by no means alters this conclusion. To the contrary, as I have argued in this essay, the majority of the former colonial powers avoided the imposition of full sovereignty on the occupied territories and created arrangements to support a form of control which was devoid of legal sovereignty. It is this deployment of 'exceptional' practices by 'democracies' that is one of the most challenging aspects of current political theory and practice.

References

Agamben, G. (1998), *Homo Sacer: Sovereign Power and Bare Life*, trans. D. Heller-Roazen. Stanford: Stanford University Press.

—(2000), *Means Without End: Notes on Politics*, trans. V. Binetti and C. Casarino. Minnesota: University of Minnesota Press.

—(2005), *State of Exception*. Chicago: Chicago University Press.

Arendt, H. (1951), *The Origins of Totalitarianism*. New York: Harcourt, Brace and World.

—(1958), *The Human Condition*. Chicago: Chicago University Press.

—(1970), *On Violence*. New York: Harvest.

Benjamin, W. (1978), 'Critique of Violence', in *Reflections*. New York: Schocken Books, 277–300.

Benton, L. (2002), *Law and Colonial Cultures*. Cambridge: Cambridge University Press.

Burroughs, P. (1999), 'Imperial Institutions and the Government of Empire', in A. Porter (ed.), *The Oxford History of the British Empire: The Nineteenth Century*. Oxford: Oxford University Press, 170–97.

Cohn, S. B. (2004), *The Bernard Cohn Omnibus*. New Delhi: Oxford University Press.

Comaroff, J. and J. Comaroff (2006), *Law and Disorder in the Postcolony*. Chicago: University of Chicago Press.

Fanon, F. (1967a), *Black Skin, White Masks*. New York: Grove Press.

—(1967b), *The Wretched of the Earth*. New York: Grove Press.

Fieldhouse, D. K. (1967), *The Colonial Empires: A Comparative Survey from the Eighteenth Century*. New York: Delacorte Press.

Fontana, B. (ed.) (1988), *Constant: Political Writings*. Cambridge: Cambridge University Press.

Foucault, M. (2004), *Security, Territory, Population*. New York: Palgrave Macmillan.

Gendzier, I. (1973), *Frantz Fanon: A Critical Study*. London: Wildwood House.

Goldberg, T. D. (2008), 'Racial Palestinization', in R. Lentin (ed.), *Thinking Palestine*. London and New York: Zed Books, 25–45.

Gourevitch, P. and E. Morris (2009), *The Ballad of Abu Ghraib*. New York: Penguin Books.

Hardt, M. and A. Negri (2004), *Multitude: War and Democracy in the Age of Empire*. New York: Penguin Press.

Hussain, N. (2003), *The Jurisprudence of Emergency: Colonialism and the Rule of Law*. Ann Arbor: University of Michigan Press.

Johnston, R. (1973), *Sovereignty and Protection: A Study of British*

Jurisdictional Imperialism in the Late Nineteenth Century. Durham: Duke University Press.

Judt, T. (2005), 'The New World Order', *New York Review of Books*, 14 July, 17.

Kalyvas, A. (2005), 'The Sovereign Weaver: Beyond the Camp', in A. A. Norris (ed.), *Politics, Metaphysics, and Death: Essays on Giorgio Agamben's* Homo Sacer. Durham: Duke University Press, 107–34.

Lentin R. (2005), '"Femina Sacra": Gendered Memory and Political Violence', *Women's Studies International Forum*, 29: 463–73.

—(2011), 'Palestinian Women from *Femina Sacra* to Agents of Active Resistance'. Paper presented at the International Colloquium, WWW. World Wide Women: Globalisation, Genders and Languages, Research Centre for Women's and Gender Studies (CIRSDe), Università degli studi di Torino, 10–12 February.

—(ed.) (2008), *Thinking Palestine*. London and New York: Zed Books.

Macey, D. (2000), *Frantz Fanon: A Life*. London: Granta Books.

Mitchell, T. (1991), *Colonizing Egypt*. Berkeley: University of California Press.

—(2002), *Rule of Experts: Egypt, Techno-Politics, Modernity*. Berkeley: University of California Press.

Naimark, N. M. (2001), *Fires of Hatred: Ethnic Cleansing in Twentieth-Century Europe*. Cambridge, MA: Harvard University Press.

Neuman, F. ([1930] 1987), *Social Democracy and the Rule of Law*, ed. Keith Tribe. London: Allen and Unwin.

Priest, D. (2005), 'CIA Holds Terror Suspects in Secret Prisons', *The Washington Post*, 2 November, available at http://www.washingtonpost.com/wp-dyn/content/article/2005/11/01/AR2005110101644.html, accessed 15 September 2011.

Scheuerman, E. W. (1997), *Between the Norm and the Exception*. Cambridge, MA: MIT Press.

Schmitt, C. (1988), *Political Theology: Four Chapters on the Concept of Sovereignty*. Cambridge, MA: MIT Press.

—([1950] 2003), *The Nomos of the Earth*. New York: Telos Press.

—(2007), *Theory of the Partisan: Intermediate Commentary on the Concept of the Political*, trans. G. L. Ulmen. Ann Arbor: Telos Press.

Sharif, H. (2003), *Approaching Palestinian Liberation with the Theory of Franz Fanon*. Unpublished MA Thesis, Mansfield College, Oxford University.

Shenhav, Y. (2006), *The Arab Jews*. Stanford: Stanford University Press.

Spektorowski, A. (2000), 'The French New Right: Differentialism and the Idea of Ethnofilian Exclusionism', *Polity*, XXXIII (2 Winter): 383–403.

Stoler, A. L. (2006), 'On Degrees of Imperial Sovereignties', *Public Culture*, 18: 117–39.

Weiss, Y. (2004), 'Ethnic Cleansing, Memory and Property: Europe 1944–1948', *Historia: Journal of the Israeli Historical Society*, 13: 43–74. (In Hebrew.)

Weitz, D. E. (2003), *A Century of Genocide: Utopias of Race and Nation*. Princeton: Princeton University Press.

Notes

A previous version of this essay first appeared in Hebrew in *Theory and Criticism*, 29(Fall) 2006: 205–18 and is reproduced with permission of the Van Leer Jerusalem Institute.

1. Hardt and Negri (2004) suggest that the institutionalisation of the exception as a global paradigm is based on the juxtaposition of two traditions: the exception in German legal thought and the American ideology of exceptionalism.

2. Palestinians comprise 15 per cent of the Israeli population after the ethnic cleansing of Palestinians in the 1948 war and thereafter.

3. To be sure, ethnic cleansing is not genocide. For the distinction between genocide and ethnic cleansing see Weitz (2003: 10) and Weiss (2004). For a different position see Naimark (2001).

4. Schmitt (1988). On Schmitt's text as a response to Benjamin's *Critique of Violence,* see Agamben, *State of Exception* (2005), chapter 4.

5. Schmitt himself was not oblivious to the exceptional implications of imperialism. In *The Nomos of the Earth* (2003) he criticised imperialism as a pseudo-secular strategy, which leads to the de-politicisation and de-theologisation of the European nomos.

6. Ronit Lentin (2005; 2011) also provides a feminist critique of Agamben, speaking particularly about what she labels as 'femina sacra'.

7. In *Homo Sacer*, Agamben refers in passing to the Spanish colonial history in Cuba and to the British in South Africa, as two cases in which 'the camp' was born.

8. For example, Agamben echoes the distinction that Arendt borrowed from Aristotle between *zoē* and *bios* as two forms of life (Arendt 1958), or her analysis of stateless people (Arendt 1951).

9. In his *Political Theology*, Schmitt has already pointed to Hobbesian theory of the state as theological moment which enabled the creation of modern Europe.

10. One of the striking facts about Fanon's two major books is the manner in which they influenced racial and national struggles in the Middle East. For example, in Israel, *Black Skin, White Masks* has become a founding book for the Mizrahi struggle (that of Arab Jews; see Shenhav 2006), whereas *The Wretched of the Earth* remained outside of the discourse. In the Arab world, the opposite situation occurred. Whereas *The Wretched of the Earth* was translated into Arabic in the 1960s and arguably fuelled the Palestinian national struggle (Sharif 2003), *Black Skin, White Masks* was never translated into Arabic (Gendzier [1973] made this argument in the 1970s, and as far as I know this is still the situation).

11. I use the term 'partisan' following Schmitt (2007). According to Schmitt, the partisan uses pure violence. It marks politics as war rather than peace.

12. Martial law was a frequent manifestation of the 'exception' in the colonies. As Hussain (2003) persuasively argues in his excellent analysis, it carried different meanings in Europe and in the colonies. Based on cases from Punjab and St. Thomas, Hussain shows how their use in the colonies were suffused, both in practice and in theory, with racialised definitions and interpretations.

13. Some of Schmitt's students, such as Neuman and Kirshcheimer, criticised the liberal rule from the leftist ranks (Neuman 1987; see Scheuerman 1997). They launched a sharp critique of the big monopolies and show how the distinction between a friend and a foe is organised also in the economic sphere.

2

The Management of Anomie: The State of Exception in Postcommunist Russia

Sergei Prozorov

On 4 November 2010 a mass murder took place in the village of Kuschevskaya, population 35,000, in the Krasnodar Region of the Russian Federation. Intruders broke into the home of a local farmer, Server Ametov, killing his entire family as well as the two families visiting the Ametovs on the evening of the public holiday, the Day of Russian National Unity. A total of twelve people, including four little children, died of numerous stab wounds, burns or suffocation. Within a week three suspects were apprehended by the local police. Yet following pressure by the national media, the investigation of the case was pursued further, eventually culminating in the arrest on 17 November of two members of the District Council, Sergei Tsapok and Sergei Tsepovyaz, who were subsequently indicted as the organisers of the murder.

After these arrests, the local authorities were overwhelmed by complaints about the crimes committed by the gang led by Tsapok and Tsepovyaz, going back as long as fifteen years and including racketeering, robbery, extortion and gang rape. Current membership of the gang is estimated at 400 people. According to reports by investigative journalists (see for example Sokolov-Mitrich 2010; Lebedeva 2010), from 1998 the gang consolidated itself into a major agricultural holding company and gradually took control of the entire law enforcement apparatus in the district, including the police, the courts and the procuracy. Indeed, at the moment of his arrest, one of the suspects, Alexander Khodych, served as the Head of the Organised Crime Unit of the regional police and was responsible for combating 'political extremism'. According to Attorney General Yuri Chaika, the ongoing investigation of the situation in the district has revealed that over 1,500 crimes committed by the gang were covered up by local and regional police and the courts (Gazeta.ru Editorial 2011).

This is not to say that the rule of this gang over Kuschevskaya unfolded in isolation from regional and federal politics. Both Tsapok and Tsepovyaz served as members of the District Council elected on the ballot of the United Russia party, chaired federally by Prime Minister Putin and regionally by Governor Aleksander Tkachev, who is reported to have known Tsapok personally and to have praised his efficient business activities (Tirmastae 2010). Moreover, according to the investigation of the opposition movement Solidarity, Mr Tsapok was observed in attendance at the official inauguration of President Medvedev in 2008, an honour rarely bestowed on regional politicians or businessmen. Responding to the demands for his resignation, Governor Tkachev justified his unwillingness to resign by claiming that 'the situation, similar to that of Kuschevskaya, where the police and the gangs work together, is typical for many districts of the region' (Tirmastae 2010). Judging by the absence of comments on this case from either Prime Minister Putin or President Medvedev, as well as by the shift of media attention to other gruesome murders in neighbouring regions, Tkachev's claim met with widespread agreement.

What are we to make of this reduction of the exceptionally gruesome murder to a 'typical case' in postcommunist Russia? What is this political order, in which the exception becomes the rule, not merely in the sense of playful logical paradoxes but in the sense of a brutal indistinction between law and crime, authority and violence, government and gang? From the beginning of the Putin presidency in 1999, contemporary Russian politics has been frequently interpreted in terms of the resurgence of 'authoritarianism' (see Anderson 2007; Baker and Glasser 2005; Gudkov 2001; Sakwa 2004; Truscott 2005). However, the precise nature of this authoritarianism has remained occluded by facile analogies with Soviet or Imperial eras, whereby the Putin era is understood either as a de-ideologised version of Soviet socialism ('Stalinism-lite') or a superficially 'modernised' resurgence of Russian autocracy. Both of these analogies are highly problematic insofar as they ignore the genealogical point of descent of the current regime in the process of the *demise* of the Soviet order and pay insufficient attention to the way the *ruins* of the old order form the basis of the new regime (cf. Magun 2008; Prozorov 2009: chapter 1). The fundamental feature of the postcommunist condition is its origin in the experience of the dissolution of Soviet socialism in the three senses of the political order, economic system and the Soviet state.

It is in this sense that the postcommunist condition connects with the condition of colonialism that is the main focus of this book. In contrast to the practice of overseas colonisation, characteristic of European colonial powers, the Russian Empire emerged by mainland expansion into the Eurasian heartland and beyond into the Far East. As a consequence, while European colonial powers could be said to *have* colonies as external entities distinguished from the metropole, in Russia the metropole and its colonies could not be distinguished so easily, which resulted in important differences in the process of decolonisation. While, for example, Great Britain *had* an Empire that it could lose without ceasing to be what it was (though of course not remaining the same either), Russia *was* an Empire and decolonisation could therefore only be equivalent to its dissolution as an entity. This process of internal decolonisation, which began with the revolution of 1905 and reached its peak with the Bolshevik Revolution of 1917, was gradually halted by the Bolshevik government itself, which managed to reconstitute almost the entire Empire under the veneer of the anti-imperialist ideology of Marxism–Leninism. The Soviet period could therefore be understood as the temporary halting of the process of decolonisation through the full assumption of its ideology: during the seventy years of Soviet rule decolonisation was restrained in reality by being symbolically asserted in an unrestrained and hyperbolic celebration of 'Soviet internationalism'. The demise of the Soviet order in 1991 entailed the resumption of the degradation of the Empire, which continues to this day; not merely in the areas of separatist conflicts in the North Caucasus (see King and Menon 2010), but also, in a no less violent manner, within whatever we understand as 'Russia proper', of which the village of Kuschevskaya is, as we are told, a typical case.

The understanding of the contemporary condition as the process of degradation of previous forms of rule, either Imperial or Soviet, provides us with a new perspective on contemporary 'authoritarianism'. While conventional accounts of authoritarianism, modelled on the theory of dictatorship (Schmitt 1994), attribute to authoritarian rule a plenitude (*pleroma*) of power, the full realisation of its forces, its unlimited unfolding, and so forth, our approach to postcommunism rather proceeds from the fundamental suspension, deactivation and inoperativity of power, its *keno-matic* state, which Giorgio Agamben associates with the state of exception (Agamben 2005a: 48). This is the condition in which the legal order is in force but is deprived of all significance (Agamben 1998: 51).

> The state of exception is not a dictatorship (whether constitutional or unconstitutional, commissarial or sovereign) but a space devoid of law, a zone of anomie in which all legal determinations – and above all the very distinction between the public and the private – are deactivated. (Agamben 2005a: 50)

The application of Agamben's political theory to the postcommunist condition yields both theoretical and empirical benefits. On the one hand, as we shall see, the postcommunist experience provides empirical support for many of Agamben's claims that might appear excessively hyperbolic in contemporary Western contexts (cf. Laclau 2007; Passavant 2007). On the other hand, Agamben's approach provides the analysis of postcommunism with a theoretical framework adequate for grasping the Russian state of exception other than in the merely negative sense of 'disorder', 'instability' or 'illegality', characteristic of Western analyses of postcommunist Russia during the 1990s. In this chapter we shall rely on Agamben's political thought to elucidate the specificity of the contemporary mode of rule in Russia. In the following section we shall introduce the Russian concept of *bespedel* that emerged in the early 1990s to designate the postcommunist condition and serves as the best crosscultural translation of Agamben's notion of the state of exception. We shall then proceed to the analysis of the transformation of the condition of *bespedel* in the Putin presidency, whereby the postcommunist anomie became ordered and stabilised by the regime that nonetheless remains within the anomic terrain – a paradoxical configuration that we shall term *cratocracy*. In the fourth section we shall elaborate this logic of the anomic management of anomie with reference to Walter Benjamin's theory of baroque sovereignty. Despite its self-presentation as a constructive alternative to the 'wild' and 'chaotic' 1990s, the contemporary Russian regime persists in its nihilistic paradigm, all the more so as long as it keeps negating it. The chapter concludes with a discussion of the possibilities of overcoming this mode of power.

Bespedel: Between Potentiality and Actuality

Let us return to the gruesome scene of the Kuschevskaya massacre. According to the investigation of *Argumenty i Fakty*, the information on the implication of the Tsapok gang in the murder was passed to the authorities by the leaders of the underworld of the neighbouring city of Rostov, who were dismayed by the fact that four children, including an infant, had been brutally murdered in this incident (Artemov 2010). While murder as such is generally held to be an acceptable instrument of conflict resolution in the underworld, the murder of children falls outside the informal code of conduct, which is called '*ponyatia*' (literally, 'concepts'). If something is done 'not according to the concepts' ('*ne po ponyatiam*'), then the situation justifies exceptional measures in response. The cooperation of criminal gang leaders with the police investigation is an example of one such exceptional response, not usually part of the criminal code of conduct.

This expression from the underworld slang is also well suited for attempts to theorise the postcommunist condition. Various approaches to Russian postcommunism, from liberal transitionalism to cultural traditionalism (Prozorov 2009: chapter 1), face a perpetual problem of the inapplicability of the conventional conceptual apparatus of social sciences to postcommunist Russian reality, which seems bent on behaving 'not according to the concepts'. As a result, the postcommunist condition is routinely conceptualised in a purely negative manner, as the *lack* of democracy, *absence* of solidarity, *insufficient* participation, *weakness* of tradition, and so forth. Indeed, it is easy to see how familiar concepts work poorly in grasping a situation like the one in Kuschevskaya, which as we recall, was pronounced 'typical' by the authorities. The familiar oppositions between the public and the private, the legal and the illegal, the norm and the exception appear inoperative in the territory ruled by an organised criminal gang that includes the Head of the Organised Crime Unit, which exercises its authority through a combination of the selective use of legal mechanisms by corrupt police and courts and arbitrary violence, including rape and murder of apparently random victims. Can the Tsapok gang be distinguished from the postcommunist state reconstituted and run by Prime Minister Putin, and how is this distinction phenomenologically accessible to the residents of Kuschevskaya? As a result of this collapse of all distinctions we are resigned to the construction of oxymorons such as 'mafia state', the designation of Russia in the US diplomatic cables made publicly available in 2010 by WikiLeaks (see Harding 2010). However, insofar as this term conflates what we hold to be distinct and even opposite entities, its operation only reproduces a negative conceptualisation, whereby a mafia state is neither a proper 'mafia' nor a proper 'state'. Accessible only in the mode of what it is not, the postcommunist condition is mystified even further.

One solution to this problem, guided by Agamben's refusal of mystifying and mythologising tendencies in the history of law and religion (Agamben 1998: 71–80; 2011: 8–17), is to take as the sole point of departure in conceptualising postcommunism the sheer fact of its being 'not in accordance with the concepts'. Evidently, this does not mean the refusal of conceptualisation on the part of the analyst. On the contrary, we shall take as our point of departure the concept, immanent to postcommunist Russian history, which refers to precisely this condition of 'inaccordance with the concepts', the indistinction prior to all distinctions. In the Russian context, such a paradoxical concept of 'inaccordance with the concepts' is readily available to us in the form of a late-Soviet neologism, 'bespedel'.

As opposed to a neutral noun 'bespedelnost' with the same denotation of 'limitlessness', the abridged form 'bespedel' entered the popular lexicon in the late 1980s with a sharply negative connotation. Originally this term emerged as part of the criminal slang, in which it referred to the practices that violated the tacit rules of conduct in the ritualised hierarchical structure of the Soviet underworld. It is important to stress that in its original meaning bespedel does not designate 'illegality' per se and is thus entirely distinct from the corresponding Russian term 'bezzakonie', which is literally translated as 'without-law' and refers to acts or phenomena that violate established legal norms or statutes. In contrast, bespedel designates not the illegality of acts but rather their inaccordance with the tacit and informal norms that may well be themselves illegal. For instance, it is common for drivers stopped for speeding or other traffic violations to pay a bribe directly to the police officer rather than go through the trouble of paying the fine through official channels and having the violation registered in their record. According to the tacit 'concepts', the bribe in question must be lesser than or equal to the official fine. It is only when the policeman demands a greater amount, frequently threatening to pin additional violations on the hapless driver, that we leave the domain of illicit regularity and enter the perilous zone of *bespedel*, where no rules apply.

Thus, *bespedel* refers to a meta-illegality or second-degree anomie that is characterised by the radical impossibility of adjudication. In the late-Soviet and postcommunist period, *bespedel* became the favourite term to describe the socioeconomic disorder and rampant criminality that characterised the later years of perestroika and particularly the 'market reforms' of the Yeltsin presidency. In various enunciative contexts, *bespedel* may refer to the utter disrespect for traditional authorities, the acceptability of physical violence in the resolution of conflicts, the politicians' disregard for public opinion, the radical reversal of moral values, the disappearance of ethical standards in professional practices, the domination of private entrepreneurship by criminal protection rackets, and so forth.

The limitlessness of the postcommunist socio-political field is a direct effect of the threefold collapse of the Soviet political system, the economy and the state. Once the Soviet order unravelled, revealing not only the contingency of its own foundations but the radical contingency of every positive order, all ordering principles – be they Soviet or anti-Soviet – were rendered inoperative, depriving social praxis of any limitations. In other post-revolutionary contexts, including Central and East European postcommunism, this limitlessness whose momentary eruption is the feature of any genuine revolution, was quickly effaced by the institution of a new hegemonic delimitation that took the form of a 'return to Europe' and the institutional process of NATO and EU accession. A similar installation of limits took place in the Central Asian republics of the former USSR, albeit in an explicitly anti-democratic and traditionalist manner. In contrast to other post-Soviet states whose new-found independence enabled a relatively quick return to order, for Russia the postcommunist condition entailed the resumption of post-Imperial decolonisation, with its attendant fragmentation, disintegration and destabilisation, whereby all attempts at installing a positive form of postcommunist order appeared to be thwarted in advance. As I have argued in detail in *The Ethics of Postcommunism* (2009: chapters 2–4), the collapse of the Soviet order did not merely result in the demise of one historical project among others, but rather illuminated the contingency of the historical dimension as such. This deactivated from the outset any attempt to replace the project of 'building socialism' by the alternative project of 'building capitalism', 'building the Russian nation', or other forms of reconstructive transformation. It is the very idea of *building* a social order that has been rendered inoperative in the postcommunist condition, hence the lingering of the limitlessness of *bespedel*.

During the early years of postcommunism the lament about *bespedel* would typically proclaim that 'everything has become possible', with a melancholic caveat 'but not for us'. In his analysis of Russian postcommunism as a 'minimal' or 'negative' revolution, Artemy Magun has demonstrated that lamentation, melancholy and mourning are the dominant moods of the post-revolutionary period (Magun 2008: 66–84). These function as the symptoms of the failure of the revolution to fully actualise its negative potential, which could take place only through the complete annihilation of the symbolic order of human society as such. Since such annihilation does not take place and every revolution is, in this sense, a failure, its aftermath entails nothing other than the materialisation of its negativity in our everyday existence as simultaneously an experience of radical liberty and utter disempowerment. *Bespedel* is both a dizzying experience of freedom from all limitations and a nauseating experience of the impossibility of freedom as a practice; it signifies both a wide expanse of potentiality for being whatever one wants to be and a sense of actual powerlessness in the face of the reign of brute force and universal corruption. In this experience, potentiality and actuality are radically separated, whereby the absence of all limits bars and forecloses the actualisation of the very possibilities enabled by it.

We may therefore conclude that *bespedel* is ultimately the best Russian translation for what Agamben terms the 'state of exception' (Agamben 2005a). Indeed, this notion immediately recalls two of the most controversial paradigmatic figures in Agamben's work: *homo sacer* and the Muselmann (Agamben 1998; 1999) and also permits us to differentiate between them, contrary to the frequent conflation of these figures in the interpretations of Agamben's work (cf. Laclau 2007; DeCaroli 2007). Insofar as *bespedel* designates the dissolution of all structures of authority and the inoperative status of all norms, its subjects evidently inhabit the state of exception, in which they are all *homines sacri*, beings abandoned by the sovereign power that withdrew from the social realm after the demise of the Soviet Union. Moreover, given the rampant criminality of early postcommunism, its subjects indeed dwelled in the harrowing condition of being 'capable of being killed with impunity'. And yet, like the objects of what Agamben calls the 'ban' (Agamben 1998: 104–11), who have undergone a 'civil death' and are ostracised or banished from the community, postcommunist subjects may also experience their banishment as a matter of freedom, an extreme potentiality that has done away with any positive authority. It is this potentiality, which may of course be completely barred from empirical actualisation, that ultimately differentiates *homo sacer* from the Muselmann, the utterly desubjectified inhabitant of the camp (see Agamben 1999: 41–86; 1998: 166–80). For the Muselmann, confinement rather marks the withdrawal of all potentiality in the materialisation of the impossible as 'absolute necessity' (Agamben 1999: 148). From this perspective, the condition of *bespedel* must be rigorously distinguished from Agamben's figure of the camp, which, after all, is defined precisely by the limits that *bespedel* lacks.

At the same time, it would certainly be facile to celebrate the postcommunist condition in terms of liberation from the camp-like condition of Soviet 'totalitarianism'. In the condition of *bespedel*, freedom exists as a paradoxical conjunction of extreme potentiality and utter impossibility, whereby the absence of limits to the practice of freedom consumes the experience of freedom itself in the perpetual deferral of its actualisation. As Agamben remarked, 'nothing is bitterer than a long dwelling in potential' (Agamben 1995: 65). It is this bitter dwelling in the gap between potentiality and actuality that defines the postcommunist condition.

Cratocracy: The Stabilisation of *Bespedel*

Is there a way out of this bitter experience? A self-evident solution to the problem of extreme potentiality posed by the condition of *bespedel* would consist in its gradual overcoming through the institution of a hegemonic project that actualises certain of its infinite possibilities and proscribes others. This might proceed in the name of some teleological end-state of a 'bright future', in which all potentiality is expected to find fulfilment. The Russian politics of the 1990s was marked by a veritable explosion of such soteriological solutions to the problem of *bespedel*, none of which was able to attain the hegemonic status they aspired to (see Prozorov 2008). Nonetheless, it is impossible to deny the widespread temptation in the early 1990s to escape *bespedel* by a retreat into the security of a teleological project, even if the latter could only be conceivable as a simulacrum.

It is from this perspective that we must understand the phenomenon of Putinism as a highly effective, if also uncanny, solution to the problem of *bespedel*. The reason why Putinism triumphed over all its adversaries across the ideological spectrum (socialists, liberals and nationalists) is that its design for overcoming *bespedel* did not involve the imposition of any positive ideological hegemony, but rather invoked a promise of stabilisation devoid of substantive content that I have elsewhere addressed in terms of 'absolute conservatism' (Prozorov 2008: 220–2). While the neo-liberal 'conservative' reformers vainly attempted to conserve what was not yet created (the liberal order), and the nostalgic left strove to conserve what no longer existed (the Soviet system), Putinism simply conserves *what there is*, that is, the ruins of the Soviet order. Putinism thereby institutes an apparently immutable system, which carries no historical project but *for this very reason* functions very effectively in a society founded on the experience of the contingency of all historical teleologies.

This is what distinguishes Putinism from all hitherto known forms of authoritarianism of the left and the right, which limit themselves to the repertoire of *some* ideological orientations that are deployed against *others* in the manner of a Schmittian friend-enemy distinction. In terms of Ernesto Laclau's (2005) theory of populism, which he presents as a transcendental structure of the political, politics necessarily involves the process of articulation of particular demands into equivalential chains around 'empty signifiers', whose polysemy permits them to serve as quilting points for diverse and frequently divergent values, interests or ideologems. Yet, every process of articulation must presuppose the existence of signifiers that do *not* enter the equivalential chain, but rather function as the 'other' or even the 'enemy' of the newly constituted political unity. Thus, in the late 1980s the anti-communist movement in the Soviet Union was constituted by the articulation around the empty signifier 'democrats', personified by Boris Yeltsin, of such disparate political identities as monarchists, neo-liberals, anarchists, social democrats and environmentalists, whose unity was momentarily enabled by their opposition to all things 'communist'. The indisputable advance of Putinism over this logic of populism is precisely its utter indifference to the contents of

ideological maxims, which are incessantly combined into most
bizarre constellations without any need for the construction of the
antagonistic frontier and the determination of the 'other'. What
Putinism achieves is something that is barely possible to grasp in
the terms of Laclau's theory: a situation of *total* equivalence of
diverse demands or, better, their radical indistinction.

And yet, this deactivation of ideology in the reign of pure stability entails that what Putinism conserves must be identical to
what it claims to overcome. Insofar as the Putin regime does not
introduce any positive ideological content, what its policy of stabilisation achieves is logically nothing other than the stabilisation
of this ruinous scene of *bespedel* itself. What was decried, toler-
ated or barely survived in the 1990s as a 'transitional moment',
an exceptional condition on the way to something positive or
substantial, became in the Putin presidency reinscribed as the
substance of contemporary Russian social life as such, as *all there
is*. In this manner, corruption, social inequality or police brutality became normalised as stable forms of life, without of course
losing any of their negativity. Thus, the Putinite negation of the
negativity of the post-historical condition of the 1990s does not
lead to any affirmation whatsoever. Despite its self-presentation as
a positive and constructive alternative to the 'wild' and 'chaotic'
1990s, the contemporary Russian regime persists in its nihilistic paradigm, all the more so as long as it keeps negating it.
Moreover, in its 'stabilised' form *bespedel* paradoxically ends up
a bounded terrain, a limited zone of limitlessness that begins to
approximate Agamben's figure of the camp, insofar as the perils
of abandonment are multiplied by the impossibility of flight. The
Kuschevskaya village, in which arbitrary rule and random violence coexisted for over a decade with the rhetoric of stabilisation
under the aegis of Putin's United Russia party, is a paradigm of
this paradoxical situation, in which the sole substance of order is
disorder itself.

In the late nineteenth century, the period of the accelerated
capitalist development in Russia, marked by revolutionary societal
dislocations, the conservative philosopher Konstantin Leontiev
famously suggested that 'Russia must be frozen in order not to
rot'. The solution to the problem of the dissolution of the Empire
– that is, the 'internal decolonisation' of Russia – was found in the
suspension of every immanent social process and the reign of pure
synchrony. Yet, as every variant of conservatism eventually finds

out to its disappointment, what 'must be frozen in order not to rot' has always *already begun* to rot, hence the anxiety about its 'conservation', which would hardly arise, were the phenomenon in question safe in its proper and authentic existence. *Reconstituting* what is already *destitute*, the Putin regime remains as nihilistic as Yeltsin's in its evacuation of all historical meaning from the sphere of politics, yet, unlike the Yeltsin presidency, ventures to order the field of *bespedel* through the proliferation of purely ritualistic manifestations of authority that maintain a semblance of order amid anomie. Rather than overcome the anomie of *bespedel* through the institution of a new nomos, the Putin regime exemplifies the uncanny rule *of* anomie *over* anomie, the attempt to manage the condition of *bespedel* to its advantage. Rather than ward off the dissolution of the Empire in the manner of the Pauline *katechon*, this regime claims its sovereignty over the scene of post-imperial degradation and enacts this sovereignty by persevering in this ruinous scene of Russia's internal decolonisation. The task of the regime is not to overcome the post-imperial decay, fragmentation and disintegration but to make this very condition and its own standing in it permanent.

It is in this context that we may understand the reign of violence in the Kuschevskaya village as the paradigm of the management of anomie. From the beginning of the Putin presidency numerous commentators have argued that the Putinite mode of rule, devoid of any ideological or developmental project, consists simply in the reign of *power as such*, of power as brute force rather than authority. In April 2007 Putin's former economic advisor Andrei Illarionov published an article entitled 'The Force Model of the State' (Illarionov 2007), in which he argued that the current regime is sustained by the use of brute violence, unlimited by any legal mechanisms. Similarly, Mikhail Delyagin (2007) has described the existing regime as a 'force oligarchy' (*silovaya oligarkhia*) that comprises the representatives of the repressive apparatus of the state who control the key sectors of Russia's economy and are more prone to the direct recourse to violence than the 'commercial' oligarchy of the 1990s. In a less sensationalist manner, the same thesis is presented in the studies of Olga Kryshtanovskaya (2005), which demonstrate the tendency towards the composition of the Russian political and business elite from the representatives of law enforcement and security services, as well as Vadim Volkov's (2002) work on the formation of the postcommunist elite from the representatives of what was once known as 'organised crime' or, in Volkov's terminology, 'violent entrepreneurship'.

The elevation of extra-juridical violence to a distinct 'model' of the state in these analyses enables the criticism of the Putin regime from the conventional perspective of an apparently 'normal' state, founded on rule of law, constitutional principles, and so on. Yet, there is no such thing as a 'normal' state that does not contain at its foundation the state of exception that alone gives it access to its object, that is, the life of its subjects. As Agamben has demonstrated, the state of exception is the 'secret ark' at the foundation of every state (Agamben 2005a: 84–8). Thus, the difference of the Putin regime from Western liberal democracies or, for that matter, the Soviet Union does not amount to a separate alternative 'model' but rather consists in the *reduction* of state power to its pure form, whereby positive governmental interventions into social life are rendered inoperative and all that remains is the ceremonial display by power of its own power that endlessly glorifies its potentiality of self-cancellation through recourse to brute force. In the absence of any positive project in the post-Soviet condition of the resumption of internal decolonisation, authority in postcommunist Russia manifests itself through a redoubling of its own power, as the power of those who hold power or, to use Andrei Fursov's (1991) fortunate neologism, as *cratocracy*. Thus, rather than view the contemporary regime in terms of plenitude of power in its sovereign majesty, we should rather approach it as an effect of a radical *kenosis* of power, whereby it is split between its own unproductive glorification and its degradation into brute violence.

The Intrigant: Postcommunist Anomie and Baroque Sovereignty

Uncanny as this mode of power might appear, its paradigm has actually been developed by an author whose influence on Agamben's work cannot be overestimated – Walter Benjamin, whose theory of baroque sovereignty resonates strikingly with the postcommunist state of exception. Similarly to the analysis of the logic of *bespedel* in terms of the suspension of the historical process in the aftermath of the demise of socialism, Benjamin's point of departure in his *Origin of German Tragic Drama* is the transformation in the perception of history during the Baroque period, whereby the eschatological dimension was blocked and the historical world was perceived as 'nature deprived of grace' (Benjamin 2003: 81). In this world of history-as-nature, transcendence is emptied of any possible content but remains present as an 'ultimate heaven', a 'vacuum' that is capable of one day 'destroying the world with catastrophic violence' (81). It is from this perspective that we should understand Benjamin's minimal yet profound amendment to Carl Schmitt's famous definition of sovereignty as the decision on the exception (Schmitt 1985: 5–15): 'the baroque concept emerges from a discussion of the state of emergency and makes it the most important function of the prince to exclude this' (Benjamin 2003: 81). While Schmitt's sovereign consummates his sovereignty by deciding on the exception and thus bringing it into being in the manner of the miracle, Benjamin's baroque sovereign is rather faced with a more prosaic yet also more difficult task of excluding the exception that has always already taken place and even 'become the rule'. Similarly, as we have argued, the political rationality of Putinism in contemporary Russia is only intelligible as an attempt to stabilise one's standing and authority in the general state of exception coextensive with the entire social order, the limitlessness of *bespedel*.

The evacuation of the eschatological dimension ruptures the systematic analogy that Schmitt's political theology established between the sovereign and God (Schmitt 1985: 36–52): 'However highly he is enthroned over subject and state, his status is confined to the world of creation; he is the lord of creatures but he remains a creature' (Benjamin 2003: 85). To the extent that the sovereign is 'itself a creature', it is necessarily itself contaminated by the general anomie of 'history deprived of grace'. Hence, the only possible task of the baroque sovereign is to persevere in its own being without being consumed by the very state of exception it is always already caught up in. By the same token, the postcommunist regime in the Putin presidency is best grasped as the anomic management of anomie, whereby exceptional measures of the kind associated with the condition of *bespedel* are deployed to order and stabilise this condition itself.

Benjamin introduces three figures of power, the relations between which permit us to understand the transformation of sovereign power in the Baroque age. Faced with the task of self-preservation in the general state of anomie, the sovereign may seek to accumulate as much power as possible and in this manner becomes a *tyrant*, who acts on the basis of hubris, as a 'deranged creation', 'erupting into madness like a volcano and destroying himself and his entire court' (Benjamin 2003: 70). Falling victim to the 'disproportion between the unlimited hierarchical dignity with which he is divinely invested and the humble estate of his human-ity' (70), the fearful tyrant is at the permanent risk of turning into a pitiful *martyr*. There is only one possibility to exit the endless oscillation between tyranny and martyrdom in Benjamin's con-ceptual constellation, which consists in the transformation of the sovereign into the intriguer (*Intrigant*). Contrary to the tyrant, who violently tries to exclude the state of exception and falls victim to it, the intriguer – usually represented in the baroque drama by the servant to the prince – is perfectly aware that the state of exception is all there is, and rather than vainly attempt to exclude it, tries to *make use* of it through ceaseless plotting and scheming: 'Baroque drama knows no other historical activity than the corrupt energy of schemers' (88). While the Schmittian sovereign enacts its transcendence through the decision on the exception, the intriguer renounces all transcendence in favour of a purely immanent governance by staging plots and conspiracies, which, in accordance with the general reduction of history to nature, are grounded in the 'anthropological, even physiological knowledge' of human beings (95). Evidently, this immanentist modality of rule is the only possible one in the postcommunist condition, which permits us to understand the process of depoliti-cisation that began in Russia almost immediately after the demise of the Soviet order, when the process of internal decolonisation was resumed, rendering inoperative all sovereign transcendence and unleashing the immanent forces of schemers. Unwilling to risk becoming martyrs in the case of failure of their hubristic claims to tyranny, the entire Russian political elite, from President Yeltsin downwards, transformed politics into a technology of scheming, which in the Putin presidency was perfected to a degree unprec-edented in modern history. While in the early 1990s we observed the diffuse proliferation of charlatans exploiting the societal shock of *bespedel* (astrologists, messiahs, urinotherapists, faith healers, impostors, pyramid schemers, and so forth), the stabilisation of *bespedel* entails the concentration of 'corrupt energy' in the figure of the sovereign.

Conclusion

The understanding of the postcommunist mode of rule in terms of the baroque-like degradation of transcendent sovereignty into immanent intrigue in the anomic space of *bespedel* poses numerous problems for rethinking the possibilities of resistance to this form of power. Nothing would be easier than thinking up an alternative form of nomos (liberal, socialist, nationalist or any combination thereof) to oppose the anomie which the Putin regime conserves and manages, yet nothing would be less effective, as countless oppositional groups and movements (*Another Russia, National Assembly, Solidarity, Party of Popular Freedom*) have discovered to their disappointment. However, it would be a mistake to infer from these failures the societal support for the existing regime. What we observe is rather a *lack* of support for any project that seeks to exit the condition of *bespedel* by the imposition of a new hegemonic historical task, to whose realisation in the future one's existence must be sacrificed in the present. Any oppositional project that ventures to overcome the state of *bespedel* through the construction of an alternative order is likely to be met with societal indifference.

Nonetheless, this indifference must not become the object of vacuous moralising that blames those caught up in the state of exception for insufficient resistance to it. Instead, we must recognise that the pathway out of anomie into a new nomos is not merely empirically problematic but conceptually inconsistent. As long as we search for the way out of *bespedel* through the negation of its negativity, we are bound to remain within its nihilistic coordinates: nothing is more nihilistic than a negation of nihilism (Esposito 2008: 45–76). The passage from anomie to nomos is exactly the *same* passage that leads from nomos to anomie. Reversing the direction merely ensures that we remain literally in the same place and the possibility of a relapse back into anomie remains safe, as the residents of Kuschevskaya who have lived through over a decade of campaigns for the rule for law and against corruption know all too well. In the case of the postcommunist *bespedel* we are not dealing with an externally induced disorder that could be eliminated by a return to order, grounded either in the depths of tradition or in rational design, but with the actualisation of the potentiality at work in any form of constituted order. If, as we have seen, anomie is not the opposite of the nomos but is inscribed within it as the potentiality of its self-suspension that remains amenable to management by scheming and intrigue, then there is little sense in fighting anomie with any nomological politics.

Nor is it possible to evade the condition of *bespedel* by retreating from the degraded and inoperative nomos into a pre-nomological state of nature, since in the condition of *bespedel*, history merges irreparably with nature and there is no longer a possibility of distinguishing between the two (Agamben 2005a: 87–8; 1998: 188). It is at this point of apparent impasse that Agamben deploys his characteristic move of finding the possibility of redemption in the conditions of utmost hopelessness and despair. In accordance with Hölderlin's famous phrase, Agamben finds 'saving power' where we are accustomed to see only danger (Agamben 1998: 187–8; 1991: 108; see also Prozorov 2010). We have no hope of evading the state of exception by opting for the uncontaminated normativity of *bios* or the naturalism of *zoē*. What we can do, however, is appropriate this condition for a different, profane *use*, whereby anomie stops being the privilege of the sovereign, authorising its recourse to violence, but is rather extended to the entire domain of social praxis (see Agamben 2007: 73–92; 2005b: 26–9, 134–7).

This reappropriation of anomie, whose logic in the postcommunist context we have analysed elsewhere, resonates with Benjamin's notion of the 'real state of exception' which differs from the sovereign state of exception in its severing all ties with the law and the state form, even the purely formal ties that we have described in terms of the cratocratic management of anomie through scheming and violence:

> Only if it is possible to think the Being of abandonment beyond every idea of the law (even that of the empty form of law's being in force without significance) will we have moved out of the paradox of sovereignty towards a politics freed from every ban. (Agamben 1998: 59)

In this appropriation of abandonment, *bespedel* no longer functions as the condition of separation and disempowerment but is rather the site of potential emancipation that, moreover, is entirely of our own making as the effect of the dissolution of Soviet socialism. The extreme potentiality that characterises *bespedel* must therefore not be effaced, minimised or regulated, but rather brought wholly into actuality as the concrete experience of freedom (see Agamben 1991: 84–98; 1995: 73–82).

In this process of reappropriation, the postcommunist state must be approached neither as a privileged object of struggle nor as the omnipotent obstacle to emancipation, but simply as one among many hazards that surround us in this limitless domain in which no norms may be expected to apply. Precisely because *bespedel* is defined by the suspension of every norm, any elaboration of the logic of its reappropriation in normative terms is entirely beside the point. What is needed and presently lacking in postcommunist Russia is rather an immanently developed form of practical reason, a *phronesis* for *bespedel* that seeks to evade the powers of the schemers that presently manage it. Only by out-scheming the schemers of the state of exception will it become possible to transform what is now an anomic zone of abandonment and disempowerment into the site of emancipatory social praxis: 'The prison must imprison itself. Only thus will the prisoners be able to make their way out' (Agamben 1995: 99). While Agamben's theory firmly establishes the possibility of this mode of emancipation, it is neither a matter of historical necessity nor of yet another historical project, but remains entirely contingent on the concrete practices that apply the logic of anomie to anomie itself, thereby overcoming our separation from our own limitless potentiality.

References

Agamben, G. (1991), *Language and Death: The Place of Negativity*. Minneapolis: University of Minnesota Press.

—(1995), *The Idea of Prose*. New York: State University of New York Press.

—(1998), *Homo Sacer: Sovereign Power and Bare Life*, trans. D. Heller-Roazen. Stanford: Stanford University Press.

—(1999), *Remnants of Auschwitz: The Witness and the Archive*, trans. D. Heller-Roazen. New York: Zone Books.

—(2005a), *State of Exception*, trans. K. Attell. Chicago: University of Chicago Press.

—(2005b), *The Time That Remains: A Commentary on the Letter to the Romans*, trans. P. Dailey. Stanford: Stanford University Press.

—(2007), *Profanations*. New York: Zone Books.

—(2011), *The Sacrament of Language: An Archaeology of the Oath*. Stanford: Stanford University Press.

Anderson, P. (2007), 'Russia's Managed Democracy', *London Review of Books*, 29(2): 3–12, available at http://www.lrb.co.uk/v29/no2/andeo1_.html, accessed 14 March 2010.

Artemov, A. (2010), 'Organizator Rezni v Kushevskoi Ustroil Isteriku', *Argumenty i Fakty*, available at http://www.aif.ru/society/article/39101, accessed 14 March 2010.

Baker, P. and S. Glasser (2005), *Kremlin Rising: Vladimir Putin's Russia and the End of Revolution*. New York: Simon and Schuster.

Benjamin, W. (2003), *The Origin of German Tragic Drama*. London: Verso.

DeCaroli, S. (2007), 'Boundary Stones: Giorgio Agamben and the Field of Sovereignty', in M. Calarco and S. DeCaroli (eds), *Giorgio Agamben: Sovereignty and Life*. Stanford: Stanford University Press, 43–68.

Delyagin, M. (2007), 'Chekizm: Silovaja Oligarkhia kak Rodimoe Pyatno Yeltsinizma', *APN*, available at http://www.apn.ru/publications/article18498.htm, accessed 14 March 2008.

Esposito, R. (2008), *Bios: Biopolitics and Philosophy*. Minneapolis: University of Minnesota Press.

Fursov, A. (1991), 'Kratokratia', *Sotsium*, 8: 111–17.

Gazeta.ru Editorial (2011), available at http://www.gazeta.ru/news/lenta/2011/01/11/n_1651206.shtml, accessed 16 September 2011.

Gudkov, L. (2001), 'Russia: A Society in Transition?' *Telos*, 120: 9–30.

Harding, L. (2010), 'WikiLeaks Cables Condemn Russia as "Mafia State"', *Guardian*, 1 December, available at http://www.guardian.co.uk/world/2010/dec/01/wikileaks-cables-russia-mafia-kleptocracy?INTCMP=SRCH, accessed 16 September 2011.

Illarionov, A. (2007), '"Silovaya Model" Gosudarstva', *Kommersant*, 53: 4.

King, C. and R. Menon (2010), 'Prisoners of the Caucasus: Russia's Invisible Civil War', *Foreign Affairs*, 89(4): 20–34.

Kryshtanovskaya, O. (2005), *Anatomia Rossiyskoi Elity*. Moscow: Zakharov.

Laclau, E. (2005), *On Populist Reason*. London: Verso.

—(2007), 'Bare Life or Social Indeterminacy', in M. Calarco and S. DeCaroli (eds), *Giorgio Agamben: Sovereignty and Life*. Stanford: Stanford University Press.

Lebedeva, A. (2010), 'Mezhdu Tsapkom i Tsepovyazom', *Russkiy Reporter*, 45(173), available at http://rusrep.ru/article/2010/11/16/kuban/, accessed 16 September 2011.

Magun, A. (2008), *Otritsatelnaja Revolutsia: K Dekonstruktsii Politicheskogo Subjekta*. St Petersburg: European University Press.

Passavant, P. A. (2007), 'The Contradictory State of Giorgio Agamben', *Political Theory* 35(2): 147–74.

Prozorov, S. (2008), 'Russian Postcommunism and the End of History', *Studies in East European Thought*, 60: 207–30.

—(2009), *The Ethics of Postcommunism: History and Social Praxis in Russia*. Basingstoke: Palgrave.

—(2010), 'Why Giorgio Agamben is an Optimist', *Philosophy and Social Criticism*, 36: 1053–73.

Sakwa, R. (2004), *Putin: Russia's Choice*. London: Routledge.

Schmitt, C. (1985), *Political Theology: Four Chapters on the Concept of Sovereignty*. Cambridge, MA: MIT Press.

—(1994), *Die Diktatur*. Berlin: Duncker and Humblot.

Sokolov-Mitrich, D. (2010), 'Zakon Tsapka', *Russkiy Reporter*, 47(175), available at http://rusrep.ru/article/2010/12/01/kuschevskaya/, accessed 16 September 2011.

Tirmastae, M. L. (2010), 'Sergeja Tsapka Zapisali v Edinuju Rossiu', *Kommersant*, 230(4530), available at http://www.kommersant.ru/doc-y.aspx?DocsID=1556538, accessed 16 September 2011.

Truscott, P. (2005), *Putin's Progress*. New York: Simon and Schuster.

Volkov, V. (2002), *Violent Entrepreneurs: The Use of Force in the Making of Russian Capitalism*. Ithaca, NY: Cornell University Press.

3

The Cultural Politics of Exception

Marcelo Svirsky

> The profanation of the unprofanable is the political task of the coming generation.
>
> (Agamben 2007: 92)

By focusing on the ontological notion of 'exceptionality' present in Agamben's *oeuvre*, rather than on 'states of exception', I adhere to the claim that Agamben's conceptual tools are relevant to the cultural analysis of settler-colonial societies. At its core, his work is sensitive to anxieties about decolonisation, though his concepts require some philosophical adaptation if this relevance is to be made explicit. My reading aims to supplement and expand Agamben's conceptual apparatus with insights from two sources: one is Esposito's 'immunitarian' paradigm; and the other is Deleuze and Guattari's politics of desire.

Exception and Exemption

A sincere and real concern for European downfall into dictatorship is present in Agamben's works.[1] What sustains this concern is both an assumption about, and a lament for, a democratic canon under crisis. Exception, *homo sacer*, bare life, the camp are all signs of this decline. But the fault has no origin: it cannot be found in a sort of self-deteriorating political culture crystallised in draconic laws, nor in a reverse trajectory led by opportunistic leaderships. Glocal events and processes – such as migration, unemployment and terrorism – lash the spheres of culture, law and politics, actualising new xenophobic demons. It is in the conjunction of these actual selections that we find the fault. All in all, Agamben's concern is about a fault in a canon, and a lament. However, joy and distress cohabit in the form of the lament, the former pointing to past glories and to their appreciation, the latter to coming horrors.

Such a lament is not possible everywhere. It is geo-culturally bounded; in many aspects, it is enviable. In active settler-colonial societies such as Israel, for instance, there is no desirable democratic tradition, now undergoing a decay that is cause for lament. As Ilan Pappe states, Agamben is right that Europe 'should regain its canon, but it is a canon that can be retrieved. Israel's anti-democratic canon, however, is still alive and kicking' (Pappe 2007: 157). From the point of view of exception, an important distinction arises in regard to the object of critique and resistance: while in Europe the fault to be addressed is exception as a form of treacherous disequilibrium, in active settler-colonial societies the malady lies in the normative ways of existence, in the equilibrium itself. So, while in the first case resistance should be launched to disarm the exception to the rule, in the second case it should attack the rule itself. To put this more clearly: Europe must retreat from states of exception to fly over pluralistic horizons which somehow engage, through novel ways, with its democratic and liberal genealogies. In Israel, resistance needs to bring the state to cede on *what it is* – an active settler-colonial entity – to give way to new democratic compositions: it is Israel's normal ways of life that need to be abandoned, profaned. Europe and Israel are two different entities, two different milieus, and what is exceptional in one is not necessarily so in the other.

It seems Pappe is right that Agamben's paradigm of exception is just not applicable to places such as Israel. Worse, 'the very discussion of Israel within the parameters of this debate assumes that Israel is another case of a Western liberal democracy dangerously deteriorating into the abyss dreaded by Agamben' (Pappe 2007: 149). Nothing can please Zionists more: to have their little machines of cleansing, segregation and discrimination catalogued as 'democratic'. In this respect, the democratic charade of pseudo-heroic attempts by liberal Zionist politicians, allegedly to halt exception, is no more than that, a posturing spectacle, staged as an integral part of the real drama of ethnocracy (Yiftachel 2006). This is not to say that Israeli rule cannot deteriorate, but rather that it cannot 'deteriorate' into that which resembles its very history, composition and aspirations. Israel might free itself totally from its democratic procedures, it may continue restricting freedom of expression, it can strengthen ethnic segregation, employ more forcefully its emergency laws and so on. This deterioration does not express its alienation from a previously democratic state, but rather signals a halt to the democratic spectacle; as such, it cannot be measured with the methods provided by Agamben's concept of the state of exception.

However, there is something about the idea of exceptionality, and specifically in the way Agamben uses it, which makes us search for exceptionalism everywhere a wrong is committed. As this volume demonstrates, the paradigm of exception is applicable to other settler-colonial societies, including Australia, the United States and Argentina. The latter is an especially interesting case because on the one hand Argentina lacks the sort of European democratic tradition which may feed a lament for its loss, while on the other hand the analysis of exception that Grinberg's chapter advances points to a dimension which Agamben's legal-political paradigm does not encompass directly: that of specifically colonial ways of abandonment that perpetuate urban poverty and are implicated in contemporary practices of legal and political exception. This focus adds a further dimension of analysis – that of ways of existence – which enriches Agamben's work on the distinction between determinate 'forms of life', and a 'form-of-life' that stresses the character of potentiality in life itself (Agamben 2000: 3–14).

Ways of existence refer to what is socio-politically and culturally normal or regular in a society, and to their alternatives. So, we have two terms in juxtaposition: settler-colonial ways of existence and Agamben's states of exception. But the chapters on Australia, the US and Argentina in this volume show that the relation between these two terms is not one of juxtaposition but one of intersection, they appear as transvers-able. Therefore, we need to analyse how exceptionality, broadly understood, is akin to settler-colonialism: in Agamben's claim about 'the suspension of the norm', what sort of norm is assumed?

My contention is that Agamben's paradigm of exception is limited if considered in isolation from a local political culture and its formative history. In itself – as an analytical device of the legal-political sphere – the paradigm might appear to omit crucial aspects of social, cultural and political life that define the historical background in which legal and political measures (those defined by Agamben as exceptional) are implemented. Even Agamben's critique of the structure of the law cannot square the circle.

According to Agamben, exception is not something 'outside' of the law; rather, it 'is the originary form of law' (1998: 26). In other words, its regulative and self-referential nature (grounding the command inherent in the law) contains and tolerates its own transgression, and thus it virtually anticipates legal and political devaluations such as those adopted by Western countries after 9/11 (cf. de la Durantaye 2009: 338–45). For this reason Agamben claims that the state of exception holds together a normative and an anomic element (Agamben 2005: 86). But this structural exceptionality did not impede Europe in its development of some positive forms of democratic life. There remains a need to supplement – or perhaps to filter – Agamben's paradigm with a theory that takes account of historically and culturally distinct ways of existence, and which might enable a wider applicability of that paradigm.

Keeping the preoccupation with exceptionality central to the discussion, I turn to another Italian philosopher of exceptionality, Roberto Esposito. Three of Esposito's works are fundamentally relevant in this sense: *Immunitas* (2005), *Bios* (2008) and *Communitas* (2010).[2] The line of thought in these works is an investigation of the role played by the idea and practice of 'immunisation' in 'the principles on which communities are founded' (Campbell 2006: 2). As I will show in a moment, Esposito's immunitarian paradigm is useful in the context of the colonial encounter and indeed adds historical context to Agamben's theory of exception. In distinction to Derrida, who reduced the category of immunity into the concept of auto-immunity to depict American geopolitics of 'homeland security' after 9/11 (Borradori 2003), Esposito relies on the immunitarian paradigm to envisage a political relationality that – by bypassing the ruse of otherness – escapes from immunisation into a communitised life. For this very reason, it provides a way of thinking that allows movement from a dichotomising political language obsessed with oppressors and subaltern subjects, into one that is sensitive to the ways of existence stolen from us by the colonial encounter.

Esposito roots his analysis of what a community has in common in the common etymology of community and immunity, *munus*, the 'substance that is produced by their union' (Esposito 2010: 2). The *munus* establishes a reciprocal gift between those forming the union and so founding a people, and 'he who has been freed from communal obligations or who enjoys an originary autonomy or successive freeing from a previously contracted debt [and thus] enjoys the condition of immunitas' (Campbell 2006: 3). Immunity, then, appears as a condition of exceptionality, a move that extraordinarily opens a distance of negation that releases a subject from a commitment. The *immunitas* thus constructed 'is not only the exemption from commitment but something that interrupts the social circuit of reciprocal donation' (Esposito 2005: 16), and therefore the perfect opposite of *immunitas* is not the absent *munus* but the *communitas* of its potential carriers (15). Principally, Esposito applies this logic to explain how modern immunisation functions to preserve antinomies in the self-other relation, and for its most part, in *Immunitas* he employs the immunity category to interpret biopolitical policies of restoration that respond to intrusive dangers – policies that, according to Esposito, nowadays approximate dangerous thresholds. For Esposito, the first element that stands out in the immunitarian paradigm

> is that it presents itself not in terms of action but of reaction; more than a force in itself, it is a kickback, a counterforce, impeding the manifestation of another force. This means that the immunitary mechanism presupposes the wrong it confronts. (Esposito 2005: 17)

However, towards the end of the book, Esposito joins Alfred Tauber in considering the constitution or foundation of the collective subject, in contrast to its reaction and conservation, as the fundamental function of immunity. According to Tauber, 'the conservation of the organic integrity is only a secondary function of the immunitary system, if compared with the principal function which is to define the identity of the subject' (Esposito 2005: 236).[3] This conceptual relocation of what is prior in immunity (thereby making conservation dependent on foundation) is especially helpful when applied in the context of the colonial encounter.

I have explained elsewhere that from the early twentieth century Zionist settlers in Palestine produced a Jewish society totally separated from the native Palestinian society in housing, labour, education, social welfare, culture and politics (Svirsky 2010; 2012; cf. Shafir 1989; Smith 1993; Lockman 1996; Bernstein 2000). By exonerating itself from the dynamics of reciprocity with the native Palestinian, Zionism refused the gift of the common presence (Simmel 1950: 45). This has been defined by Veracini as 'the settler colonial non-encounter, a circumstance fundamentally shaped by a recurring need to disavow the presence of indigenous others' (Veracini 2011: 2). As is well acknowledged, this disavowal was, and is still, accompanied by a logic of replacement: 'racism never detects the particles of the other; it propagates waves of sameness until those who resist identification have been wiped out' (Deleuze and Guattari 1987: 178). In rejecting contiguity, proximity and familiarity, Zionism materialised a certain version of what is *not in common* as its mode of engagement with the concrete other. Importantly, what is at stake in the ungrateful rejection of a human encounter is the a priori cancellation of the reciprocal alterity inherent in it, the separation of bodies from the possibility of opening subjectivities to alteration by concrete others, and their distancing from collaborative and shared ways of existence. If anything characterises the embryonic Jewish settler society during the first half of the twentieth century and the formation of Israel as a state, it is the consolidation of a new political society that affirms identity as crucially based on ethnic separatism. This double refusal – of collaborative ways of existence and of the alterity implicated in them – constructed by Zionism as its own 'wrong', is the way Zionism immunised itself from intercultural life. The Jewish society in Palestine built itself up as a political immunity: a closed polity, a fortress that from its outset cultivated an oppositional and 'cleansing' attitude towards the indigenous Palestinian. However, the displacement of alterity, its repositioning afar, becomes the strategy of the *immunitas* as it simultaneously becomes its unavoidable horizon of resistance. In other words, if truly leading to structural political change, the struggle over Palestine needs to be seen first and foremost as a struggle to de-immunise Israel's space of control, as a commitment to community.

Immunity insinuated itself in the workings of the Zionist project at the formative level of constitution of the structure; however, it was not out of an original fear and insecurity Zionism built itself in Palestine around the principle of immunity. Paranoiac-persecutory machines evolved only when the stress and pressure of incomplete ethnic cleansings induced collective anxiety – or 'social phobia' as Stravynski (2007) defined it – and this eventually dominated inter-communal relationships in Palestine. Perhaps, as Piterberg explains, the very first indication of this collective anxiety is to be found right after the 1948–9 ethnic raid, in the decision '*to prevent Palestinian Arabs at all costs from returning to their homes*' (Piterberg 2001: 34, original emphasis; see Pappe 2006). It is a fact that immunitarian mechanisms are present in settler-colonial societies as a force of political conservation, but they fundamentally work as part of a historically developing, immunitary structuring dynamic.

In 2003 the Knesset (the Israeli parliament) amended the Law of Citizenship (revision 5763), so as to avoid the naturalisation of Palestinians from the occupied territories of the West Bank and Gaza by their marrying Israeli citizens. The amendment, ratified four years later by the Supreme Court, could have been considered in relation to Agamben's idea of exception as an application of the latest Western trends of securitisation and anti-migration. In another case, in July 2011 the Knesset passed the Law for the Prevention of Harm to the State of Israel by Means of Boycott which criminalises individual citizens of Israel who support the Palestinian call for boycott, divestment and sanctions (BDS). Again, the political implications of this law may easily be analysed using Agambenian categories. In the first case, the law aims at keeping apart two of the three sectors of the Palestinian people, those holding Israeli citizenship and the residents of the occupied territories (the third sector is comprised of the Palestinian diaspora). In so doing, tendencies to jeopardise the Jewish majority are regulated. In the second case, it is no secret that the Israeli government aimed at crushing the political collaboration between Israeli citizens, Jews and Palestinians, and the Palestinian organisations leading the BDS movement. In both cases, the state continues to immunise itself from shared ways of life. In comparison with the anti-migration and 'homeland security' types of law mushrooming in the West, it is more precise to conflate these two Israeli laws with another law, also recently enacted (in March 2011). This is the Admission Committees Law, which screens and excludes Palestinian families from rural housing on state-owned land. Its aim is to preserve and expand Jewish homogeneity in areas in which the state is interested in counterbalancing Palestinian presence. Perhaps this law has indirect connections with current globalising white anxieties, but its immunitarian machine fundamentally epitomises the genealogy and hopes of the Jewish state and its Jewish majority. What unites these three laws is the exemptive demographics at work, resonating with the core ambition of the Zionist political culture that has been evolving since the historical encounter with the Palestinians became colonial. To express this more clearly: the historical exemption from a commitment to community (the *immunitas* the Zionist enclave thus built) became a commitment to an exemption from intercultural and collaborative ways of existence shared by all communities. It should be clear that this exemption thus conceived does not express a lack or an object of craving; rather, its absence is a historical result of a collective production.

As said before, the preoccupation with exceptionality in ways of life, or forms of life, is not alien to Agamben. In the section titled 'Form-of-Life' in *Means Without End*, he designates '*form-of-life* [. . . as] a life in which it is never possible to isolate something such as naked life' (2000: 2.3–3.4, original emphasis), a sort of virtuality which can never be exhausted. The concept associates actual ways of life, or what I termed here ways of existence, with the idea of the possibility – or better, possibilities – that remain permanently unrealised within them, 'always and above all power' (3.4). Exemption, in Esposito's parlance, encapsulates the separation Agamben points to here of specific spheres of life, or 'forms of life' as revolving around, or developing as actualised forms, from the foundational 'form-of-life' as 'naked life'. Importantly, Agamben stresses that it is in the sovereign separation itself that we find the birth of the regularisation of the state of exception. Esposito's immunity is congruent with the foreclosure of the immanent potentiality of the 'form-of-life', and Agamben's call for the removal of that which separates and divides in order to retain the character of the possibility (in forms of life) likewise shares similar concerns with Esposito's articulation of 'de-immunisation'.

However, expanding the preoccupation with exceptionality through Esposito's immunitarian paradigm makes an important gain. As is well known, a too-close reading of Agamben's exceptionality has led scholars to vest on subaltern subjects the jacket of exception, making them the very carriers of it. Undoubtedly, some of Agamben's concepts invite such conceptualisation. This is especially true with the notion of the camp, a spatiality that hosts only well-defined subjects, and with *homo sacer* as an individualised form of subjectivity. This is problematic for at least two reasons. First, vesting subaltern subjects with the mark of exception reterritorialises their underprivileged place in language and emotion, so we find ourselves struggling twice: initially to rescue a perception of rebellion out of the dark image of oppression; and then additionally, for a better life. Second, the vest of exception brings scholars to feature 'subjects to whom all manner of things are done, often in arbitrary and violent ways, but [who are] rarely agents in their own right' (Walters 2008: 188). Passivity is the common denominator of these two types of discursive construction. The gain in theoretical insight afforded by the viewpoint of immunity, on the other hand, is that it desubjectivises the operation of exceptionality. It opens the study of exceptionalism from the production of collective subjects placed beyond the lines of exception, into an analysis of the ways of life denied to us as a result of exclusionary historical processes. In other words, exception interpreted solely through the eyes of exemption places the problematic at the level of constitutive problem, rather than at the level of the subject and its identity.

With Esposito's concept of immunitary exemption in the background, we may now rearticulate the critical claim made about the inapplicability of Agamben's paradigm to settler-colonial societies such as Israel. The claim is fair as long as exception is understood as a 'juridical situation', its prosaic legal-political application stripped of any historical and cultural consideration. But in fact, it will not be right to apply the paradigm in this way in any case, not just in settler-colonial societies. Agamben's appreciation of European democracy as that which anchors the lament already offers a strong historical and cultural consideration. The most significant aspect of Agamben's paradigm is its preoccupation with exceptionality, and in Esposito's exemption we find the conceptual viaduct through which this preoccupation might reach other analytical shores.

The Active Foundation

The denial of intercultural life that Zionist colonialism brought upon Palestine was born from the interruptions to the 'social circuit of reciprocal donation' (Esposito 2005: 16) between natives and newcomers, which in spite of the colonial divide have prospered in the past (Bernstein 2000; Campos 2011) and do exist in the present (Svirsky 2012).[4] The growth of these interruptions of potential intercultural connections *is* the growth of the Zionist immunitarian social circuit of reciprocal donation: both are one and only one production. Importantly, the crescendos and decrescendos in the vitality of a social circuit cannot remain 'unnoticed by the citizens', as Agamben claims with respect to the latest transformations of the constitutional order in the West (Agamben 2005: 14), but rather depend on their everyday commitment. The point is that the Zionist immunitarian binding, the daily execution of exemption, cannot be understood only in terms of leadership decision making, particularly in Israel where the majority of the Jewish population 'is aware of the oppression and fully endorses and supports it' (Pappe 2007: 151). David Hare's stupefied commentary on the massive support for the Wall separating Israel proper and the West Bank is telling:

> Have you ever known anything of which 84 percent of people were in favour of? And yet there it is, over four fifths of a nation – can you imagine that figure? – saying something completely bizarre. The Berlin Wall was built to keep people in. This one, they say, is being built to keep people out. (Hare 2009: 8)

It is important then to bring to the fore ordinary Israelis' immunitarian habits, the trivial participations of persons who, performing their everyday lives – 'each with his little machines' (Deleuze and Guattari 1983: 1) – recurrently engage their bodies in the activation of practices of exclusion and segregation. However, most Israelis would not perceive their everyday activities as having anything to do with practices that involve strongly fascist elements such as militarism, anti-egalitarianism, demographics, historical restoration and a strong sense of blood tribalism. The story of housing discrimination in rural areas in Israel is illustrative. I mentioned above that in March 2011 the Knesset enacted the Admission Committees Law. The government of Israel had always conceptualised the internal territory as a major political target for demographic and cultural conquest. Fundamentally, this assumes the Palestinian citzenry within Israel are unwelcome and extrinsic to the major aims of the state.The flagship project of this political conception is 'Judaisation'. The Judaisation of the Galilee for instance, is an official plan (launched in the late 1960s) which since the 1980s has taken as its basic aim the settling of upper-middle-class families in new small gated communities, building a home and garden lifestyle for Jews only, fully invested with new roads, well-equipped with educational systems and cultural and sports centres, and wrapped with the warm mantle of governmental ideological and economic support (Falah 1991; Yiftachel

2006). Strategically, Judaisation projects dilute Palestinian land resources, truncate the territorial continuity of Palestinian cities and villages, and make demographics the first language of politics (Yiftachel and Carmon 1997).[5]

The new Admission Committees Law provides Regional Councils with legal power to undertake 'admission committees' through which housing applicants are screened according to a principle of social suitability – aimed to suit the particular 'texture' of the communities. In practice this principally serves the objective of screening Palestinian families. In the past, before the law was enacted, the 'admission committees' were manned by residents within the communities. The main point is that the 'admission committees' in their past and present incarnations have the sole goal of preserving a high degree of ethnic and socio-economic homogeneity in these communities.

For more than a decade, a few activist organisations have worked to eradicate the 'admission committees' and transform these rural communities, built on public land (expropriated from Palestinain owners), into open and democratic forms.[6] In 2000, the Supreme Court accepted the principle of equality and the prohibition against discrimination as a guiding principle in housing and land allocation, following a petition of Adel and Iman Qa'adan, a Palestinian family of Baqa al-Gharbiyye, who applied to live in Katzir in 1994 (Davis 2003: 189);[7] but it did not abolish the 'admission committees'. However, the Qa'adan case was seen as a first sign of an unwelcome democratic development, certainly by many residents in the gated communities, as well as in relevant state institutions such as the Israel Land Administration (ILA), the Jewish Agency and the Knesset.[8] A further event caused people and institutions to take things into their own hands: in 2006, Fatinah Abrik and Ahmed Zbeidat from Sakhnin – with the support of six different NGOs – appealed to the Supreme Court after their application for housing in Rakefet, a small Galilean community in the Misgav area, was refused (Svirsky 2012). This time, however, the petitioners did not restrict the plea to the particular case of discrimination of the Palestinain couple and instead demanded the wholesale abolition of the 'admission committees'.

The legal-political race to change and adapt the ILA regulations and eventually the enactment of the Admission Committees Law in the Knesset is the formal institutional aspect of the reaction to restore immunisatory mechanisms. But to my mind, the popular grassroots efforts of regular residents in the gated communities, who recruited themselves to save the nation from the claws of egalitarianism, deserve no less attention. Since the Rakefet plea was submitted, two communities in the Galilean Misgav Regional Council sanctioned the use of an internal code to shore up the selective system of housing admission. In Manof and Mitzpe Aviv groups of worried and panicked residents gathered, discussed and pushed for decisions in their General Assemblies. In Yuvalim, Rakefet, Ya'ad and Atzmon (all communities in Misgav) these proposals are still being discussed. These upper-middle-class citizens, the majority of whom traditionally vote for Zionist leftist political parties, join forces to assemble stronger reterritorialisations of ethnic immunity. As an example, in November 2009 the Mitzpe Aviv General Assembly accorded that the purpose of the community is, among other things: 'to promote settlement, Zionism, Jewish traditions, and the Jewish character of Israel' – and anchored these as the criteria for acceptance of new residents (Mitzpe Aviv Regulations 2009: chapter a, section 2; chapter b, section 4). We should note that it is not representative professionals or technocrats but the local people residing in these communities that staff the 'admission committees' and decide upon the families applying for admission to their communities. The Admission Committees Law certainly poses a challenge to the activist groups working for equality in housing, but more fundamentally, there is a stronger process on the ground which activism must take into account: the wide immunitarian commitment to actively refuse intercultural housing.

The way I have led this narrative leaves no room to speculate on classical Marxian 'false consciousness' or Žižekean 'cynicism' as possible explanations of the intimate fascist engagements of these Galilean residents (Buchanan 2008: 125–32). If we were to look to cynicism, the explanation for the banning attitude towards housing Palestinian families would be that the immunitarians know that what they are pushing for is wrong, but all the same . . . 'this is a Jewish state'. In fact, most of them do not acknowledge their personal wrongdoing: they do know what they do – they do not pretend – but they engage with it emotionally and discursively in a fashion that erases from consciousness any trace of wrongness. The deed is contextualised in terms of the sort of regime Israel is and the sort of political culture they maintain, which means that acts of exclusion are not about doing wrong but about securing rightful privileges, according to the norms of the regime. If asked about the rightfulness or otherwise of these practices going on elsewhere, these active immunitarians would likely condemn them. Can this misplacement be corrected? As Buchanan explains, following Deleuze, there is no truth 'out there' that can save us. Cynicism and false consciousness

> reason that if we knew the truth about our situation we would be compelled to act, therefore the fact that we do not act must mean we have disavowed the truth either by suppressing all knowledge of it from ourselves or by choosing not to acknowledge its implications. (Buchanan 2008: 132)

But how, then, may we explain exclusionary practices, if not with reference to false consciousness or cynicism?

One of the central claims in Deleuze and Guattari's *Anti-Oedipus* (1983) is that the practice of fascism is not an ideological problem but one that is related to the historical production of *desire* as a social machine. This is quite shocking for activists convinced that a thorough critique of ideology, of its negative effects in everyday life, may lead people to engage differently. In *Anti-Oedipus*, Deleuze and Guattari turn away from the traditional logic of desire that has dominated the Western philosophical tradition from Plato to Lacan and has compelled us to 'choose between *production* and *acquisition*' (Deleuze and Guattari 1983: 25, original emphasis). They conceptualise desire alternatively, as 'desiring-production' carried out by 'desiring-machines'.[9] According to the factory model of 'desiring-production', desire invests the social landscape with forces of construction: 'the production is itself the process of desire' (Bignall 2011: 146). Desiring-production is social production: 'there is only desire and the social, and nothing else' (Deleuze and Guattari 1983: 28–9). When I claimed in the previous section of this chapter that the *colonial* nature of the historical encounter of Palestinians and Zionist settlers produced two separated societies in Palestine (three in fact, if we take into account the British Mandate administration and its functionaries), now we may stress that this sense of the encounter – the significance of *the colonial* – was constructed as that which expresses the different libidinal connections, and refusal to begin connections, engineered in various social spheres (Svirsky 2010; 2012). 'Desire begins with connections [. . . that] eventually form social wholes;

when bodies connect with other bodies to enhance their power they eventually form communities or societies' (Colebrook 2002: 91; cf. Buchanan 2008: 95).

We live the consequences of colonisation. This is particularly painful in a society that actively reaffirms, in new ways, old colonial allegiances historically constructed. The commitment to the immunitarian exemption started with the very production of it, and it became the real infrastructure that represses our machinic desire to proliferate new 'forms of life'. People became committed to these practices and they reacted to conserve them when activism put them at risk. The politics they unfold are the politics of desire, the complex composition of a historical infrastructure of desire intersecting and capturing forces that would otherwise connect in less paranoiac ways (Deleuze and Guattari 1983: 344–8).[10] Zionism's most incisive achievement is to have built a stable commitment to its historical gains, to the point that any negation of homogeneity is thought of as a degeneration of collective life. The enormous debt thus constructed suffocates and funnels desire, forcing its creative productions to follow predetermined forms and categories (such as exceptionalism in housing), thereby reterritorialising subjectivities according to the 'us/them' mode.[11]

'Active foundation' is the denotation we can use to signify the forces feeding into the explicit behaviours involved in the production and maintenance of exceptionality (read as occlusion from shared and collaborative ways of existence), as the actualisations of the intersections between the machinic operation of bodies (read as the operations of desire) and the social field (read as the accumulative historical production of structures through desire). It is in this respect that the established colonial patterning of desire makes most Israelis willing exemptionists. Immunitarians do not fool themselves about what they do; neither are they tricked by the exigencies of hegemony. It is in this sense that Deleuze and Guattari (1983: 29) join the Austrian-American psychiatrist William Reich to claim that 'under a certain set of conditions', people want fascism. The 'active foundation' is what secures the continuity of exceptionality (again, read as a certain form of refusal of alternative ways of existence); it is simultaneously its cause and effect, its social consistency. In the context of a desirable normative tradition we lament its corruption, the 'active foundation' secures the cultural possibility and practicality of the paradox involved in states of exception, that fluidity which makes it viable that the law suspends itself: the various anti-migrationist and pro-securitisation laws and policies proliferating in the West cannot hold for long without support from the microphysics of paranoiac collective desires.

For this reason, offering to individuals alternative interpretations of their deeds (the Marxian chimera behind some forms of activism) may barely change their commitment to certain problematic social practices. Alternative connections are required and demand a project of experimentation – freeing desire from its capture in established forms – and in this process, also undoing given subjectivities. The point is that even though one might change fascist political attitudes, the change will be deceiving if one keeps existing exclusionary lifestyles intact. Thus, activism is not a problem of the interpretation of the real, but one of knowing how and what reality is being produced, and how to produce it alternatively. In other words, as Guattari suggests, we need to recognise the 'machinic dimensions of subjectivation' (Guattari 1995: 4).

Heterodoxies

Unjustly, some theoretical appropriations of Agamben's conceptual tools have rendered his work as imposing on subaltern subjects a lack of agency. In this guise, resistance appears as a non-concept in Agamben. But as de la Durantaye explains, 'the search for [. . .] "new politics" is, for Agamben, an unquestionably urgent one' (de la Durantaye 2009: 236–8). In *Means Without End* Agamben endorses the erosion of the principle of nativity and the trinity state-nation-territory as the only way to transgress actual forms of sovereignty and citizenship. 'Only in a world', writes Agamben, 'in which the spaces have been perforated and topologically deformed and in which the citizen has been able to recognize the refugee that he or she is – only in such a world is the political survival of humankind today thinkable' (Agamben 2000: 25.6). Is not that 'perforation of spaces' that which is avoided through the immunitarian cord that keeps apart communities in Israel-Palestine? In 'The Face', Agamben looks for resistance in faciality, as an interstice, a threshold through which the potentiality of de-identification is discernible:

My face is my *outside*: a point of indifference with respect to all of my properties, with respect to what is properly one's own and what is in common [. . .] the face is the threshold of de-propriation and de-identification of all manners and of all qualities [. . .] And only where I find a face do I encounter an exteriority and does an *outside* happen to me. (Agamben 2000: 98.9–99.0, original emphasis)

Article 1.2 of the first chapter of *State of Exception* opens by saying: 'One of the elements that makes the state of exception so difficult to define is certainly its close relationship to civil war, insurrection and resistance' (Agamben 2005: 2). Agamben places states of exception together with resistance to inhabit a conceptual 'zone of undecidability' (or of 'indistinction', in the work on *Homo Sacer*), a zone of thresholds and transformations. These are two forces pushing in opposite directions, one to keep anomie and nomos in substantial articulation, the other to 'loosen what has been artificially and violently linked' (87).

According to Agamben, exceptionalism grows in the juridical Petri dish that indistinguishably associates anomie and nomos. It is easier to pinpoint what exception produces – 'a killing machine' (Agamben 2005: 86) – than to fully understand the habitual that is suspended, precisely because 'such exceptional instances are not so exceptional' (de la Durantaye 2009: 336). In Agambenian terms, exceptions augur whole sets of distinctions, between anomie and nomos, between the rights of the citizen and the bare life of refugees in the camp, and so on. In the Agamben–Esposito combination, exemption explains the sets of distinctions between ways of life that capture social production to enfeeble our opposition to exceptionality in law and politics. Either way, de la Durantaye is right in stating that the main problem associated with exceptionalism is the way it produces 'the divisions and distinctions of contemporary society' (de la Durantaye 2009: 352). We have seen this in the two previous sections.

In fact, following Agamben, the main problem with exceptionalism is not the divisions and distinctions it provokes, but their consecration. Perhaps capitalist production is the holiest mode of being in our modern world. Here resides, I believe, the strongest plea for resistance in Agamben: his call 'to profane', most persuasively made in 'In Praise of Profanation' (2007). The sacred, explains Agamben, is that which is 'removed from the free use and commerce of men', and is placed in a zone of 'special unavailability' (Agamben 2007: 73), exempt from human use. In Israel, the 'sacredness' of racial segregation is anchored in the unavailability of intercultural life – a principle of organisation which is in fact the very foundation of the Zionist community. Only by profaning the sacred is the possibility of finding new social uses for housing, education, labour, and so on, returned to free experimentation. To profane, then, is to create an exception from the norm, in the form of a deterritorialisation, a flight from entrenched forms of life, that returns to life the free use of things:

> Profanation [. . .] neutralizes what it profanes. Once profaned, that which was unavailable and separate loses its aura and is returned to use [. . . it] deactivates the apparatuses of power and returns to common use the spaces that power had seized. (Agamben 2007: 77)

It is tempting to see in the magic possibility of rescuing an immolated being from its passage into the sacred, a chance to shatter the common commitment to the rite and to what it founds. On 25 June 2006, an Israeli soldier named Gilad Shalit was captured by a Hamas commando at a southern corner of the border with the Gaza Strip. Since then, the Israeli government has refused to release imprisoned Palestinians in a political exchange. Shalit's particular situation might be seen as a limbo, between his being as a living captive and his commitment to sacrifice himself as a soldier. This liminality, I shall explain, opens a magic possibility of profaning the binding and securing life. But his family, captive of the caesura that divides the profane and the sacred, has joined the government in another refusal of their own. In August 2009 Gilad's sister, Hadas, at the age of obligatory conscription, joined the army. Her parents did not hide their pride, and neither did their friends or other relatives – and the Hebrew-speaking media applauded. The sacred – the conscription into the Zionist army – thus remained sacred for the Shalit family, even with Gilad's captivity and in spite of the official refusal to cede and endorse an exchange. This leaves the power of the sacred intact (Agamben 2007: 77), sanctioning once again a religiosity that made redundant the uncountable demonstrations and acts of protest calling upon the government to negotiate with the captors. By this public refusal to profane the sacred, the government is not given reasons to reconsider its insistence on executing Gilad's sacrifice, which is itself rendered legitimate by his own conscription and, subsequently, by that of his sister.

The exceptional state of the captive soldier, framed by an

Isaac-type sacrifice to the segregated society to which he commits himself, offers a moment of reflection on the role of resistance, on profanation. The capture of soldiers may be seen as providing a transitional space in which, on the one hand, the sacred soldier 'has survived the rite that separated him from other men and continues to lead an apparently profane existence among them' (Agamben 2007: 78) – a space close to exceptional survival. On the other hand, as being in transition, the right (and the decision) over his body is still claimed by the state. The point is, however, that the zone of transition produced by this type of capture of the sacred opens up the potential to embrace resistance and to move the captive body closer to life in the process of profaning the sacred commitment.

Agamben is clear in that the dissolution of the division itself, the caesura between the sacred and the profane, is the location of resistance, the site of profanation:[12] 'To profane means to open the possibility of a special form of negligence, which ignores separation or, rather, puts it to a particular use' (Agamben 2007: 75). Agamben invokes Emile Benveniste to press home the idea of alternative uses that break the conjunction between 'the myth that tells the story and the rite that reproduces and stages it' (75). In Israel, the army is still unquestionably the most authoritative of all myths. It motorises a monstrous apparatus of whirling machines, which organise life from kindergarten to the final years of high school, making of this age a horizon towards which the system builds up an anxiety to enlist. Here we meet the double betrayal of Israeli teachers: first as mothers and fathers to their own children, and the second time as educators of society's children in general, they encourage the youth to immolate themselves. In the Hebrew-speaking society in Israel, socialisation should be read as immolation. However, maintaining a militarised society requires much effort which does not always pair global and local processes. Some studies report on the changing commitment of the Ashkenazi middle-class hegemony towards the practice of conscription (Levy and Lomsky-Feder 2007). The Israeli Defence Force reports every year on what they see as the 'alarming' descent in conscription numbers. So, it is not surprising that efforts to recruit the un-recruitable, as with the Jewish ultra-religious sector, have been in process for more than a decade. Only recently, the national-religious MK Zevulun Orlev (Habayit Hayehudi, the Jewish House Party), head of the Knesset Education Committee,

has proposed a bill to increase and expand the educational programmes to motivate recruitment in schools.

In Israel, almost-eighteen year olds from Jewish homes are never
asked about their plans to study or work; queries about their
immediate futures only concern the army unit into which they are
enlisting. Is any sentiment more disconcerting than the pride of
a parent for his or her child being recruited? Indeed, most Israeli
parents are proud to the point that they willingly miss the chance
to revert the colonial legacy of the social binding, to profane the
social bond. The communal binding offered to Jewish citizens
in Israel has only one possible trajectory, which traces its path
through conscription. In other words, the possibility of putting
the communal binding to a different use – say, in an inclusive civil
fashion – has been violently removed from free use. An organisation called New Profile, whose motto is 'Movement for the
Civil-ization of Israel Society', works precisely to deactivate the
existing 'form of life' in Israel: they help young men and women
to consider conscientious objection. In their charter, among other
things, they write:

> We will not go on being mobilized, raising children for mobilization,
> supporting mobilized partners, brothers, fathers, while those in charge
> of the country go on deploying the army easily, rather than building
> other solutions [. . .] For our part, we refuse to go on raising our chil-
> dren to see enlistment as a supreme and overriding value. We want a
> fundamentally changed education system, for a truly democratic civic
> education, teaching the practice of peace and conflict resolution, rather
> than training children to enlist and accept warfare. (New Profile 2009)

However, the attempted capture of profaning behaviours knows
no rest: in September 2008, the Attorney General of Israel ordered
a criminal investigation of New Profile, under allegations that they
were encouraging draft dodging. Since then, New Profile activists
have frequently been harassed by the police.

Nonetheless, Agamben's writing on potentiality and the return
of an entrenched 'form of life' to an open 'form-of-life' in which
life can be made profane, provides an important framework for
thinking about colonial legacies in Israel-Palestine: 'For to profane
means not simply to abolish and erase separations but to learn to
put them to a new use, to play with them' (Agamben 2007: 87).
To profane is to invoke virtuality, in the Deleuzian sense: to sup-

plant conscription with civil alternatives, to displace segregation in favour of intercultural life, to commit for community rather than to immunity.

References

Agamben, G. (1998), *Homo Sacer: Sovereign Power and Bare Life*, trans. D. Heller-Roazen. Stanford: Stanford University Press.

—(2000), *Means Without End: Notes on Politics*, trans. V. Binetti and C. Casarino. Minnesota: University of Minnesota Press.

—(2005), *State of Exception*, trans. K. Attell. Chicago: University of Chicago Press.

—(2007), *Profanations*, trans. J. Fort. New York: Zone Books.

Barzilai, G. (2005), *Communities and Law: Politics and Cultures of Legal Identities*. Ann Arbor: University of Michigan Press.

Bernstein, D. (2000), *Constructing Boundaries: Jewish and Arab Workers in Mandatory Palestine*. New York: State University of New York Press.

Bignall, S. (2011), *Postcolonial Agency: Critique and Constructivism*. Edinburgh: Edinburgh University Press.

Borradori, G. (ed.) (2003), *Philosophy in a Time of Terror. Dialogues with Jürgen Habermas and Jacques Derrida*. Chicago and London: University of Chicago Press.

Buchanan, I. (2008), *Deleuze and Guattari's Anti-Oedipus*. London: Continuum.

Campbell, T. (2006), 'Bios Immunity Life: The Thought of Roberto Esposito', *Diacritics*, 36(2): 2–23.

Campos, M. (2011), *Ottoman Brothers*. Stanford: Stanford University Press.

Colebrook, C. (2002), *Gilles Deleuze*. London and New York: Routledge.

Davis, U. (2003), *Apartheid Israel – Possibilities for the Struggle from Within*. London: Zed Books.

de la Durantaye, L. (2009), *Giorgio Agamben: A Critical Introduction*. Stanford: Stanford University Press.

Deleuze, G. and F. Guattari (1983), *Anti-Oedipus: Capitalism and Schizophrenia*, trans. R. Hurley, M. Seem and H. R. Lane. Minneapolis: University of Minnesota Press.

—(1987), *A Thousand Plateaus: Capitalism and Schizophrenia*, trans. B. Massumi. Minneapolis: University of Minnesota Press.

Esposito, R. (2005), *Immunitas: Protección y Negación de la Vida*, trans. L. Padilla López. Buenos Aires: Ammorrotu. (Spanish, all translations mine.)

—(2008), *Bios: Biopolitics and Philosophy*, trans. T. Campbell. Minneapolis: University of Minnesota Press.

—(2010), *Communitas: The Origin and Destiny of Community*, trans. T. Campbell. Stanford: Stanford University Press.

Falah, G. (1991),'Israeli "Judaisation" policy in the Galilee', *Journal of Palestinian Studies*, 20(4): 69–85.

Guattari, F. (1995), *Chaosmosis: An Ethico-Aesthetic Paradigm*, trans. P. Bains and J. Pefanis. Bloomington and Indianapolis: Indiana University Press.

Hare, D. (2009), 'Wall: A Monologue', *The New York Review*, 56(7): 8–10.

Jabareen, Y. (2008), 'Constitution Building and Equality in Deeply-Divided Societies: The Case of the Palestinian-Arab Minority in Israel', *Wisconsin International Law Journal*, 26(2): 346–400.

Jamal, A. (2011), *Arab Minority Nationalism in Israel – The Politics of Indigeneity*. London: Routledge.

Levy, Y. and E. Lomsky-Feder (2007), 'From "Obligatory Militarism" to "Contractual Militarism": Competing Models of Citizenship', *Israel Studies*, 12(1): 127–48.

Lockman, Z. (1996), *Comrades and Enemies: Arab and Jewish Workers in Palestine, 1906–1948*. Berkeley: University of California Press.

Mitzpe Aviv (2009), *Regulations*. Unpublished Community Document, Tel Aviv.

New Profile (2009), *Charter*, available at http://www.newprofile.org/english/?p=21, accessed 29 July 2011.

Pappe, I. (2006), *The Ethnic Cleansing of Palestine*. Oxford: Oneworld.

—(2008), 'The *Mukhabarat* State of Israel: A State of Oppression is Not a State of Exception', in R. Lentin (ed.), *Thinking Palestine*. London and New York: Zed Books, 148–70.

Piterberg, G. (2001), 'Erasures', *New Left Review*, 10: 31–46.

Qa'adan v Israel Land Administration, The Supreme Court of Justice, Case No. 6698/95 (2000).

Shafir, G. (1989), *Land, Labor and the Origins of the Israeli-Palestinian Conflict, 1882–1914*. Berkeley: University of California Press.

Simmel, G. (1950), *The Sociology of Georg Simmel*, compiled and trans. K. Wolff. Glencoe, IL: Free Press.

Smith, B. (1993), *The Roots of Separatism in Palestine*. London: I.B. Tauris.

Stravynski, A. (2007), *Fearing Others: The Nature and Treatment of Social Phobia*. Cambridge: Cambridge University Press.

Svirsky, M. (2010), 'The Production of *terra nullius* and the Zionist-

Palestinian Conflict', in P. Patton and S. Bignall (eds), *Deleuze and the Postcolonial*. Edinburgh: Edinburgh University Press, 220–50.

—(2012), *Arab-Jewish Activism in Israel-Palestine*. Farnham: Ashgate.

Tauber, A. I. (1997), *The Immune Self: Theory or Metaphor?* Cambridge: Cambridge University Press.

The Nation (2011), *Editorial*, 18/25 July 2011, 3.

Veracini, L. (2011), 'Introducing Settler Colonial Studies', *Settler Colonial Studies*, 1: 1–12.

Walters, W. (2008), 'Acts of Demonstration: Mapping the Territory of (Non-) Citizenship', in E. Isin and G. Nielsen (eds), *Acts of Citizenship*. London: Zed Books.

Yiftachel, O. (2006), *Ethnocracy – Land and Identity Politics in Israel/Palestine*. Philadelphia: University of Pennsylvania Press.

— and Carmon, N. (1997), 'Socio-Spatial Mix and Inter-Ethnic Attitudes: Jewish Newcomers and Arab Jewish Issues in the Galilee', *European Planning Studies*, 5(2): 215–37.

Notes

1. As an example, take the United States's decision to go to war in Libya 'without either requesting a declaration of war from Congress, as required by the Constitution, or obtaining legislative authorization, as required by the War Powers Resolution of 1973' (*The Nation* 2011).

2. Quotes from *Immunitas* are my translations from the Spanish version.

3. Importantly, Tauber stresses the open and modifiable character of this process so identity is always vulnerable to exterior forces and resistance. See Tauber 1997.

4. In my *Arab-Jewish Activism in Israel-Palestine* (Svirsky 2012) I analyse interculturalism in Israel-Palestine in political activism, bilingual education and professional sports.

5. Segregationist machines in housing became emblematic of Zionism at a very early stage of the colonisation (Shafir 1989; Bernstein 2000).

6. For a full analysis of these organisations see chapter 3 in my *Arab-Jewish Activism in Israel-Palestine* (Svirsky 2012).

7. See *Qa'adan v Israel Land Administration* (2000). Only in 2007, after renewed attempts to forestall the implementation of the ruling, did the Qa'adans receive the permit to build their house in Katzir.

For a critical reading of the ruling see Barzilai 2005; Jabareen 2008; and Jamal 2011.

8. The Jewish Agency operates in Judaisation projects such as the 'settler body'. Under formal agreements between the State of Israel and the 'national' institutions (the Jewish Agency and the Zionist World Organization) enshrined in different laws (Davis 2003: 29, 41), the Jewish Agency is invested with state functions in various areas (education, relations with the Jewish Diaspora) including the area of settlement. It has been said that this arrangement facilitates discrimination against Arab citizens in an indirect mode in order to avoid, as much as possible, verdicts such as those cited above. The Israel Land Administration (ILA) is the government agency responsible for managing 93 per cent of the land in Israel (which is legislated as national land and it is the property of either the State of Israel, the Jewish National Fund or the Development Authority) which comprises 4,820,500 acres. Ownership of real estate in Israel usually means leasing rights from the ILA for forty-nine or ninety-eight years.

9. As Bignall explains, 'when desire is conceptualised in terms of the acquisition of that which is missing or lacking, it immediately becomes separated from reality: the desired object is missing in the subject's lived experience' (Bignall 2011: 145).

10. As much as we may tend to associate the process of desire with critical creativity, it should be clear that the model explains all sorts of productions, fascists inclusive. This is because of the distinction between creative processes of desire making new connections and bringing about the existence of new assemblages, and the inhibitory processes of assembled bodies that resist transformation (Bignall 2011: 147). The project Deleuze and Guattari call 'schizoanalysis' is about the study of forms of inhibition and repression vis-à-vis the practice of liberation of desire (Deleuze and Guattari 1983: 273–382).

11. For the Deleuzian reader I point here to the illegitimate uses of the passive syntheses; see Deleuze and Guattari 1983: 68–113; cf. Buchanan 2008: 74–88.

12. I believe that Agamben's method of connecting exception and resistance is best read with Deleuze's insistence on the evental role of the infinitives: *to consecrate, to profane.*

II. Colonial Sovereignty

4

Indigenising Agamben: Rethinking Sovereignty in Light of the 'Peculiar' Status of Native Peoples
Mark Rifkin

But the relation of the Indians to the United States is marked by peculiar and cardinal distinctions which exist no where else [. . .] Though the Indians are acknowledged to have an unquestionable, and, heretofore, unquestioned right to the lands they occupy [. . .]; yet it may well be doubted whether those tribes which reside within the acknowledged boundaries of the United States can, with strict accuracy, be denominated foreign nations. They may, more correctly, perhaps, be denominated domestic dependent nations.

Cherokee Nation v Georgia (1831)

The relation of the Indian tribes living within the borders of the United States, both before and since the Revolution, to the people of the United States has always been an anomalous one and of a complex character [. . .] They were, and always have been, regarded [. . .] not as States, not as nations, not as possessed of the full attributes of sovereignty, but as a separate people, with the power of regulating their internal and social relations, and thus far not brought under the laws of the Union or of the State within whose limits they resided.

US v Kagama (1886)

Protection of territory within its external political boundaries is, of course, as central to the sovereign interests of the United States as it is to any other sovereign nation. But from the formation of the Union and the adoption of the Bill of Rights, the United States has manifested an equally great solicitude that its citizens be protected by the United States from unwarranted intrusions on their personal liberty [. . .] By submitting to the overriding sovereignty of the United States, Indian tribes therefore

necessarily give up their power to try non-Indian citizens of the
United States except in a manner acceptable to Congress.

Oliphant v Suquamish Indian Tribe (1978)

What does 'sovereignty' mean in the context of US Indian policy?
Looking at the statements above, all from US Supreme Court
decisions focused on the status of Native peoples, sovereignty at
least touches on questions of jurisdiction, the drawing of national
boundaries, and control over the legal status of persons and entities within those boundaries.[1] While one could characterise the
concept of sovereignty as a shorthand for the set of legal practices
and principles that allow one to determine the rightful scope of
US authority, it seems to function in the decisions less as a way of
designating a specific set of powers than as a negative presence, as
what Native peoples categorically lack, or at the least only have in
some radically diminished fashion managed by the US. Yet while
the decisions seem to be grasping to find language adequate to the
disturbing legal limbo in which Native nations appear to sit, they
also insist unequivocally that such peoples fall *within* the bounds
of US sovereignty, and the oddity attributed to US Indian policy
is offered as confirmation of that fact. Typifying 'the relations of
the Indians to the United States' as 'peculiar' and 'anomalous',
while also consistently presenting Native peoples as unlike all
other political entities in US law and policy, indexes the failure of
US discourses to encompass them while speaking as if they were
incorporated via their incommensurability.

In *Homo Sacer: Sovereign Power and Bare Life*, Giorgio
Agamben has described this kind of dialectic as the 'state of exception', suggesting that it is at the core of what it means for a state
to exert 'sovereignty'.[2] He argues, 'the sovereign decision on the
exception is the originary juridico-political structure on the basis of
which what is included in the juridical order and what is excluded
from it acquire their meaning', and '[i]n this sense, the exception is
the originary form of law' (Agamben 1998: 19, 26). What appears
as an exception from the regular regime of law actually exposes
the rooting of the law itself in a 'sovereign' will that can decide
where, how and to what the formal 'juridical order' will apply.
The narration of Native peoples as an exception from the regular
categories of US law, then, can be seen as, in Agamben's terms, a
form of 'sovereign violence' which 'opens a zone of indistinction
between law and nature, outside and inside, violence and law'

(64).[3] The language of exception, of inclusive exclusion, discursively brings Native peoples into the fold of sovereignty, implicitly offering an explanation for why Native peoples do not fit existing legal concepts (they are different) while assuming that they should be placed within the context of US law (its conceptual field is the obvious comparative framework).[4]

In using Agamben's work to address US Indian policy, though, it needs to be reworked. While his concept of the exception has been immensely influential in contemporary scholarship and cultural criticism, such accounts largely have left aside discussion of indigenous peoples, and attending to Native peoples' position within settler-state sovereignties requires investigating and adjusting three aspects of Agamben's thinking: the persistent inside/outside tropology he uses to address the exception, specifically the ways it serves as a metaphor divorced from territoriality; the notion of 'bare life' as the basis of the exception, especially the individualising ways in which he uses that concept; and the implicit depiction of sovereignty as a self-confident exercise of authority free from anxiety over the legitimacy of state actions. Such revision allows for a reconsideration of the 'zone of indistinction' produced by and within sovereignty, opening up analysis of the ways settler-states regulate not only proper kinds of embodiment ('bare life') but legitimate modes of collectivity and occupancy – what I will call *bare habitance*.

If the 'overriding sovereignty' of the US is predicated on the creation of a state of exception, the struggle for sovereignty by Native peoples can be envisioned as less about control of particular policy domains than of *metapolitical authority* – the ability to define the content and scope of 'law' and 'politics'. Such a shift draws attention away from critiques of the particular rhetorics used to justify the state's plenary power and towards a macrological effort to contest the 'overriding' assertion of a right to exert control over Native polities. While arguments about Euramerican racism and the disjunctions between Native traditions and imposed structures of governance can be quite powerful in challenging aspects of settler-state policy, they cannot account for the structuring violence performed by the figure of sovereignty. Drawing on Agamben, I will argue that 'sovereignty' functions as a placeholder that has no determinate content.[5] The state has been described as an entity which exercises a monopoly on the legitimate exercise of violence, and what I am suggesting is that the state of exception

produced through Indian policy creates a monopoly on the legitimate exercise of legitimacy, an exclusive uncontestable right to
define what will count as a viable legal or political form(ul)ation.
That fundamentally circular and self-validating, as well as anxious
and fraught, performance grounds the legitimacy of state rule
on nothing more than the axiomatic negation of Native peoples'
authority to determine or adjudicate for themselves the normative
principles by which they will be governed. Through Agamben's
theory of the exception, then, I will explore how the supposedly
underlying sovereignty of the US settler-state is a retrospective
projection generated by, and dependent on, the 'peculiar'-isation
of Native peoples.

The Domain of Inclusive Exclusion: The Camp and the Reservation

In introducing his argument in *Homo Sacer*, Agamben marks
while seeking to trouble the distinction between *zoē* and *bios* – 'the
simple fact of living common to all living beings (animals, men, or
gods)' versus 'the form or way of living proper to an individual or
a group' (Agamben 1998: 1). He suggests that in classical antiq-
uity the former was excluded from the sphere of politics and that
part of what most distinguishes modernity, particularly the structure of the state, is the effort to bring the former into the orbit of
governmental regulation, in fact to see it as the animating principle
of political life ('the politicization of bare life as such' [4]). The
first articulation of the book's central thesis, then, is as follows: '*It
can even be said that the production of a biopolitical body is the
original activity of sovereign power*' (6).[6] In other words, modern
sovereignty depends upon generating a vision of the 'body' – of
apolitical natural life – that is cast as simultaneously exterior
to the sphere of government and law and as the reference point
for defining the proper aims, objects and methods of governance
('[p]lacing biological life at the center of its calculations' [6]),
serving as an authorising figure for decision making by self-
consciously political institutions while itself being presented as
exempt from question or challenge within such institutions.

   Further, and more urgently for Agamben, the generation of
'bare life' makes thinkable the consignment of those who do not
fit the idealised 'biopolitical body' to a 'zone' outside of political participation and the regular working of the law but still

within the ambit of state power. Describing this possibility, he observes,

> The relation of exception is a relation of ban. He who has been banned is not, in fact, simply set outside the law and made indifferent to it but rather *abandoned* by it, that is, exposed and threatened on the threshold [. . .] It is literally not possible to say whether the one who has been banned is outside or inside the juridical order. (Agamben 1998: 28–9)

For Agamben, the Nazi concentration camp serves as the paradigmatic example of the biopolitical imperatives structuring modern sovereignty, described as 'the hidden matrix and nomos of the political space in which we are still living' (Agamben 1998: 166). The camp opens up a location within the state in which persons who are linked to the space of the nation by birth can be managed as 'bare life', as mere biological beings bereft of any/all the legal protections of citizenship.

Yet if that denial of political subjectivity and simultaneous subjection to the force of the state confuses, or perhaps conflates, 'exclusion and inclusion', to what extent is that blurring predicated on the reification of the boundaries of the 'sovereign power' of the nation? Put another way, if the person in the state of exception is considered 'bare life' and thus neither truly 'outside [n]or inside the juridical order', how does one know that the 'abandoned' comes under the sway of a given sovereign? How might the 'irreducible indistinction' enacted by sovereignty that Agamben describes itself depend on a prior geopolitical mapping that is also produced through the invocation of sovereignty, differentiating those people and places that fall within the jurisdictional sphere of a given state from those that do not?

That process of *distinction*, I contend, draws on the logic of exception Agamben theorises but in ways that cannot be reduced to the creation of a 'biopolitical body'. In describing how modern sovereignty appears to found itself on the will of the people, Agamben locates a biopolitical problematic at the core of that claim:

> It is as if what we call 'people' were in reality not a unitary subject but a dialectical oscillation between two opposite poles: on the one hand, the set of the People as a whole political body, and on the other, the subset of the people as a fragmentary multiplicity of needy and

excluded bodies; [. . .] at one extreme, the total state of integrated and sovereign citizens, and at the other, the preserve – court of miracles or camp – of the wretched, the oppressed, and the defeated. (Agamben 1998: 177)

The 'People' stands less for the actual assemblage of persons within the state than for the set of those who fit the ideal 'body', and who consequently will be recognised as 'citizens', with the rest of the resident population consigned to the realm of 'bare life' – the people who are not the People and thus are excluded from meaningful participation while remaining the objects of state control. However, when reflecting on the status of indigenous populations in relation to the settler-state, a third category emerges that is neither people nor People – namely *peoples*. The possibility of conceptualising the nation as 'a whole political body' requires narrating it as 'a unitary subject' rather than a collection of separate, unsubordinated, self-governing polities. In critiquing the approach of previous theorists to the issue of sovereignty, Agamben notes, 'The problem of sovereignty was reduced to the question of who within the political order was invested with certain powers, and the very threshold of the political order itself was never called into question', but Agamben's account itself assumes a clear 'within' by not posing the question of how sovereignty produces and is produced by place, how the state is realised as a spatial phenomenon as part of 'the very threshold of the political order itself' (Agamben 1998: 12).

I am suggesting, then, that the biopolitical project of defining the proper 'body' of the people is subtended by the geopolitical project of defining the territoriality of the nation, displacing competing claims by older/other political formations as what we might call *bare habitance*. Agamben notes, 'The camp is a piece of land placed outside the normal juridical order, but it is nevertheless not simply an external space' (Agamben 1998: 169–70), but that definition also seems to capture rather precisely the status of the reservation, a space that while governed under 'peculiar' rules categorically is denied status as 'external', or 'foreign'. Examining the reservation, and more broadly the representation of Native collectivity and territoriality in US governmental discourses, through the prism of Agamben's analysis of the state of exception helps highlight the kinds of 'sovereign violence' at play in the (re)production and naturalisation of national space.[7] The effort to think biopolitics without geopolitics, bare life without bare habitance, results in the erasure of the politics of collectivity and occupancy: what entities will count as polities and thus be seen as deserving of autonomy; what modes of inhabitance and land tenure will be understood as legitimate; and who will get to make such determinations and on what basis?[8] Focusing on the fracture between 'the People' and 'the people' imagines explicitly or implicitly either a reconciliation of the two or the proliferation of a boundaryless humanness unconstrained by territorially circumscribed polities. These options leave little room for thinking indigeneity, the existence of *peoples* forcibly made domestic whose self-understandings and aspirations cannot be understood in terms of the denial of (or disjunctions within) state citizenship.[9]

While in the next section I will address how biopolitical and geopolitical dynamics work together, specifically in the translation of Native peoples into aggregates of individual domestic subjects (as either a race or a culture), I first want to explore in greater detail how the production of national space depends on coding Native peoples and lands as an exception. Administrative mappings of US jurisdiction remain haunted by the presence of polities whose occupancy precedes that of the state and whose existence as collectivities repeatedly has been officially recognised through treaties. The Supreme Court decisions with which I began all register this difficulty. In *Cherokee Nation v Georgia*, the court explicitly finds that the 'acts of our government plainly recognize the Cherokee nation as a state', indicating they are 'a distinct political society, separated from others, capable of managing its own affairs and governing itself' (16). Yet the majority opinion also insists, 'The Indian territory is admitted to compose a part of the United States', adding, 'They occupy a territory to which we assert a title independent of their will' (17). Following a similar line of reasoning, *US v Kagama* insists, 'the colonies before the Revolution and the States and the United States since, have recognized in the Indians a possessory right to the soil [. . .] But they asserted an ultimate title in the land itself' (381), and Justice Rehnquist in *Oliphant v Suquamish* argues, 'Indian tribes do retain elements of "quasi-sovereign" authority after ceding their lands to the United States' although 'their exercise of separate power is constrained so as not to conflict with the interests of [the US's] overriding sovereignty' (208–9). Each of these formulations acknowledges a tension between the kinds of political identity and authority suggested by the ability to enter into formal agreements with the US and the claim that such otherwise (or previously) 'distinct political societ[ies]' are fully enclosed within the boundaries of the state, and thus subject in some fashion to its rule.

Presenting US–Indian relations as 'peculiar' or 'anomalous' marks that tension, but such a description depicts the treaty system and the workings of federal Indian law as neither regular domestic law nor foreign policy. The oddity can seem to inhere in the treaties themselves, a supposed irregularity which US lawmakers sought to remedy in the late nineteenth century by ending the practice of treaty making.[10] The 'peculiar'-ity of the treaty system, though, is less a function of the constitutional status it confers on Indian policy (enacting it through documents that, in the words of Article VI of the US Constitution, make it 'the supreme law of the land') than the underlying contradiction to which the treaty system points. Treaties register and mediate a structural disjunction between the continuing existence of autochthonous Native collectivities which predate the formation of the US and the adoption of a jurisdictional imaginary in which such collectivities are imagined as part of US national space. More than merely recognising Native peoples as 'distinct political societ[ies]' with whom the US must negotiate for territory, however, the treaty system also seeks to interpellate Native polities into US political discourses, presupposing (and imposing) forms of governance and occupancy that facilitate the cession of land.[11] While in one sense acknowledging Native peoples as 'separate' entities from the US, the treaty-based Indian policy of the late eighteenth and nineteenth centuries also sought to confirm the US's 'ultimate title in the land itself', thereby indicating the stresses generated by the narration of Native nations as domestic. Dispensing with treaties, though, does not eliminate such strain, or the normative difficulties it creates for validating US authority over Native populations and lands, instead simply trying to displace the problem of legitimacy which still returns insistently to trouble US legal discourses.[12]

The potential disjuncture in US jurisdiction opened by the presence of non-national entities with claims to land ostensibly inside the nation is sutured over by proclaiming a 'sovereignty' that supposedly alleviates the potential 'conflict' between US and Native mappings. Presented as simply logically following from Native peoples' residence on 'territory admitted to compose a part of the United States' (*Cherokee Nation v Georgia*: 18), the invocation of sovereignty casts them as exceptional, an aberration from the normal operation of law but one contained within the broader sphere of US national authority. 'Indian tribes' have only a 'possessory right' or 'quasi-sovereign' claims, but 'ultimate title', the decisions reassuringly indicate, lies with the US. Yet rather than providing an underlying framework in which to situate indigenous populations, sovereignty instead appears as a mutable figure that enables their occupancy to be portrayed as 'peculiar'. Discursively, it bridges the logical and legal chasm between the political autonomy indexed by the treaty system and the depiction of them as domestic subjects. US political discourses seek to contain the instability of the settler-state by repeatedly declaring the nation's geopolitical unity, but at moments when that avowal is brought into crisis by the continuing presence and operation of Native polities, the topos of sovereignty emerges, as if it exists before and beyond the specific legal questions at stake in any particular case or act of policy making. As Judith Butler suggests, 'it is not that sovereignty exists as a possession that the US is said to "have" [. . .] Grammar defeats us here. Sovereignty is what is tactically produced through the very mechanism of its self-justification' (Butler 2004: 82).[13] The citation of sovereignty in this completely open-ended, but rhetorically foundationalising, way suggests a potentially unlimited capacity to (re)define what will count as the organising framework of political order.

The performative citation of sovereignty by the US depends on the creation of a state of exception for Native peoples. The content of 'sovereignty' in the decisions is the assertion of the authority to treat Native peoples as having constrained, diminished political control over themselves and their lands, and such a contention rests on the assumption that despite their existence before and after the founding of the US as 'separate people[s], with the power of regulating their internal and social relations' (US v Kagama: 381–2), they somehow do not have equivalent status to 'foreign' nations. As Agamben observes, 'the state of exception is [. . .] the principle of every juridical localization, since only the state of exception opens the space in which the determination of a certain juridical order and a particular territory first becomes possible' (Agamben 1998: 19). The jurisdictional imaginary of the US is made possible only by localising Native peoples, in the sense of circumscribing their political power/status and portraying Indian policy as an aberration divorced from the principles at play in the rest of US law, and that process of exception quite literally opens the *space* for a legal geography predicated on the territorial coherence of the nation. Those political collectivities whose occupancy does not fit the geopolitical ideal/imaginary of the state are left abandoned by it, 'exposed and threatened on the threshold' of the juridical order that is made possible and validated by their exception (28). From that perspective, settler-state sovereignty can be viewed as producing the impression of boundedness by banning – rendering 'peculiar', 'anomalous', 'unique', 'special' – competing claims to place and collectivity.[14] This line of thought further suggests that if the validity of national policy is presented as being derived from the underlying fact of sovereignty, such a claim to legitimacy itself relies on the promulgation of an exception which rests on nothing more than the absoluteness with which it is articulated and enforced.

Dependence, Race and the Limits of Culture

Representing Native populations and lands as occupying an 'anomalous' position allows the US government to validate its extension of theoretically unlimited authority over them, rendering them external to the normal functioning of the law but yet internal to the space of the nation. The dominance perpetuated through the ongoing recreation of this state of exception, though, inheres not merely in the exercise of unhampered jurisdiction over Native peoples but in the ways that jurisdiction enables a metapolitical scripting of the terms of collectivity itself. More than circumscribing or disciplining the autonomy of Native peoples, Indian policy recodes their identities, defining and redefining the threshold of political identity and legitimacy and determining how Native peoples will enter that field, including what (kinds of) concepts and categories they will inhabit.[15] The representation of Native peoples as an exception makes possible their incorporation into US administrative discourses in any number of ways along a wide spectrum ranging from polity to bare life. In that process of inscription, the biopolitical and the geopolitical dynamics of nation-statehood discussed above enter into a dialectical relay, the former serving as a way of resolving the threatened incoherence of the latter by providing a set of tactics through which to recast Native peoples as people.[16] In seeking to cope with the presence of pre-existing polities on what it seeks to portray as domestic space, the US often translates autochthonous, self-governing Native polities as populations, as either collections of bodies in need of restraint/protection or cultural aggregations. In being interpellated into US political discourses in this way, they are managed as residents – as a kind of racialised, endangered or enculturated body – on land that self-evidently constitutes part of the nation.

Turning again to the Supreme Court cases with which I began, this dynamic can be seen in the mobilisation of the figure of dependence. The decision in *Cherokee Nation v Georgia* invents the notion of 'domestic dependent nation', and in justifying the fabrication of this unheard-of status, the court articulates what would become a (if not *the*) central trope of federal Indian law, saying of Native peoples that '[t]heir relation to the United States resembles that of a ward to his guardian.' The opinion adds, 'They look to our government for protection; rely upon its kindness and its power; appeal to it for relief to their wants; and address the president as their great father' (17). That vision of superintendence depends upon infantilisation, casting the same group referred to earlier in the decision as a 'distinct political society' as a child in need of guidance and safeguarding. This description, though, appears just in the wake of the court's insistence that 'those tribes which reside within the acknowledged boundaries of the United States' cannot, 'with strict accuracy, be denominated foreign nations' (17). The image of Native nations as hapless minors, 'ward[s]', appears retroactively to justify their status as 'domestic', but their apparent dependency *follows from* their location 'within the acknowledged boundaries' of the nation-state, 'dependent' providing a content for 'domestic' belonging other than simply the absence/disavowal of 'foreign'-ness. A particular jurisdictional mapping, 'within', then, comes to appear through the prism of dependence as a qualitatively different kind of relation; Native polities' call for the acknowledgement of their boundaries and autonomy is transfigured instead as a mass of 'wants' – a term suggestive of persistent bodily need.

This discursive transmutation of indigenous peoplehood into bare life is even more pronounced in *US v Kagama*. Rehearsing the language of 'ward'-ship, the decision expands the scope and deepens the sense of the dependency cited in the earlier opinion: 'These Indian tribes are the wards of the nation. They are communities dependent on the United States. Dependent largely for their daily food. Dependent for their political rights' (383–4).

Dispensing with the rhetoric of nationhood from the previous decision, the court here envisions 'Indian tribes' as groups whose continued existence is utterly contingent on federal care. They are an undifferentiated mass of flesh with no 'political' existence apart from whatever 'rights' may happen to be granted (or withheld) by the US. Once again, though, this corporealisation of Indians is brought back to the problems they potentially pose for national spatiality:

> The power of the General Government over these remnants of a race once powerful, now weak and diminished in numbers, is necessary to their protection, as well as to the safety of those among whom they dwell. It must exist in that government, because it never has existed anywhere else, because the theatre of its exercise is within the geographical limits of the United States, because it has never been denied, and because it alone can enforce its laws on all the tribes. (*US v Kagama*: 384–5)

While reinforcing the impression of an assemblage of exposed and endangered bodies, 'remnants' whose frailty leaves them on the verge of extinction, the passage ends up justifying US power by reference to the supremacy which is understood to be a necessary corollary of the coherence of 'the geographical limits of the United States'. The sheer vehemence of the statement that control over Indians 'must exist in that government' intimates a profound anxiety, the phrase 'anywhere else' suggesting a fear that the space of the nation might somehow be(come) alien to itself – an *elsewhere* to which US jurisdiction explicitly is 'denied' by the indigenous inhabitants. The categorisation of Indians as 'weak and diminished' bodies or a murderous threat to 'the safety' of neighbouring white communities (a 'savage race') appears to provide a reason, in a biopolitical key, for the exertion of authority over them, but it occupies the space of the exception already produced by the encompassing insistence that Native peoples fall within the 'theatre' of US governance.

Presenting Indians as bare life – dying 'remnants', helpless children and/or vicious savages – addresses their status within the regime of US policy as if it were a function of natural facts, pre-political or apolitical conditions to which US institutions respond,[17] but the biopolitical figure of dependence presumes a vision of geopolitical incorporation which precedes it, the latter appearing as if it were merely background for the former. But the background keeps coming to the fore, invested in the decisions with a force that rhetorically exceeds and logically disjoints its apparent role as simply setting as opposed to focus or aim. Viewed in this way, the critique of Indian policy as racist only addresses biopolitical tactics without dislodging the geopolitical structure of exception. Robert A. Williams takes such an approach, arguing that the vision of Indians as 'uncivilized, unsophisticated, and lawless savages' enshrined in numerous nineteenth-century Supreme Court opinions continues to serve as the basis for Indian law, given the ongoing citation of those cases as precedent: 'The stereotypes or images that the Court has thus legitimated and expanded can now be used to legally justify a rights-denying, jurispathic form of racism against those groups' (Williams 2005: xxviii, 21). Through the term 'jurispathic', Williams, following the legal theorist Robert Cover (1993), refers to the power of the court to make one tradition of law or legal interpretation the exclusive, authoritative one, thereby eliminating alternatives or denying them institutional validity by refusing to sanction them as legally or politically viable options. However, casting that dynamic in Indian policy as primarily one of a 'racism' that denies access to 'rights' leaves aside not only the question of territoriality but of Native peoples' status as independent polities. According to Williams, the Supreme Court refuses to apply the 'egalitarian principles of racial equality normally applied to all other groups and individuals in post-*Brown* America', instead 'deciding [. . .] Indian rights case[s] according to an overarching metaprinciple of Indian racial inferiority' (127),[18] but if such 'egalitarian principles' were applied so that Indians were deemed no different than any other 'groups and individuals' in 'America', that disposition in and of itself still would not reverse the linked dynamics of internalisation and individualisation through which Indians are understood as subjects of US domestic law and policy, as firmly *within* the nation and thus subjected to its metapolitical authority. While no longer positioned as savages or dependent children, cast as fully rights-bearing individuals rather than bare life, Native peoples still would signify as collections of persons within the ambit of US jurisdiction rather than as autonomous political collectivities whose identity and status cannot be managed by US institutions.

Thus, although Williams recognises the difference between Native peoples and those minorities whose horizon of legal

aspiration largely is full inclusion in the nation as citizens, offering what he describes as a 'singularity thesis' that acknowledges
'the unique types of autochthonous rights that tribal Indians want
protected under U.S. law' (Williams 2005: xxv), his indictment of
US modes of racialisation cannot fully capture the political work
performed by sovereignty, or rather the work that the citation
of sovereignty performs in (re)defining and regulating the terms
of 'political' identity. Inasmuch as the biopolitical discourse of
race helps dissimulate the violence at play in the domestication
of Native peoples by depicting the terms of US rule as due to the
'natural' qualities of Indians, the kind of anti-racist challenge
Williams suggests can help disqualify the bodily as a basis for
Indian law, thereby clearing conceptual and discursive ground so
as to draw attention back to the issue of territoriality.[19] Having
done so, though, one still needs to contest not so much the 'metaprinciple of Indian racial inferiority' as that of the jurisdictional
coherence of national space. In his interpretation of *Oliphant v
Suquamish*, for example, Williams claims that the court's denial
of the defendant's authority to prosecute non-Indians depends on
little more than a rehearsal of demeaning nineteenth-century stereotypes of Indians from previous decisions, including *Cherokee
Nation* and *Kagama*, that have been sanitised by the removal of
most of the overtly denigrating language. Yet *Oliphant* asserts,

> Upon incorporation into the territory of the United States, the Indian
> tribes thereby come under the territorial sovereignty of the United
> States and their exercise of separate power is constrained so as not to
> conflict with the interests of this overriding sovereignty. (*Oliphant v
> Suquamish*: 209)

Even if the Indian/non-Indian distinction were eliminated as a
vestige of a noxious regime of racial hierarchy, the 'territorial
sovereignty of the United States' would remain, along with the
dangerously amorphous, infinitely expansive, and uncontestable
'interests' that are said to follow from it and that provide the
means of 'overriding' any initiative by Native populations to represent and assert themselves as autonomous collectivities.

If anti-racist resistance remains urgent but still insufficient to
the task of breaking the stranglehold on the 'political' held by
the US as a result of its exceptionalisation of indigenous polities,
might the notion of 'culture' better serve to challenge settler-

state authority?[20] As Elizabeth Povinelli (2002) has illustrated, the *recognition* of indigenous cultural difference within liberal multiculturalist governance tends to reaffirm the coherence of the nation-state, fetishise an anachronising vision of Native identity and exonerate continuing forms of imperial superintendence. Focusing on Australia, she argues that

> national pageants of shameful repentance and celebrations of a new recognition of subaltern worth remain inflected by the conditional (as long as they are not repugnant; that is, as long as they are not, at heart, not-us and as long as real economic resources are not at stake). (Povinelli 2002: 17)[21]

The state's performance of its redemption from a violent colonial past depends on the embrace, or more accurately invention, of a version of aboriginality that is consistent with the moral norms of settler-state law yet still strange enough to generate the frisson of diversity/discrepancy, creating the thrill of indigenous authenticity while not validating acts or ideas 'repugnant' to the sensibilities of non-native citizens. The effort to locate and outline Native cultures occurs against the background of unquestioned settler-state jurisdiction, continuing to code Native populations as both exceptional and as collections of individual domestic subjects.

As I have been suggesting, then, the topos of sovereignty designates less a content that can be replaced (a racist vision of Indian savagery, a Eurocentric resistance to Native customs) than a process of compulsory relation, one predicated on the supposedly unquestionable fact of national territorial boundaries. While contesting the various discourses that reaffirm the validity of assorted elements of settler-state jurisdiction certainly can do powerful work in challenging and changing particular policies, creating greater tactical room for manoeuvre in a range of struggles, such an approach cannot fully address the structuring force of sovereignty, the ways in which the exceptionalisation of Native peoples works to legitimise the unconstrained metapolitical power of the US to invent, enforce and alter the statuses/categories/concepts in which Native peoples are made to signify.

The Question of (or Quest for) Legitimacy

If US Indian policy in its circulation of the figure of sovereignty has the potential to displace Native polities entirely, why not do so? Why not simply erase this ongoing threat to the jurisdictional imaginary of the nation?[22] To do so would foreground the very unilateral will – the theoretically limitless imperial violence – on which US territoriality rests, exacerbating the very structural crisis of legitimacy the topos of sovereignty works to dissimulate. In other words, the claim of sovereignty appears at moments in which a gap has opened in the operative logics of US law, offering a way of resolving legal and political questions that threaten to undo the geopolitics of the settler-state.[23] Simply to present US superintendence as a function of brute force would undercut the very legitimising aim of the arguments in which sovereignty is employed, thwarting their effort to cover the inability of US law philosophically to ground itself in the ground of the nation.

The citation of sovereignty, therefore, is less a confident and self-assured indication of untroubled control than a restless performance in which the failure to find a normative foundation on which to rest the legitimacy of national jurisdiction remains a nagging source of anxiety. Justice Clarence Thomas addresses this dynamic in his concurrence to the decision in *US v Lara* (2004).[24] Thomas observes that there is a contradiction at the heart of US Indian policy: 'In my view, the tribes either are or are not separate sovereigns, and our federal Indian law cases untenably hold both positions simultaneously' (215), and he later adds, 'The Federal Government cannot simultaneously claim power to regulate virtually every aspect of the tribes through ordinary domestic legislation and also maintain that the tribes possess anything resembling "sovereignty"' (225).[25] Despite the fact that the majority opinion describes tribes' 'inherent sovereignty' as the source of their, still circumscribed, criminal jurisdiction, it also indicates that such 'sovereignty' can be abridged, restored and reconfigured at will by Congress, thereby cloaking US imperial modes of exception as something other than, in Agamben's terms, 'sovereign violence' and covering the degree to which Native peoples are left 'exposed and threatened on the threshold' of national territoriality (Agamben 1998: 64, 28).

The attempt to locate legitimacy for US jurisdiction in something other than its own imposed, circular obviousness can be found even in the most strident declarations of sovereignty. In *Oliphant*, for example, the majority opinion suggests that 'Indian tribes do retain elements of "quasi-sovereign" authority after ceding their lands to the United States' and that they 'give up their power to try non-Indian citizens' after 'submitting to the overriding sovereignty of the United States' (208, 210). Such moments suggest a point at which Native peoples voluntarily surrender certain forms of political authority. While quite doubtful as a way of characterising the actual workings of the treaty system or the ways it was understood by Native signatories (assuming that sale or lease of particular plots of land is tantamount to a wholesale acceptance of unconstrained regulation by the US over every aspect of Native life), this description does predicate federal power on consent ('ceding', 'submitting'), seeking to cast US sovereignty as encompassing yet fundamentally non-coercive.

This effort to find a way to ameliorate the force of settler-state jurisdiction suggests that part of the metapolitical generation of categories, concepts and statuses is the attempted simulation of legitimacy as well. In this vein, the legal positing of Native sovereignty provides a discursive entry point that can be occupied by Native peoples in ways that expose the domination at play in the deployment of the topos of sovereignty by the settler-state. Exploiting the kind of logical incoherence and underlying normative crisis towards which Thomas points, the discourse of sovereignty can be mobilised to deconstruct US rule by illustrating how the settler-state exerts a monopoly on the production of legitimacy – the ways statuses are imposed on Native peoples in the context of their axiomatic yet constitutionally indefensible subjection to US authority. The countercitation of sovereignty can reveal and contest the operation of such a monopoly by drawing attention to the organising indistinction between force and law in Indian policy – the operation of a geopolitical state of exception.

This position, though, runs against the grain of two understandings of Native articulations of 'sovereignty' prominent in indigenous political theory: as the adoption of a specific set of principles of governance imposed by settler-states; or as a pragmatic attempt to make indigenous concepts intelligible within state terminologies and to state institutions.[26] The first, presented perhaps most forcefully by Alfred in his essay 'Sovereignty', envisions sovereignty as a particular form of government, one derived from alien conventions. The problem for Native peoples in utilising the discourse of sovereignty is that doing so reifies a 'European notion of power and governance' which is fundamentally at odds with Native beliefs and practices: 'Sovereignty itself implies a set of values and objectives that put it in direct opposition to the values and objectives found in most traditional indigenous philosophies' (Alfred 2005: 43).[27] In describing 'sovereignty' as 'a set of values' at odds with 'indigenous philosophies', Alfred presents 'retraditionalisation', eschewing settler-state terminologies and ideologies in favour of the 'wisdom coded in the languages and cultures of all indigenous peoples', as the vehicle for 'achiev[ing] sovereignty-free regimes of conscience and justice' (40, 49). What I have been arguing, however, is that 'sovereignty itself' is empty, a topological placeholder through which to displace, or contain, the paradox of asserting 'domestic' authority over populations whose existence as peoples precedes the existence of the state. Thus, adopting a different set of principles – an indigenous rather than European 'notion [. . .] of governance' – does not secure 'autonomy' from settler-state superintendence, from being coded as an 'anomaly' axiomatically subject to the metapolitical authority of the settler-state.

Alfred's argument relies on the juxtaposition of indigenous political models with European ones without addressing how the settler-state narrates its jurisdiction over national space and justifies its extension of regulatory control over Native peoples. He suggests that 'sovereignty' designates 'a conceptual and definitional problem centered on the accommodation of indigenous peoples within a "legitimate" framework of settler state governance' (Alfred 2005: 34–5), adding that they 'must conform to state-derived criteria and represent ascribed or negotiated identities' (43), but he stops short of investigating the ways in which the topos of sovereignty works to validate a range of discrepant (kinds of) 'identities' which Native peoples at various times have been and are called on to inhabit.[28] An insistence on difference cannot unsettle the state's assertion of the authority to adjudicate the status of indigenous polities, because 'sovereignty' is the vehicle not of implementing a stable set of 'values and objectives' but of repudiating any challenge to the territorial imaginary of the nation. Moreover, articulations of difference can be refracted back through the prism of Native 'peculiar'-ity, possibly reinforcing the process of exceptionalisation. Put another way, Alfred draws attention to a particular type of identity (liberal bureaucracy) imposed by the state rather than the state's fraught and uneven effort to generate legitimacy for its management of Native identities.

As against Alfred's call for eschewing the framework of 'sovereignty', Dale Turner insists that the protection of Native peoples involves making their concerns and representations intelligible within the legal and political structures of the settler-state. In *This is Not a Peace Pipe*, Turner argues that the political terrain on which Native peoples must move has been mapped by the settler-state, and that if they are to gain greater traction for their land claims and assertions of governmental autonomy they will need to express them in ways that non-native people and institutions can understand. '*As a matter of survival*, Aboriginal intellectuals must engage the non-Aboriginal intellectual landscapes from which their political rights and sovereignty are articulated and put to use in Aboriginal communities' (Turner 2006: 90, original emphasis). Given that non-native political processes already are active in shaping the terms of indigenous governance and social life, Native peoples cannot afford simply to ignore them or to insist on the significance of 'traditional' knowledge in ways that speak past non-native modes of articulation. However, to what extent does Turner's notion of *reconciling* knowledges also present the struggle over sovereignty as a function of cultural dissonance between indigenous peoples and the settler-state? The central question he poses is 'how do we explain our differences and in the process empower ourselves to actually change the state's legal and political practices?' (101), but does transposing indigenous concepts into non-native terminologies intervene in the logic structuring 'the state's legal and political practices'? Does such a conversion challenge the jurisdictional imperative and imaginary driving the settler-state assertion of authority over Native peoples? The idea of 'explain[ing]' indigenous 'differences' acknowledges the imperial force exerted under the sign of sovereignty, but it does not contest the state's monopoly over the legitimate exercise of legitimacy, nor does it prevent those 'differences' from being reified, regulated and subordinated as 'culture' in the ways discussed earlier.

However, in a more deconstructive mode, Turner also calls for a thorough accounting of the violences of settler-state imperialism. 'The project of unpacking and laying bare the meaning and effects of colonialism will open up the physical and intellectual space for Aboriginal voice to participate in the legal and political practices of the state' (Turner 2006: 30–1). Later, he suggests that indigenous intellectuals should pursue three goals:

> (a) they must take up, deconstruct, and continue to resist colonialism and its effects on indigenous peoples; (b) they must protect and defend indigeneity; and (c) they must engage the legal and political discourses of the state in an effective way. (Turner 2006: 96)

What kind of 'participat[ion]' and 'engage[ment]' do such strategies yield? Although Turner tends to answer this question by focusing on the possibility of explaining indigenous intellectual traditions, making them comprehensible to non-natives, the above comments offer another option, namely deconstructing the dynamics of settler-state power – problematising the ways it seeks to generate legitimacy for itself. He describes such intervention as 'understanding [. . .] how colonialism has been woven into the normative political language that guides contemporary Canadian legal and political practices' (Turner 2006: 30). In other words, the kinds of 'normative' claims made by the settler-state are not simply distinct from indigenous ones but are aporetic, themselves predicated on the (thread)bare insistence that the state maintains an 'overriding sovereignty'. By 'unpacking and laying bare' the logical and legal emptiness of sovereignty, the 'space' opened is precisely that which has been placed in the state of exception, illustrating how Native 'peculiar'-ity – and the various statuses derived from it – are less a function of a mistranslation of indigenous difference than the marker of an enforced structural relation.

Emphasising the normative crisis over which the topos of sovereignty is stretched does not so much make room for indigenous principles within Euramerican terminologies and institutions as refuse *en toto* the right claimed by the state to assess and adjudicate Native governance, drawing attention to the state's inability to ground Indian policy in anything but the forced incorporation of Native persons and lands into the nation. As Agamben suggests in *Means Without End*, sovereignty 'is the guardian who prevents the undecidable threshold between violence and right [. . .] from coming to light' (Agamben 2000: 113). In the three cases on which I have focused, the assertion of Native autonomy threatens to disrupt the US territorial/jurisdictional imaginary and that potential rupture is contained by the citation of 'sovereignty' – a concept whose substance keeps shifting and out of which emerge statuses and classificatory schemes that determine the institutional intelligibility of Native identities and claims. That process of exceptionalisation has no check – the 'plenary power' or 'overriding sovereignty' of the US is taken to license complete control over Native collectivities, including in what ways and to what extent, if any, they in fact will be recognised as collectivities (never mind as self-determining polities). To leave uncontested the topology of settler-state sovereignty, then, is to allow for Native peoples to remain abandoned to, in Agamben's terms, a 'zone of indistinction between [. . .] outside and inside, violence and law' (64). Moreover, that 'zone' is less a function of a self-confident exercise of power than a sign of the normative tenuousness of US authority. As Clarence Thomas's comments suggest, the creation of a concept like 'inherent sovereignty' works to cover while not unsettling the 'overriding' and potentially limitless authority exerted by the US government, specifically Congress, in Indian affairs, providing the impression of a legal logic that can guide or legitimise US actions.

I am suggesting, however, that it might be possible to occupy the contradiction embedded in a formulation like 'inherent sovereignty' in ways that neither endorse the category as (continually re)formulated within US Indian policy, disown it as the imposition of an alien norm, nor translate indigenous traditions into its terms. Instead, the status can be used as a discursive entry point through which to highlight the groundlessness of US claims to Native land and the impossibility of reconciling Indian policy with the principles of constitutionalism, drawing attention to the difficulty of validating the incorporation of Native peoples into the mapping of the jurisdictional geography of the state except through recourse to violence. Such a strategy emphasises the coercive imposition of domesticity on Native peoples who neither sought nor desired it, foregrounding the ways in which the narration of indigenous polities as subjects of domestic law depends on a process of exceptionalisation in which they axiomatically are consigned to a 'peculiar', and thus regulatable, internality that forcibly disavows their autonomy and self-representations.[29]

If such a deconstructive argument were successful, in Turner's terms 'open[ing] up the physical and intellectual space for Aboriginal voice' (Turner 2006: 30–1), what might the resulting relationship look like? The disjunction between the supposed fact of Indians' domesticity and their existence as independent political collectivities prior to the formation of the US appears perhaps most visibly in the negotiation of treaties, and that tension supposedly is allayed by the assent of Native peoples to these documents. Although certainly less unilateral than the declaration of authority over Native populations contained in *Kagama* and *Oliphant*, treaties were not free from US efforts to regulate what would constitute viable forms of political subjectivity, representing Native governance and land tenure in ways that facilitated the project of settler expansion. That being said, as the process within US constitutionalism most suited to the recognition of extraconstitutional entities, treaty making seems the most viable vehicle for a 'sovereignty-free' politics. Rather than trying to contain the geopolitical difficulties that indigenous occupancy generates for the imaginary of the settler-state, treaties can serve as sites of negotiation, not simply over particular concrete issues but over the terms of engagement themselves.[30] When no longer subordinated to the assertion of an overriding, underlying, pre-emptive or plenary authority, such dialogue could perform the kind of translation Turner describes between different traditions or frameworks of governance, displacing sovereignty in favour of politics. In *Means Without End*, Agamben suggests, '*Politics is the exhibition of a mediality: it is the act of making a means visible as such*. Politics is the sphere neither of an end in itself nor of a means subordinated to an end' (Agamben 2000: 116–17, original emphasis), and in this vein, treaties freed from the end of securing the obviousness of national territoriality become a 'mediality' of negotiation. The forms of recognition emerging from that process would not function as part of a mode of regulation and would not be predicated on casting Native peoples as an exception *within* the sphere of US politics and law.

What I have sought to do, then, is to use Agamben's analysis of the violence of sovereignty in its reliance on the production of a state of exception to suggest the absence of a normative framework for US Indian policy, and more broadly for the geopolitics of the settler-state. The coding of Native peoples as 'peculiar' within US governance depends on the assertion of a territorially based jurisdiction over them that further licenses the regulation of their entry into the shifting field of national politics, generating various (kinds of) categories that they are called on to occupy. While offering rigorous critique of such statuses, including their racialising premises and inability to engage with traditional philosophies and practices, indigenous political theory largely has not contested the broader ways in which violence is transposed into legitimacy through the circulation of the enveloping yet empty sign of 'sovereignty'. Exposing that transposition, potentially through the countercitation of Native sovereignty (giving deconstructive force to what largely operates as a placeholder within settler-state governance), can work to disrupt the attendant metapolitical matrix through which Native identities are produced and managed. As Justice Thomas suggests in his opinion in *US v Lara*, 'The Court should admit that it has failed in its quest to find a source of congressional power to adjust tribal sovereignty' (225). Emphasising that failure and thus the location of Native peoples at the threshold between law and violence, between 'ordinary domestic legislation' and imperialism, opens the state of exception to the possibility of self-determination, in which indigenous polities cease to be axiomatically enfolded within the ideological and institutional structures of the settler-state.

References

Agamben, G. (1998), *Homo Sacer: Sovereign Power and Bare Life*, trans. D. Heller-Roazen. Stanford: Stanford University Press.

—(2000), *Means Without End: Notes on Politics*, trans. V. Binetti and C. Casarino. Minnesota: University of Minnesota Press.

—(2005), *State of Exception*, trans. K. Attell. Chicago: University of Chicago Press.

Alfred, T. (1999), *Peace, Power, Righteousness: An Indigenous Manifesto*. New York: Oxford University Press.

—(2005), 'Sovereignty', in J. Barker (ed.), *Sovereignty Matters: Locations of Contestation and Possibility in Indigenous Strategies for Self-Determination*. Lincoln: University of Nebraska Press, 33–50.

Allen, C. (2000), 'Postcolonial Theory and the Discourse of Treaties', *American Quarterly*, 52(1): 59–89.

Anaya, S. James (1996), *Indigenous Peoples in International Law*. New York: Oxford University Press.

Appadurai, A. (1996), *Modernity at Large: Cultural Dimensions of Globalization*. Minneapolis: University of Minnesota Press.

Barker, J. (2005), 'For Whom Sovereignty Matters', in J. Barker (ed.), *Sovereignty Matters: Locations of Contestation and Possibility in Indigenous Strategies for Self-Determination*. Lincoln: University of Nebraska Press, 1–31.

Biersteker, T. J. and C. Weber (eds) (1996), *State Sovereignty as Social Construct*. Cambridge: Cambridge University Press.

Brown v the Board of Education, 348 US 886 (1954).

Butler, J. (2004), 'Indefinite Detention', in *Precarious Life: The Powers of Mourning and Violence*. New York: Verso, 50–100.

Byrd, J. A. (2007), '"Living My Native Life Deadly": Red Lake, Ward Churchill, and the Discourses of Competing Genocides', *American Indian Quarterly*, 31(2): 310–32.

Calarco, M. and S. DeCaroli (eds) (2007), *Giorgio Agamben: Sovereignty and Life*. Stanford: Stanford University Press.

Cherokee Nation v Georgia, 30 US 1 (1831).

Cheyfitz, E. (2000), 'The Navajo-Hopi Land Dispute: A Brief History', *Interventions*, 2(2): 248–75.

Clech Lâm, M. (2000), *At the Edge of the State: Indigenous Peoples and Self-Determination*. Ardsley, NY: Transnational Publishers.

Connolly, W. E. (2007), 'The Complexities of Sovereignty', in M. Calarco and S. DeCaroli (eds), *Giorgio Agamben: Sovereignty and Life*. Stanford: Stanford University Press, 23–42.

Cover, R. (1993), *Narrative, Violence, and the Law: The Essays of Robert Cover*, ed. M. Minow, M. Ryan and A. Sarat. Ann Arbor: University of Michigan Press.

Cramer, R. A. (2005), *Cash, Color, and Colonialism: The Politics of Tribal Acknowledgment*. Norman: University of Oklahoma Press.

DeCaroli, S. (2007), 'Boundary Stones: Giorgio Agamben and the Field of Sovereignty', in M. Calarco and S. DeCaroli (eds), *Giorgio Agamben: Sovereignty and Life*. Stanford: Stanford University Press, 43–69.

Deloria, V., Jr. and C. M. Lytle (1998), *The Nations Within: The Past and Future of American Indian Sovereignty*. Austin: University of Texas Press.

Enns, D. (2004), 'Bare Life and the Occupied Body', *Theory and Event*, 7(3): 1–24.

Field, L. W., with the Muwekema Ohlone Tribe (2003), 'Unacknowledged Tribes, Dangerous Knowledge: The Muwekema Ohlone and How Indian Identities are "Known"', *Wicazo Sa Review*, 18(2): 79–94.

Fitzpatrick, P. (2005), 'Bare Sovereignty: *Homo Sacer* and the Insistence of Law'", in A. Norris (ed.), *Politics, Metaphysics, and Death: Essays on Giorgio Agamben's* Homo Sacer. Durham: Duke University Press, 49–73.

Foucault, M. (1990), *The History of Sexuality*, vol. I, trans. R. Hurley. New York: Vintage Books.

Friedberg, L. (2000), 'Dare to Compare: Americanizing the Holocaust', *American Indian Quarterly*, 24(3): 353–80.

Garroutte, E. M. (2003), *Real Indians: Identity and the Survival of Native America*. Berkeley: University of California Press.

Gilroy, P. (1993), *The Black Atlantic: Modernity and Double Consciousness*. Cambridge, MA: Harvard University Press.

Gunter, D. (1998), 'The Technology of Tribalism: The Lemhi Indians, Federal Recognition, and the Creation of Tribal Identity', *Idaho Law Review*, 35: 85–123.

Hardt, M. and A. Negri (2000), *Empire*. Cambridge, MA: Harvard University Press.

Harring, S. L. (1994), *Crow Dog's Case: American Indian Sovereignty, Tribal Law, and United States Law in the Nineteenth Century*. New York: Cambridge University Press.

Ivison, D., P. Patton and W. Sanders (eds) (2000), *Political Theory and the Rights of Indigenous Peoples*. Cambridge: Cambridge University Press.

Jaimes, M. A. and T. Halsey (1992), 'American Indian Women: At the Center of Indigenous Resistance in North America', in M. A. Jaimes (ed.), *The State of Native America: Genocide, Colonization, and Resistance*. Boston: South End Press, 311–44.

Kaplan, A. (2005), 'Where is Guantánamo?', *American Quarterly*, 57(3): 831–58.

Kiesow, R. M. (2005), 'Law and Life', in A. Norris (ed.), *Politics, Metaphysics, and Death: Essays on Giorgio Agamben's* Homo Sacer. Durham: Duke University Press.

Konkle, M. (2004), *Writing Indian Nations: Native Intellectuals and the Politics of Historiography, 1827–1863*. Chapel Hill: University of North Carolina Press.

Laclau, E. (2007), 'Bare Life or Social Indeterminacy', in M. Calarco and S. DeCaroli (eds), *Giorgio Agamben: Sovereignty and Life*. Stanford: Stanford University Press, 11–22.

McCulloch, A. M. and D. E. Wilkins (1995), '"Constructing" Nations Within States: The Quest for Federal Recognition by the Catawba and Lumbee Tribes', *American Indian Quarterly*, 19(3): 361–88.

Niezen, R. (2003), *The Origins of Indigenism: Human Rights and the Politics of Identity*. Berkeley: University of California Press.

Norgren, J. (1996), *The Cherokee Cases: The Confrontation of Law and Politics*. New York: McGraw-Hill.

Norris, A. (ed.) (2005), *Politics, Metaphysics, and Death: Essays on Giorgio Agamben's* Homo Sacer. Durham: Duke University Press.

Oliphant v Suquamish Indian Tribe, 435 US 191 (1978).

Pease, D. E. (2003), 'The Global Homeland State: Bush's Biopolitical Settlement', *boundary 2*, 30(3): 1–18.

Plessy v Ferguson, 163 US 537 (1896).

Povinelli, E. A. (2002), *The Cunning of Recognition: Indigenous Alterities and the Making of Australian Multiculturalism*. Durham: Duke University Press.

Prucha, F. P. (1994), *American Indian Treaties: The History of a Political Anomaly*. Berkeley: University of California Press.

Raibmon, P. S. (2005), *Authentic Indians: Episodes of Encounter from the Late-Nineteenth-Century Northwest Coast*. Durham: Duke University Press.

Ramirez, R. K. (2007), *Native Hubs: Culture, Community, and Belonging in Silicon Valley and Beyond*. Durham: Duke University Press.

Rancière, J. (2004), 'Who is the Subject of the Rights of Man?', *South Atlantic Quarterly*, 103(2): 297–310.

Rasch, W. (2003), 'Human Rights as Geopolitics: Carl Schmitt and the Legal Form of American Supremacy', *Cultural Critique*, 54(Spring): 120–47.

Rifkin, M. (2008), 'Documenting Tradition: Territoriality and Textuality in Black Hawk's Narrative', *American Literature*, 80(4): 677–705.

Saunt, C. (2003), *A New Order of Things: Property, Power, and the Transformation of the Creek Indians, 1733–1816*. New York: Cambridge University Press.

Smith, A. (2005), *Conquest: Sexual Violence and American Indian Genocide*. Cambridge: South End Press.

—(2008), 'American Studies without America: Native Feminisms and the Nation-State', *American Quarterly*, 60(2): 309–16.

—and J. Kēhaulani Kauanui (2008), 'Native Feminisms without Apology', *American Quarterly*, 60(2): 241–316.

Sparke, M. (2005), *In the Space of Theory: Postfoundational Geographies of the Nation-State*. Minneapolis: University of Minnesota Press.

Stoler, A. L. (1995), *Race and the Education of Desire: Foucault's History of Sexuality and the Colonial Order of Things*. Durham: Duke University Press.

Trask, H.-K. (1999), *From a Native Daughter: Colonialism and Sovereignty in Hawai'i*. Honolulu: University of Hawai'i Press.

Turner, D. (2006), *This is Not a Peace Pipe: Towards a Critical Indigenous Philosophy*. Toronto: University of Toronto Press.

US v Lara, 541 US 193 (2004).

US v Kagama, 118 US 375 (1886).

Wilkins, D. E. (1997), *American Indian Sovereignty and the United States Supreme Court*. Austin: University of Texas Press.

—and K. Tsianina Lomawaima (2001), *Uneven Ground: American Indian Sovereignty and Federal Law*. Norman: University of Oklahoma Press.

Williams, R. A., Jr. (1997), *Linking Arms Together: American Indian Treaty Visions of Law and Peace, 1600–1800*. New York: Oxford University Press.

—(2005), *Like a Loaded Weapon: The Rehnquist Court, Indian Rights, and the Legal History of Racism in America*. Minneapolis: University of Minnesota Press.

Womack, C. S. (1999), *Red on Red: Native American Literary Separatism*. Minneapolis: University of Minnesota Press.

Notes

I would like to thank Colin (Joan) Dayan for initially suggesting that my thoughts on this topic could be an essay. A longer version of this essay was published under the same title in *Cultural Critique*, 73(Fall) 2009: 88–124, Copyright 2009 Regents of the University of Minnesota, and is reproduced with permission of the University of Minnesota Press.

1. *Cherokee Nation v Georgia*: 16–18; *US v Kagama*: 381–2; *Oliphant v Suquamish*: 208–10. These three cases are central precedents for federal Indian law which continue to be cited within contemporary decisions. In *Cherokee Nation v Georgia*, the plaintiffs were suing to get an injunction against the operation of a series of laws passed by Georgia annexing Cherokee territory to state counties. The court found that 'Indian tribes' are not 'foreign nations', but instead 'domestic dependent nations', so they are not one of the entities that can bring a suit to the Supreme Court under its constitutionally regulated original jurisdiction. The case, therefore, was dismissed for want of jurisdiction. *US v Kagama* concerned the murder of one Indian by two others on the Hoopa Valley Reservation, and the issue at stake was the constitutionality of the Major Crimes Act (1885), which made murder on reservation – as well as several other acts – a federal crime regardless of the race of the perpetrators or victims. The court found that Congress had the authority to limit the jurisdiction of Native governments on Native lands due to the presence of the latter within the boundaries of the US In *Oliphant v Suquamish*, the issue was whether an Indian tribe, specifically the government of

the Port Madison Reservation, had the authority to try non-Indian residents, and the court found that tribes do not due to the limits, both explicit and implied, placed on tribal jurisdiction by Congress as well as the general loss of 'inherent jurisdiction' over certain matters of governance due to tribes' supposed 'status'. For discussion of these cases, see Harring (1994); Norgren (1996); Wilkins (1997); and Williams (2005).

2. For commentary on Agamben and examples of the circulation of his work, particularly *Homo Sacer*, see Butler (2004); Calarco and DeCaroli (2007); Enns (2004); Friedberg (2000); Norris (2005); Pease (2003); Rancière (2004); and Rasch (2003).

3. In distinguishing Indian policy from the constitutional principles structuring US law, I am neither suggesting that the latter provides a normative framework towards which Indian policy should aspire, nor that dissolving Indian policy into the rest of US law would erase or ease the violence I describe. Rather I am arguing that the production of a national territoriality for 'domestic' law depends on the abandonment of Native polities to a state of exception. Conversely, while many scholars have suggested that violence is endemic to the operation of law, a position theorised perhaps most eloquently in the work of Robert Cover, I am suggesting that such violence is different from the imperial force at play in the domestication of Native peoples in that the latter brackets the Constitution in seeking to produce the supposedly self-evident space of US jurisdiction. In this vein, marking the difference between the state of exception and the ubiquitous gap between legal norm and application, Agamben suggests that in the exception 'the lacuna does not concern a deficiency in the text of the legislation that must be completed by the judge; it concerns, rather, a *suspension* of the order that is in force in order to guarantee its existence' (Agamben 2005: 31). For critiques of Agamben that present what he refers to as 'exception' as actually framed by law, see Fitzpatrick (2005); Kiesow (2005); and Laclau (2007). For a different discussion of the problems of invoking the 'rule of law' in light of US Indian policy, see Smith (2008).

4. In 'For Whom Sovereignty Matters', Joanne Barker suggests, 'There is no fixed meaning for what *sovereignty* is', that it 'is embedded within the specific social relations in which it is invoked and given meaning' (Barker 2005: 21). While acknowledging the multiplicity of the term's uses, I want to suggest, via Agamben, that there is a regularity to its citation in settler-state governance, particularly US

Indian policy, and that the variability of its apparent meanings is part of the topological work it performs.

5. David Wilkins observes, 'We see [. . .] that "federal Indian law" as a discipline having coherent and interconnected premises is wholly a myth' (Wilkins 1997: 2).

6. On 'biopolitics' see Foucault (1990). Some scholars when writing about Agamben, though, seem to confuse his notion of 'bare life' with an actual pre-political, natural state rather than seeing it as a way of designating the biopolitical process by which states employ discourses of nature and the body to various ends. See Connolly (2007); Fitzpatrick (2005); and Laclau (2007).

7. I should clarify that I am not trying to compare the Nazi Final Solution to US Indian policy, but gesturing towards the ways in which taking the camp as paradigmatic of modern statehood can efface the geopolitics of statehood and thus the dynamics of settler-state imperialism. For such a comparison, which utilises Agamben, see Friedberg (2000). On the problems that attend trying to put different genocides into dialogue, see Byrd (2007). In discussing the Nazi concentration camp, Agamben acknowledges that it can be traced to earlier Spanish and British tactics in which 'a state of emergency linked to a colonial war is extended to an entire civil population' (Agamben 1998: 166–7), yet he does not explore how the German programme of extermination might arise out of imperial ambitions/projects. For discussion of the ways European nationalities (in terms of space and citizenship) were carved out of broader imperial fields through the employment of shifting discourses of race, see Stoler (1995).

8. On Agamben's tendency to fetishise the relation between individuals and the state and to overlook challenges to the latter by collectives/communities, see Laclau (2007) and Rancière (2004).

9. For prominent examples of these dynamics, see Appadurai (1996); Butler (2004); Gilroy (1993); Hardt and Negri (2000); and Kaplan (2005). For discussion of the problem of space in contemporary theory, see Sparke (2005). The process I am describing can be illustrated by the tendency, in *Homo Sacer* and the work of many other contemporary scholars, to make the refugee/migrant paradigmatic in critiquing the state-form. In *Homo Sacer*, Agamben argues that the figure of the refugee, the stateless person, 'who should have embodied the rights of man par excellence [. . .] signals instead the concept's radical crisis' since the rights that ostensibly derive from being human 'show themselves to lack every protection and reality

at the moment in which they can no longer take the form of rights belonging to citizens of a state' (Agamben 1998: 126). Humanitarian efforts predicated on the pre-political status of the human 'can only grasp human life in the figure of bare or sacred life and therefore, despite themselves, maintain a secret solidarity with the very powers they ought to fight' (133), reinforcing the very logic of biopolitical exception through which sovereignty is exercised. Supposedly 'breaking the continuity between man and citizen, *nativity* and *nationality*', the figure of the refugee serves for Agamben as 'a limit concept that radically calls into question the fundamental categories of the nation-state' (131, 134), but can that example of the proliferation of 'bare life', of persons denied access to the rights of citizenship and thus made vulnerable to unrestrained state violence, speak to collectivities who have 'had their nationality *forcibly changed in their own homeland*' (Trask 1999: 30, original emphasis), who have seen themselves and their lands be subsumed by the state?

10. Congress did so through an amendment to an appropriations bill in 1871, although treaty-like 'agreements' continued to be negotiated with Native peoples but they did not have the same constitutional status as treaties. On the history of US treaty making, see Prucha (1994); Williams (1997).

11. Assumptions central to the treaty system include the existence of a centralised government with the power to enforce its decisions on the population and a clearly delimited land-base separate from that of other peoples, parts of which can be sold as property. For discussion of this process of translation, see Alfred (1999); Cheyfitz (2000); Rifkin (2008); and Saunt (2003). For accounts that emphasise treaties' recognition of Native populations as polities, while underplaying the ways in which the treaty system seeks to script the meaning/contours of political identity, see Allen (2000); Konkle (2004); and Womack (1999). I should be clear that I am in no way suggesting that existing treaties simply can be dispensed with as charades. Treaties under the Constitution are the 'supreme law of the land', and when the government seeks to ignore them by presenting them as merely a historical expediency, it vitiates its own claims to be governed by the rule of law.

12. As Joanne Barker notes, the nation defined by the Constitution 'was contingent upon it being recognized as legitimate by other already recognized nations', and Indian treaties emerged as 'a mechanism for both the exercise of nationhood and the recognition of national sovereignty', showing other countries that the US could function as

a state (Barker 2005: 4). Although beyond the limits of this essay, then, the assertion of settler-state jurisdiction also needs to be situated within international formations which while in many ways still reaffirming the absolute territoriality of states against indigenous claims also suggest another scale at which sovereignty is cited, circulated and can be contested. On the production and circulation of notions of 'sovereignty' within supra-state formations, see Biersteker and Weber (1996).

13. In the phrase elided by my use of ellipses, she also suggests that 'sovereignty' is not 'a domain that the US is said "to occupy"', but I am suggesting that sovereignty appears in the service of constituting just such a 'domain' – national space itself.

14. As Steven DeCaroli argues, 'when the edges of the sovereign field are made to appear arbitrary, the challenge is directed at the heart of sovereignty itself, and [. . .] those actions that warrant banishment share the characteristic of having called into question the legitimacy of this boundary' (DeCaroli 2007: 51). Yet he, like Agamben, treats the 'boundary' as a figure for the organising logic of law rather than as designating its literal spatial field of exercise.

15. For discussion of the various statuses created and managed by US Indian policy, especially the judiciary, see Wilkins (1997); Wilkins and Lomawaima (2001).

16. The importance of this distinction is suggested by the ongoing struggle of global Indigenous movements to have the phrase 'indigenous peoples' rather than 'indigenous people' included in international covenants, as well as the continuing effort by settler-states (especially anglophone) to block that usage. See Anaya (1996); Clech Lâm (2000); and Niezen (2003).

17. As Agamben argues in his discussion of the dynamics of banishment/abandonment through which bare life is constituted as such, 'the state of nature is not a real epoch chronologically prior to the foundation of the City but a principle internal to the City' (Agamben 1998: 105).

18. The reference here is to *Brown v the Board of Education* (1954) which struck down the principle of 'separate but equal' which had legalised segregation for nearly fifty years, since the phrase first was propagated by *Plessy v Ferguson* (1896).

19. It is worth noting that race is not the only biopolitical tactic/mode through which US sovereignty operates. Ideologies of gender also have been and are crucial to the organisation and validation of settler-state dominance. For examples of Native feminist work that

108   Agamben and Colonialism

explores this relation, see Smith (2005); Smith and Kauanui (2008); Jaimes and Halsey (1992); Ramirez (2007).

20. A discussion of Agamben's use of the concept of 'taboo', and the ways in which he uses it to exceptionalise 'culture' as that which cannot be 'politics', appears here in the longer version.

21. The dynamic Povinelli describes is perhaps most visibly at play in US Indian policy within the process of attaining federal recognition. See Cramer (2005); Field (2003); Garroutte (2003); Gunter (1998); and McCulloch and Wilkins (1995).

22. The US has at times adopted policy designed to eliminate the existence of tribes as legally recognised entities, but the government subsequently has changed course as a result of challenges to the legitimacy of such actions by other US officials, Native leaders and intellectuals, and concerned non-native organisations. For an overview of the history of US Indian policy, see Deloria and Lytle (1998).

23. In this vein, Agamben observes that 'exceptional measures' are 'juridical measures that cannot be understood in legal terms', such that 'the state of exception appears as the legal form of what cannot have legal form' (Agamben 2005: 1).

24. Finding that tribes have the power to prosecute non-member Indians, the case turned on whether such authority is one that tribes hold by themselves or one delegated to them by the federal government.

25. While Thomas ultimately is trying to argue that Native peoples are merely subjects of US law and not distinct sovereigns, the trajectory of his logic heads in the opposite direction. He observes that 'tribes [. . .] are not part of this constitutional order, and their sovereignty is not guaranteed by it', and if Native polities are extra-constitutional entities, their authority over themselves and their lands cannot be defined or circumscribed by reference to constitutionally licensed principles and institutions. Extra-constitutional entities cannot simply become objects of regular constitutional power ('ordinary domestic legislation') by congressional will, otherwise the Constitution is reduced to simply the unrestricted/unrestrictable operation of governmental fiat. On the 'extraconstitutional status of tribal nations', see Wilkins (1997).

26. Both of the scholars addressed below, Taiaiake Alfred and Dale Turner, are addressing Native relations with the Canadian state rather than the US. However, they offer versions of arguments also made by those focused on US policy, many referencing Alfred in particular, and engaging with their work helps frame the issues I

consider as relevant beyond the US context while also contextualising the US as a settler-state.

27. For a more extensive elaboration of Alfred's critique of the concept of 'sovereignty', see Alfred (1999).

28. See Field (2003); Garroutte (2003); Gunter (1998); Ivison, Patton and Sanders (2000); Niezen (2003); Povinelli (2002); and Raibmon (2005).

29. In many ways, such a strategy already is at play in Indigenous internationalism, particularly the movement to have Indigenous self-determination recognised as a fundamental right by international institutions like the UN. See Anaya (1996); Clech Lâm (2000); Niezen (2003); Trask (1999); and Williams (2005: 170–95).

30. David Wilkins (1997: 309) offers a similar formulation, calling for the repudiation of the 'plenary power' doctrine and the reaffirmation of a policy predicated on Native consent. His argument, though, underplays the metapolitical power exerted over the terms of 'consent' through the citation of 'sovereignty', whether expressed specifically as plenary power or not.

5

Reading Kenya's Colonial State of Emergency after Agamben

Stephen Morton

In June 2009 the London lawyers Leigh Day filed a legal case against the British government on behalf of five Kenyans representing the Mau Mau War Veterans' Association, for atrocities and human rights violations committed during the state of emergency in Kenya between 1952 and 1960. In a letter addressed to the then British Prime Minister, Gordon Brown, the former detainees begin by invoking the Kikuyu proverb '*Muingatwo na kihoto dacokago; muingatwo na njuguma niacokaga*' ('He who is defeated with unjust force will always come back; he who is dealt with justly will never come back'). By framing their demand for justice within the rhetorical structure of a Kikuyu proverb, the detainees situate their public address to the British government within the ethical and legal frame of reference of Kikuyu society. The proverb is significant, in other words, because it legitimates the detainees' claim with reference to the legal values and codes of Kikuyu society and culture, and defines the authority of the former detainees as legal subjects with the right to address the figure of British Parliamentary sovereignty, the prime minister. In the letter, the former detainees proceed to explain how they are Kenyans in 'our 70s and 80s who have travelled to London from our rural villages to tell the world of the torture and trauma we have lived through at the hands of the British colonial regime'. The former detainees are careful to emphasise that their claim is not 'a case about colonialism or politics'. Yet their assertions that 'thousands of Kenyans were detained during the Kenyan emergency', that 'thousands were tortured and treated inhumanely', and 'that this violence was known about and authorised at the highest levels of Government in London at the time' clearly link the traumatic aftermath of Britain's state of emergency in Kenya with the violence of colonial rule ('Letter to Gordon Brown'). In so doing, the former detainees foreground the way in which the violence associated with the colonial state of emergency in Kenya has been normalised by the British colonial state. Moreover, by demanding that the British government publicly acknowledge the historical wrongs committed against the Kikuyu population, the five Mau Mau veterans – Ndiki Mutua, Paulo Nzili, Jane Muthoni Mara, Wambugu Wa Nyingi and Susan Ngondi – seek redress for the British colonial government's systematic torture, brutalisation and detention without trial of thousands of Kenyans during the state of emergency.

Such a demand for truth and justice is not without precedent. After all, writing letters to leading colonial administrators and senior British government officials was a crucial part of the political campaign for many suspected Mau Mau terrorists detained without trial in British concentration camps during the 1950s (Elkins 2005: 205–8). In one letter held in the Kenya National Archives, Albert Mbogo Njoroge, a detainee at the Gutundu Works Camp at Kiambu, poses the following two questions: 'What is the meaning of the word emergency? Is emergency inhuman deeds?' (cited in Elkins 2005: 206). By asking these questions, Njoroge can be seen to address the British colonial authorities from the standpoint of a Kikuyu detainee, who understands the meaning of the word 'emergency' in terms of the very 'inhuman deeds' of violence of which he had direct physical experience, rather than in the terms of an abstract legal definition of a state of emergency as a law which suspends the normal rule of law. In doing so, Njoroge unmasks the very *raison d'être* of the British colonial state of emergency: to discipline and punish the anti-colonial resistance movement in Kenya, and to reassert British colonial sovereignty in Kenya.

Such letters from Kikuyu detainees also shed significant light on the colonial genealogy of the state of emergency as a quasi-legal technique of governmentality, and, in so doing, offer an important supplement to Giorgio Agamben's account of the state of exception. He has argued that 'the state of exception [*Ausnahmezustand*] tends increasingly to appear as the dominant paradigm of government in contemporary politics' (Agamben 2005: 2). By drawing on the German term *Ausnahmezustand*, or 'state of exception', rather than the English term 'state of emergency', Agamben suggests that the state of exception is not reducible to an official legal declaration by a state that temporarily suspends existing rights, rules and regulations, but also involves multiple actors, institutions and techniques of power to sustain this state of emergency. Agamben's argument that there are structural similarities between the use of emergency measures in post-revolutionary France, Britain during the First World War, and Nazi Germany during the 1930s has far-reaching implications for understanding the claims of liberal democratic societies to protect the rights and freedoms of the human subject, and raises provocative questions about the putative differences between liberal democratic states and totalitarian governments. Yet his comparative analysis of a range of different states of emergency not only overlooks the precise historical connections between these states of exception and the proliferation of new laws, regulations and agents that are involved in contemporary states of emergency (Hussein 2007); it also elides the concatenation of civil, military and police powers specific to political sovereignty in the European colony. The wide powers that were granted to the police and to the military in former European colonies such as Kenya certainly challenged the liberal rhetoric of the civilising mission, but these powers were buttressed by the founding violence of European colonial sovereignty that denied the civil and political rights to the colonised that European nation-states guaranteed for its own citizens, as well as for European colonial settlers (Mbembe 2001: 24–65). What Agamben's analysis of the state of exception fails to consider, in short, is how colonial sovereignty was experienced as a permanent state of emergency from the standpoint of the colonised.

To further elucidate these limitations in Agamben's account of the state of exception, this chapter considers how the state of emergency in Kenya from 1952–60 has been codified in the rhetoric of British colonialism, and criticised by postcolonial African writers and intellectuals as a sign of the inherent violence and injustice of European colonial rule. Beginning with a discussion of Ngũgĩ wa Thiong'o's critique of colonial narratives of the emergency period, the chapter proceeds to consider how the colonial government used the deaths of white settlers and Kenyan Loyalists to justify its recourse to emergency legislation and the detention of an estimated 1.5 million Kikuyu people, who were suspected by the colonial authorities of being involved with the Land and Freedom movement, more commonly known as the Mau Mau. As a counterpoint to such colonial narratives of the emergency period in Kenya, the chapter concludes by assessing how Ngũgĩ's novel *Weep Not, Child* (1964) both foregrounds and contests the human rights abuses in military courts and detention camps that emergency legislation made possible. In so doing, I suggest that the narrative of emergency in *Weep Not, Child* not only discloses the colonial genealogy of the state of exception that Agamben elides; the novel also highlights the forms of agency and resistance to the racial and ethnic frames of the British colonial administration that attempted to reduce the Kikuyu people to a form of bare life.

Ngũgĩ, Fanon and the Colonial State of Emergency in Kenya

If Agamben's theory of the state of exception elucidates the complex legal and extra-legal procedures by which European and North American states have been able to exercise their sovereign power through the use of force, the extent to which such theories can account for the political and legislative formation of the European colony is an open question, as the political philosopher Achille Mbembe has suggested. For Mbembe, 'the colony' is 'the site where sovereignty consists fundamentally in the exercise of power outside the law (*ab legibus solutus*) and where "peace" is more likely to take on the face of a "war without end"' (Mbembe 2003: 23). In light of Mbembe's argument, the very idea of an exception to the rule of law would appear to be beside the point in the context of the European colony. This is not to suggest that the law did not exist in the European colony, but rather that the colony was the place where the tensions between the rule of law and the absolute sovereignty of the European state were played out (Hussain 2003: 6–7). Indeed, it was the bureaucratic forms of colonial government by decrees rather than by the rule of law in late nineteenth-century sub-Saharan Africa that formed a prototype for the political formation of National Socialism, as Hannah Arendt has powerfully argued in *The Origins of Totalitarianism* (Arendt 1986: 221). What Arendt crucially foregrounds here is the colonial genealogy of the state of exception, and the racist logic that underpins it.

As Agamben has suggested, states of exception draw on a range of legal and non-legal techniques of power to assert sovereignty. In the colonial context, European colonial governments mobilised a repository of narratives and metaphors to mask, obfuscate and justify the violent techniques of colonial sovereignty, particularly during national independence struggles. The colonial rhetoric surrounding the state of emergency in Kenya is no exception to this tendency. The case for the declaration of a state of emergency in Kenya was predicated in part on the colonial stereotype of the Mau Mau. This stereotype was based on the myth surrounding the oathing ceremonies in the colonial imagination. The oathing ceremonies were a tactic of political organisation in which resistance fighters swore an oath of unity to the political cause of *ithaka na wiyathi* (land and freedom) (Elkins 2005: 21; Anderson 2005: 27). But these ceremonies were represented in the British press and in popular literary representations of the Mau Mau as a sign of African savagery. The colonial stereotype of the Mau Mau was also linked to the violent attacks carried out by some members of the Land and Freedom Army against white settlers and against Kikuyu chiefs and their followers who were loyal to the British colonial state (Anderson 2005: 87).

It was this failure of the European imagination to comprehend that the violent acts of the Land and Freedom Army were an expression of political opposition to the policies of the British colonial state that prompted European settlers and government officials to frame such acts of violent anti-colonial insurgency as a kind of illness or psychological disease brought on by the corrupting effects of oathing ceremonies (Anderson 2005: 88). For the oathing ceremonies were associated in the European mind with a racist stereotype of African religion and culture as atavistic and anti-Western. Such stereotypes could certainly be understood to disavow the role of the oath in Western societies. As Agamben has argued in *The Sacrament of Language* (Agamben 2011), the oath functions as a particular kind of speech act in which a human subject puts his or her own life at stake before a figure of legal or religious authority. By disavowing the significance of the oath in the political culture of Western societies, colonial stereotypes of Mau Mau oathing ceremonies also disavow the constitutive role of the oath in defining the subject's relationship to competing forms of sovereignty. Indeed, the counter-oathing ceremonies that the British colonial administration introduced in the detention camps to 'rehabilitate' Kikuyu detainees suspected of being Mau Mau insurgents during the colonial state of emergency in Kenya foreground the way in which British colonial sovereignty also depended on the performance of an oath that put the subject's life at stake in a way that mirrored the violence that the rhetoric of

British colonialism attributed to Mau Mau oathing rituals. What is more, such colonial stereotypes of the 'savagery' of Mau Mau oathing rituals served to deny the social and economic significance of the Kikuyu's grievances: the systematic expropriation of Kikuyu land by white settlers in the first half of the twentieth century; the increasing control and regulation of Kikuyu labour; and the levying of unpopular forms of taxation, such as the hut tax and the poll tax (Elkins 2005: 16–17). In this way, the recourse to a colonial state of emergency in Kenya was justified through the use of a metalepsis, or a rhetorical manipulation of causes and effects, in which the 'evil savagery' of Mau Mau is presented as the cause of the colonial state of emergency, rather than a political response to the violent system of colonial sovereignty, race labour and the forced dispossession of Kikuyu land.

It is precisely the rhetorical manipulation of causes and effects in the dominant colonial narrative of the Kenyan state of emergency that the Kenyan writer Ngũgĩ wa Thiong'o contests in his essay 'Mau Mau: Violence, and Culture'. First written in 1963 (the year of Kenya's independence) and published in his 1972 essay collection *Homecoming*, this essay is ostensibly a review of Fred Majdalany's historical monograph *State of Emergency* (1962). But Majdalany's book also provides Ngũgĩ with an example of how some European historians as well as colonial administrators and white settlers distorted the meaning of the colonial state of emergency in Kenya. It is for this reason that Ngũgĩ begins his essay with an account of the economic, political and cultural conditions of British colonialism in Kenya that precipitated the political revolt against colonial rule in the 1950s. In Ngũgĩ's account, the

> white settler came early in the century and he immediately controlled the heart of the economy by appropriating the best part of the land for himself. Alienation of land, after all, was then the declared British colonial policy for the region which later became Kenya. (Ngũgĩ 1972: 26)

The only way in which white settlers were able to consolidate this 'economic position', Ngũgĩ continues, was by forcing 'black men to work in labour gangs' and rationalising this 'exploitation of African land and labour by claiming he was civilising a primitive people' (Ngũgĩ 1972: 26). By beginning his critique of Majdalany's *State of Emergency* with an account of the colonial expropriation of land, the exploitation of African labour power, and the colonial rhetoric that was mobilised to justify this expropriation, Ngũgĩ implies that the 'Mau Mau revolution of 1952' was grounded in a political struggle over land and labour (26). Such an argument is made plain later in the review when Ngũgĩ explicitly states that the 'basic objectives of Mau Mau revolutionaries were to drive out the Europeans, seize the government, and give back to the Kenya peasants their stolen property and land' (28).

In highlighting the rational political objectives of the Land and Freedom Army, Ngũgĩ also challenges the colonial stereotype of Mau Mau as atavistic and primitive, and emphasises that the Mau Mau oath 'was a commitment to sabotage the colonial machine and to kill if necessary' (Ngũgĩ 1972: 28). Significantly, his analysis of the violent acts of anti-colonial insurgency echoes Frantz Fanon's assertion in *The Wretched of the Earth* that 'At the individual level, violence is a cleansing force' (Fanon 2004: 51). In Ngũgĩ's argument, the crucial point about acts of violence – as with oaths – is 'the nature of the particular historical circumstances that make them necessary and the cause they serve' (Ngũgĩ 1972: 28). By framing the use of violence in terms of its particular historical circumstances, Ngũgĩ judges the use of violence according to a moral logic of means and ends: 'Violence in order to change an intolerable, unjust social order is not savagery: it purifies man. Violence to protect and preserve an unjust, oppressive social order is criminal and diminishes man' (28). This suggestion that violence 'purifies man' borrows from Fanon's suggestion that violence is a 'cleansing force' for the psychic life of the colonised. What is more, Ngũgĩ can be seen to develop Fanon's point that the 'praxis' of violence through liberation 'enlightens the militant because it shows him the means and the ends' (Fanon 2004: 44). By linking the violent means of anti-colonial struggle to the specific political goals of the Land and Freedom movement in colonial Kenya, in other words, Ngũgĩ implies that anti-colonial violence has a political and moral, as well as a psychotherapeutic, purpose. Just as Fanon suggested that violence is 'the perfect mediation' because the 'colonized man [sic] liberates himself in and through violence' (Fanon 2004: 44), so for Ngũgĩ violence is a means for the colonised to assert sovereignty over both their land and their lives.

Ngũgĩ's rethinking of Fanon in the context of the Kenyan state of emergency in the 1950s is important also because it helps to clarify how the use of violence by the European colonial government was not an exceptional measure specific to the circumstances of the state of emergency, but was rather part of the repressive apparatus of the colonial state. The state of emergency, Ngũgĩ contends, only 'intensified' the violence that the British colonial government had already 'perpetrated' on the 'African people for fifty years' (Ngũgĩ 1972: 29). It is precisely this history of violent colonial sovereignty and dispossession that colonial narratives of the state of emergency in Kenya sought to distort by framing the state of emergency as a necessary and measured response to the 'savage' attacks on European settlers and Kenyan loyalists by Mau Mau guerrillas, and by effacing the brutal methods of counter-insurgency that the British colonial administration mobilised to suppress the resistance movement. Such a gross historical distortion is exemplified for Ngũgĩ in Fred Majdalany's reliance on the records of 'the Colonial Office, the Kenya government officials, members of the administration at the time of the Emergency, the generals and the chiefs – who were all anti-Mau Mau' (28), and by his failure 'to tell the full story of several crucial incidents'. For Ngũgĩ, this failure is exemplified in Majdalany's account of the Lari massacre:

> Majdalany recounts what is generally called the Lari massacre in colonial records, but does not add that many of the killed were collaborators with the enemy and hence traitors to the African cause: that many innocent men and women were afterwards led to the forest and summarily executed by the government forces. I know six who were taken from my village, which was miles from Lari. The relatives of the six murdered people tried to take the case to the courts, but this never came to anything. Such was the nature of colonial justice in Kenya, even before this period of war. (Ngũgĩ 1972: 29)

Ngũgĩ's critique of *State of Emergency* is significant because it identifies a broader tendency in histories of the emergency period in Kenya to elide and distort the rational political grievances of the Land and Freedom movement, and to downplay the violent practices that the colonial government encouraged and legitimated through its range of emergency measures. It is this historical elision and distortion in dominant colonial narratives of the emergency that Ngũgĩ attempts to address in his literary fiction, as we will see later in the chapter. Before doing so, however, the following section considers the predominant colonial narrative of emergency in Kenya, and analyses the ways in which the state of emergency was framed and justified in the rhetoric of empire.

Writing the State of Exception in Colonial Kenya

The formal declaration of a state of emergency in Kenya took place on 20 October 1952 after several exchanges between senior government officials, such as the colonial secretary in London, Oliver Lyttelton and the colonial governor of Kenya, Sir Evelyn Baring. The emergency regulations, together with Baring's proclamation, were published in an *Official Gazette Extraordinary* on 21 October 1952. These emergency powers were framed with reference to the British Emergency Powers (Defence) Act 1939, a statute which had given the British government unrestricted power to detain individuals deemed dangerous to the state in a time of war, following the outbreak of the Second World War (Simpson 1992). But the correspondence between senior colonial officials in Kenya also raised questions about the limitations of the British Emergency Powers (Defence) Act 1939 to detain individuals deemed dangerous to the stability of the colonial government. In one exchange between colonial officials dated 11 October 1952, there is a suggestion that the Malayan Emergency Regulations Ordinance 1948, which had been used to suppress communist resistance to the colonial government in Malaya, provided a more robust legal framework for the Kenyan state of emergency. The reason for this is that the Malayan state of emergency had empowered the state to detain suspected insurgents indefinitely, and that the period of detention would not expire at the end of the colonial state of emergency. The British Emergency Powers (Defence) Act 1939, by contrast, had 'no such provision' (Public Records Office 1952). Despite such reservations, the published declaration of 20 October 1952 would seem to indicate that the emergency regulations were perfectly adequate for the purposes of the colonial government's counter-insurgency strategy. According to Part II, Section 6 (I) of the *Official Gazette Extraordinary*, the United Kingdom Emergency Powers Order in Council 1939 empowered the Governor of Kenya to

> make such Regulations as appear to him to be necessary or expedient for securing the public safety, the defence of the territory, the main-tenance of public order and the suppression of mutiny, rebellion and

riot, and for maintaining supplies and services essential to the life of the community. (Colony and Protectorate of Kenya 1952: 487)

These regulations included making 'provision for the detention of persons and the deportation and exclusion of persons from the territory', authorising the seizure of 'any property or undertaking', 'the entering and search of any premises', providing for the amendment of 'any law, for suspending the operation of any law and for applying any law with or without modification'. The emergency regulations also provided for the 'apprehension, trial and punishment of persons offending against the Regulations', but they did not authorise 'the making of provisions for the trial of persons by Military Courts' (Colony and Protectorate of Kenya 1952: 487). The *Official Gazette Extraordinary* also included a separate Government Notice subtitled 'Emergency Regulations 1952', which defined in detail Baring's interpretation of these broad emergency powers as they appeared 'necessary or expedient' to him for maintaining political order in British Kenya. These regulations detailed the terms of detention orders and police powers to detain suspected persons, as well as outlawing acts likely to cause 'mutiny, sedition or disaffection', public meetings or processions likely to 'give rise to grave disorder', the 'publication of alarming reports', subversive publications, and the possession of firearms and explosive substances, as well as a 'sword, spear, cutlass, *panga*, *simi*, axe, hatchet, knife or other dangerous weapon' (Colony and Protectorate of Kenya 1952: 491–4). Such regulations certainly highlight the wide powers afforded to the Governor of Kenya to assert sovereignty over the British colony. And these powers are further evidenced in the amendments to the emergency regulations passed in April and May 1953, which made the unlawful possession of firearms, explosives and ammunition 'a capital offence' (339); and created 'emergency zones', or geographical areas in which 'scheduled offences' such as possession of offensive weapons, consorting with armed persons or persons 'acting prejudicially to public safety' could be tried immediately in a Court of Emergency Assize (523–8). These latter amendments also included clear guidelines on the punishment and treatment of detainees in the detention camps (395–407). Yet even though the regulations empowered the Governor of Kenya and various other agents and institutions of the colonial state to detain, torture, violate and execute the Kikuyu population with impunity, this violent exercise of colonial sovereignty was not self-evident from the text of the emergency regulations themselves.

At the time that the state of emergency was declared, the colonial government had determined that they would arrest, try and detain the leader of the Kenyan African Union, Jomo Kenyatta, for his role in aiding and abetting the violent acts carried out by the Land and Freedom movement. This strategy would ultimately prove to be counterproductive, for it made Kenyatta into a symbol of political resistance, even though he had more moderate political leanings and did not support the violent methods of resistance employed by the Land and Freedom movement (Elkins 2005: 36; Anderson 2005: 67). What is crucial, however, is that the emergency regulations consolidated the sovereignty of the colonial government, and allowed it to exercise greater and greater control over the life and death of the Kikuyu population.

As in the colonial spaces of South Africa, India and Ireland, the effects of the colonial state of emergency cannot be understood with reference to the letter of the law alone. For although the colonial government gazettes contain detailed information defining the specific legal powers accorded to colonial governments, they tend to occlude any discussion of the constitutive role of cultural representation and cultural stereotypes in framing the Land and Freedom Army as savage, inhuman figures, who could be tortured and killed with impunity. Indeed, it was in texts such as F. D. Corfield's official history of the origins and growth of Mau Mau (Kenya 1960), J. C. Carothers's report *The Psychology of Mau Mau* (Kenya 1954), and Louis Leakey's analysis of the Mau Mau's political demands and tactics (1952; 1954) that the political activities of the Land and Freedom movement were framed in terms of colonial stereotypes of the Mau Mau. These colonial stereotypes were reiterated in British newspaper reports of Mau Mau atrocities; in historical accounts of the state of emergency in Kenya, such as Fred Majdalanay's *State of Emergency*; and in popular novels, such as Robert Ruark's *Something of Value* (1954) and *Uhuru* (1960), and Elspeth Huxley's *A Thing to Love* (1954).

Such stereotypes were used to justify the rehabilitation of Mau Mau detainees to an international public, and to mask the use of detention and torture as a means of disciplining the civilian population and punishing the Mau Mau. In the special detention camp at Manyani reserved for prisoners labelled as 'hardcore', sadistic public spectacles of torture such as forced anal penetration and

rolling detainees in barbed wire were used to punish Mau Mau
detainees, and to terrorise and subdue other detainees in the camp
(Elkins 2005: 156–7). Other forms of physical punishment and
forced labour in the British colonial detention camps in Kenya may
seem banal by comparison with such extreme forms of violence,
but they were no less effective in controlling the population. In his
account of life in the Manda Island detention camp, for instance,
the writer Gakaara wa Wanjau describes how the camp provided
an extra-legal space in which the camp officer forced the detainees
to comply with the colonial government's demand that the detainees work. While the officer states that 'the law of Kenya had now
made a provision for forced labour for detainees' and that 'all
detainees would now work whether or not they volunteered for
it', he also refuses to show the prisoners the confidential document
containing the order (Gakaara 1988: 64). In this respect, Gakaara
suggests that the colonial detention camp is a space beyond the
normal rule of law, a view that is confirmed by the camp officer's
assertion that 'we had gone beyond the regard of the law courts
of the British Government' (64). The ambivalent legal space
of the detention camp also allows the camp commanders and
prison guards to control the bodily lives of the prison population.
Gakaara details this biopolitical function of the detention camp
by documenting the ways in which the prison guards torture some
of the detainees, police their diet, regulate their access to prison
education and sentence the detainees to solitary confinement. On
a superficial reading, Gakaara's narrative of the colonial detention
camp may seem to exemplify Agamben's account of the state of
exception, a space which relegates the detainee to an extra-legal
position in which she or he can be tortured or killed with impunity. Indeed, the British colonial state's demand that Mau Mau
detainees 'confess' to having taken an oath would seem to confirm
Agamben's suggestion that sacred forms of power continue to
underpin modern forms of sovereignty that are deemed to be
secular. But what such a reading crucially overlooks is the agency
and social organisation of detainees in prison camps such as that
at Manda Island. For, as Gakaara repeatedly suggests, it was the
prisoners' networks that allowed them to win small concessions
within the detention camp.

Postcolonial Literary Narratives of Kenya's Colonial State of Exception

Gakaara's prison diary offers a vivid first-hand testimony of the conditions within Manda Island detention camp during the emergency in Kenya, and for this reason can be seen to offer an insight into the shared historical experiences of the state of emergency from the standpoint of Kikuyu detainees. Like Gakaara, Ngũgĩ wa Thiong'o draws on his autobiographical experience of the state of emergency in colonial Kenya in novels such as *Weep Not, Child* and *A Grain of Wheat* (2002a). The specific details of Ngũgĩ's experiences of the emergency and his elder brother's involvement in the Land and Freedom struggle are detailed in his memoir *Dreams in a Time of War* (2010). As a child during the emergency, Ngũgĩ did not have direct experience of the detention camps. Yet he weaves together family stories and memories of the emergency in his postcolonial fiction to articulate the relationship between the state of emergency and the broader history of British colonialism in Kenya. In so doing, Ngũgĩ encourages us to read the emergency in Kenya as a continuation and intensification of violent colonial sovereignty and dispossession under the guise of the colonial rhetoric of the civilising mission.

The 'civilising' process of rehabilitation in the detention camps that was unmasked by Gakaara as a lesson in violent colonial subjection is also explored by Ngũgĩ in his first novel, *Weep Not, Child*. By working with and against the resources of the European *bildungsroman*, Ngũgĩ raises important questions about the ideological function of colonial education, and its relationship to colonial sovereignty. The genesis of the *bildungsroman* as novelistic form is associated with the rise of the bourgeois individual in the late eighteenth and early nineteenth centuries, and by an attempt to contain conflict between the two dominant economic classes of the epoch. In Franco Moretti's account of the genre, the *bildungsroman* has 'accustomed us to looking at normality *from within* rather than from the stance of its exceptions' – a fictional way of looking at the world that may seem to elude the violence and conflict associated with the French Revolution (Moretti 1987: 11, original emphasis). Yet, as Moretti goes on to suggest through a passing reference to Michel Foucault, normality is an effect of power that is produced though social institutions. Significantly, Moretti adds that the 'literary expression' of normality is 'nineteenth-century mass narrative: the literature of states of exception, of extreme ills and extreme remedies' (12). Moretti does not elaborate on what he means by 'the literature of states of exception' (12). Yet if this phrase is mapped onto the techniques of Western colonial sovereignty, it becomes possible to see how the aesthetic form of the *bildungsroman* is marked by the imperialist determinants of European aesthetics, and by the civilising mission of English literature (Redfield 1986: viii). In a gloss on the meaning of the term *bildung*, Marc Redfield identifies a 'profound homology between pedagogy and aesthetics, the education of a subject and the figuration of a text' (38–9). In Redfield's account, the project of aesthetic education underpinning the *bildungsroman* has 'enormous political utility and is in fact inseparable [. . .] from the rhetoric of class struggle and colonial administration'. Citing David Lloyd, Redfield argues that the '"individual narrative of self-formation is subsumed in the larger narrative of the civilizing process, the passage from savagery to civility, which is the master narrative of modernity"' (51).

It is precisely this connection between the '"individual narrative of self-formation"' and the '"larger narrative of the civilizing process"' that Ngũgĩ wa Thiong'o interrogates in his first published novel *Weep Not, Child*. By working with and against the generic codes of the *bildungsroman*, Ngũgĩ gradually reveals how the civilising mission of education serves to further alienate the colonised from their land and their culture. The novel begins with an account of the male protagonist's desire for an education. Although it is Njoroge's mother, Nyokabi, who facilitates Njoroge's education, Ngũgĩ frames his protagonist's education in relation to the nationalist rhetoric of Jomo Kenyatta. As his brother Kamau explains: 'Your learning is for all of us. Father says the same thing. He is anxious that you go on, so you might bring light to our home. Education is the light of Kenya. That's what Jomo says' (38). In this passage, Njoroge and his family are interpellated by the belief that education will lead to their emancipation. Following the imprisonment of Jomo Kenyatta, the death of Ngotho (Njoroge's father), and Njoroge's own torture in the wake of the state of emergency, however, Ngũgĩ suggests that colonial education is a myth designed to preserve colonial sovereignty.

By reframing the *bildungsroman* in the context of Kenya's colonial state of emergency, Ngũgĩ demonstrates how the civilising mission of colonial education alienates the colonised from their land and their culture. If *Weep Not, Child* exemplifies what Franco Moretti calls the literature of states of exception, it is a literary text that also reveals how the colonial state of emergency is a continuation and intensification of the violence of colonial sovereignty. For the European colony, as Achille Mbembe has argued, can itself be understood as 'the location par excellence where the controls and guarantees of judicial order can be suspended – the zone where the violence of the state of exception is deemed to operate in the service of "civilization"' (Mbembe 2003: 23). The paradox of the narrative process of self-formation in *Weep Not, Child* is that it leads the male protagonist to lose 'faith in all the things he had earlier believed in, like wealth, power, education, religion' (Ngũgĩ 1964: 134). This is not to suggest, however, that the novel simply reinforces the subordination of Ngũgĩ's Kikuyu characters to the wretched condition of bare life. To be sure, Njoroge considers taking his own life at the end of *Weep Not, Child* following the death of his father, the imminent execution of his brother, Boro, and the uncertain fate of Kori, whose detention prompts Njoroge to ask whether 'He might be killed like those who had been beaten to death at Hola Camp' (134). Yet it is Njoroge's mothers Nyokabi and Njeri who persuade him against suicide. Njoroge regards his failure to take his own life as a sign of his cowardice. But this is to overlook the important role of women in Ngũgĩ's fictional depiction of the emergent postcolonial nation. Such a role may be limited by the narrow, patriarchal view of women presented in some of Ngũgĩ's fiction (Ngũgĩ 2002b; Boehmer 1991; Nicholls 2010). But what Njeri and Nyokabi's transgression of the curfew imposed during the colonial state of emergency at the end of the novel also gestures towards is a form of agency and collectivity that circumvents the violence of colonial sovereignty. By circumventing the spatial and temporal restrictions imposed by the emergency, Njeri and Nyokabi's trangression of the curfew offers a counterpoint to the necropolitical form of resistance, which Njoroge imagines as the only available means of effective resistance to the colonial state.

The forms of political agency and collectivity that Ngũgĩ articulates in his writing may seem to illuminate the limitations of Giorgio Agamben's reflections on the state of exception to account for the formation of sovereign power in the European colony, and the forms of resistance to it. As this essay has tried to suggest, Agamben's account of the state of exception does not offer a sustained account of the particular ways in which the state of exception has become normalised in formations of colonial sovereignty through cultural stereotypes of 'African savagery' that have been mobilised by the colonial state to justify the use of coercive techniques of governmentality. Yet, as the recent challenge that the Mau Mau War Veterans' Association presented to the British government indicates, there are also ways in which Agamben's reflections on sovereignty and the state of exception can be recalibrated to account for the spatial and temporal 'dis-application' between the colonial laws of emergency that granted executive powers to a colonial governor or administrator and the techniques of violent colonial governmentality that such laws enabled. In their attempt to bring the British government to justice for the historical legacy of colonisation and violent forms of counter-insurgency during the emergency period, the Mau Mau War Veterans' Association prompted the British Foreign Office to disclose 2,000 boxes of documents that may implicate the British Government in the violent practices of the colonial administration during the emergency period in Kenya (Macintyre 2011: 14). In so doing, the Mau Mau veterans used the legal space of the British High Court to highlight and contest the ways in which the violence of the colonial power of exception is buried in the archives of colonialism. Such tactics offer a powerful example of the way in which the subjects of colonial violence have used the juridical techniques associated with colonial power against the institutions of colonial sovereignty in order to demand justice and recognition for past wrongs committed. Just as Ngũgĩ uses the codes and conventions of the European *bildungsroman* to foreground the process by which the rhetoric of the civilising mission worked to normalise the violence of colonial sovereignty, so the Mau Mau War Veterans' Association use the juridical codes of the British legal system to disclose the systematic violence of colonial governmentality. In this respect, both Ngũgĩ and the Mau Mau War Veterans' Association offer an important supplement to Agamben's gesture towards another more radical use of the law, which seeks both to study and play with the law in order to deactivate it (Agamben 2005: 64).

References

Agamben, G. (2005), *State of Exception*, trans. K. Attell. Chicago: University of Chicago Press.

—(2011), *The Sacrament of Language: An Archaeology of the Oath*, trans. A. Kotsko. Cambridge: Polity.

Anderson, D. (2005), *Histories of the Hanged: Britain's Dirty War in Kenya and the End of Empire*. London: Weidenfeld and Nicolson.

Arendt, H. (1986), *The Origins of Totalitarianism*. London: George Allen and Unwin.

Boehmer, E. (1991), 'The Master's Dance to the Master's Voice: Revolutionary Nationalism and the Representation of Women in the Writing of Ngũgĩ wa Thiong'o', *The Journal of Commonwealth Literature*, March, 26(1): 188–97.

Colony and Protectorate of Kenya (1952), *Official Gazette Extraordinary*, 21 October.

Elkins, C. (2005), *Britain's Gulag: The Brutal End of Empire in Kenya*. London: Jonathan Cape.

Fanon, F. (2004), *The Wretched of the Earth*, trans. R. Philcox. New York: Grove Press.

Gakaara wa Wanjau (1988), *Mau Mau Author in Detention*. Nairobi: Heinemann Kenya.

Hussain, N. (2003), *The Jurisprudence of Emergency: Colonialism and the Rule of Law*. Ann Arbor: University of Michigan Press.

Hussein, N. (2007), 'Beyond Norm and Exception: Guantánamo', *Critical Inquiry*, 33(Summer): 734–47.

Huxley, E. (1954), *A Thing to Love*. London: Chatto and Windus.

Kenya (1954), *The Psychology of Mau Mau by Dr J.C. Carothers*. Nairobi: Government Printer.

— (1960), *The Origins and Growth of Mau Mau: An Historical Survey*, Cmnd. 1030. London: HMSO.

Leakey, L. (1952), *Mau Mau and the Gikuyu*. London: Methuen.

—(1954), *Defeating Mau Mau*. London: Methuen.

'Letter to Gordon Brown from the Mau Mau Veterans', available at http://www.leighday.co.uk/documents/Letter%20to%20Gordon%20 Brown%20from%20the%20Mau%20Mau%20veterans.pdf, accessed 27 July 2009.

Macintyre, B. (2011), 'Secret Colonial Files May Show More Blood on British Hands', *The Times*, 7 April, 14.

Majdalany, F. (1962), *State of Emergency: The Full Story of Mau Mau*. London: Longmans.

Mbembe, A. (2001), *On the Postcolony*. Berkeley: University of California Press.

—(2003), 'Necropolitics', trans. Libby Meintjes, *Public Culture*, 15(1): 11–40.

Moretti, F. (1987), *The Way of the World: The Bildungsroman in European Culture*. London: Verso.

Ngũgĩ wa Thiong'o (1964), *Weep Not, Child*. London: Heinemann.

—(1972), *Homecoming: Essays on African and Caribbean Literature, Culture and Politics*. London: Heinemann Educational Books.

—([1967] 2002a), *A Grain of Wheat*. London: Penguin.

—(2002b), *The River Between*. London: Penguin and Heinemann.

—(2010), *Dreams in a Time of War*. London: Harvill Secker.

Nicholls, B. (2010), *Ngũgĩ wa Thiong'o, Gender, and the Ethics of Postcolonial Reading*. Farnham: Ashgate.

Public Records Office (1952), Colonial Office 822/ 443.

Redfield, M. (1986), *Phantom Formations: Aesthetic Ideology and the Bildungsroman*. Ithaca, NY: Cornell University Press.

Ruark, R. (1954), *Something of Value*. London: Hamish Hamilton.

—(1960), *Uhuru*. London: Hamish Hamilton.

Simpson, A. W. B. (1992), *In the Highest Degree Odious: Detention Without Trial in Wartime Britain*. Oxford: Clarendon Press.

6

Colonial Sovereignty, Forms of Life and Liminal Beings in South Africa
Stewart Motha

Giorgio Agamben has said little or nothing about colonialism per se. Nonetheless, this volume is dedicated to the possibility and potential of Agamben's thought contributing to thinking a range of problems, theoretical and practical, that might be encountered in the colonial context. Agamben is a philosopher known for elaborating transhistorical concepts and paradigm shifts, and is thought to be a theorist of a new, often ineffable, politics. His philosophical writings address sovereignty, biopolitics, transformations in the nature and character of the state, the 'camp' as paradigm of modernity, the fragility and contingency of the rule of law, and the exposure of various 'forms of life' to the vicissitudes of violence and power. These are all pertinent to the colonial and postcolonial context. Notwithstanding this potential, there is a strong conviction among many, including myself, that colonialism necessarily demands some close attention to history, to context, to the local and specific – elements that are conspicuously absent in scholarship inspired by Agamben.[1] This is not to say that I do not find Agamben's own writing evocative and stimulating, pushing me again and again to combine thinkers, genres and materials – leading me to seek openings for thought when academic disciplines often want to close them down.

Nevertheless, I want to begin with this note of caution and surprise that European philosophers continue to make grand claims about the relationship between sovereignty and law, the camp, biopolitics, the human/animal distinction, the concept of 'the people', or declarations on the 'rights of man' without sustained reference to how Europeans learned to govern themselves by governing others during half a millennium of imperial expansion, violence and rule. This kind of European theory often attempts to insulate itself from the criticism I have just made by prefixing its theories and claims as being specific to the 'West'.[2] To claim that one speaks from or of the 'West' is no alibi (see Motha 2009a). Imperialism and capitalism are the globalisation, or *mondialisation* as Jacques Derrida and Jean-Luc Nancy have insisted on putting it, of what is called the 'West' (Derrida 2002; Nancy 2007). There is then a process of having-become-world, of becoming-world, that goes hand in hand with imperialism and capitalism. It is precisely that co-emergence of the 'West', imperialism and the 'world' (and its sovereign biopolitical formations) that makes the paucity of reference by Agamben to colonialism so surprising, and the intervention made by the present volume so necessary.

More specific suspicions about Agamben's grandiose claims are tackled by Paul Patton (2007) in a thoughtful and critical treatment of the former's suggestion that he is 'correcting' and 'completing' Foucault's work on biopolitics (Agamben 1998: 9). As Patton suggests, in the end

> the difference between [Agamben's] approach and that of Foucault is not so much a matter of correction and completion as a choice between epochal concepts of biopolitics and bare life and a more fine-grained, contextual, and historical analysis intended to enable specific and local forms of escape from the past. (Patton 2007: 218)[3]

The concern of this volume is with the colonial past and present, and the possibilities of an anti-colonial and postcolonial future. This must necessarily entail attention to the specific context of colonialism and neo-colonial formations. But it must also involve the risk of thinking afresh, asking new questions, and deploying concepts where they are strange or estranged.

My focus in this chapter is on the potential significance of Agamben's thought in considering the colonial legacies and post-colonial possibilities in South Africa. South Africa is regarded by many as a paradigmatic instance of successful anti-colonial rebellion. Despite the terms of the post-apartheid settlement being disputed, and questions being asked about the persistence of white, colonial and capitalist formations, South Africa is nonetheless emblematic of human struggle and resistance against unjust and undemocratic political and legal regimes. It is, moreover, a state that is now founded and administered through an elaborate liberal, and some would suggest 'post-liberal' constitution (see Klare 1998). However, the transition from apartheid to 'post-apartheid' is not a linear movement. Many query how much of the colonial social and economic structures and formations have been undone by the move to 'post-apartheid' (Ramose 2007; Madlingozi 2007). That is, the apartheid state was only one juridical and political episode in a longer colonial usurpation and appropriation. It is thus possible to claim that while the apartheid legal order has been dismantled, a postcolonial social, economic and political order is yet to be inaugurated, or else that postcolonial becoming is necessarily fluid, emergent and incomplete.

Beginning in 1994, a new constitutional dispensation ushered in an era of representative democracy, juridical equality and constitutional supremacy in South Africa. The most obvious aspects of apartheid-era violence and excess, and emergency rule, have been highly circumscribed by the Constitution.[4] All of this presents a paradox regarding the relevance of Agamben's thinking for South Africa as a colonial or postcolonial order. How readily can Agamben's thought on a variety of juridico-political formations – sovereignty, the 'camp' as paradigm of the modern, a 'form of life' liberated from its enfoldment in citizen/subject and accompanying categories of exclusion, the structure of the 'ban', bare life or 'abandoned being' – be regarded as pertinent to South Africa? It would of course be trite and simplistic to think that the point of philosophical discourses, languages or concepts is to find a place for their 'application'. The point, to put it bluntly, is not to find 'bare life' in South Africa as a precursor to considering the relevance of Agamben's thought for that setting.

In the discussion that follows I focus on the proliferation of 'forms of life' in philosophical discourses that tackle contemporary political and legal problems. I consider the political implications of Agamben's thinking in that wider context of reliance on the notion of a 'form of life' by many thinkers. A great deal of political thinking informed by continental philosophy has focused on forms of life such as *bare life* (Agamben 1998), *precarious, vulnerable* and *grievable life* (Butler 2004; 2009), and *creaturely life* (Santner 2007). The theologico-political phenomenon that spawns this thinking on various 'forms of life' is sovereignty. Sovereignty and its relationship to the political is a key progenitor of why various theorists have found it necessary to attend to ethical, political and juridical problems through a 'form of life'. I will establish the connection between sovereignty, the political and political discourses about a 'form of life' with particular reference to South Africa. I will then consider the wider implications of how and why Agamben and Butler tackle the juridico-political problem of sovereignty through 'forms of life'. I will close with a shift in genre to literature and the post-apartheid novel by discussing Marlene van Niekerk's *Agaat* (2006). The novel presents the possibility of attending to the singularity of being, and is a site for imagining life not within the constraints of juridical and political forms which might be relatively closed or open, but for attending to everyday existence. The character of being in the postcolonial setting, I suggest, is a *liminal* one. In *Agaat* we encounter the liminal existences of post-apartheid beings.

The Problem of Sovereignty and Colonialism in South Africa

Sovereignty presents a particular conundrum in the postcolony. The usurpation of territory, subordination of populations, degradation of all forms of life and appropriation of land are among the key features of colonial sovereignty. The attempt to address and redress these imperial excesses – that is, the attempt to depart from colonial sovereignty – often adopts the language, symbolism and practices of sovereignty. Elsewhere I have identified this as the problem of *archiving* colonial sovereignty (Motha 2009b). I use the term 'archive' after Jacques Derrida (1997). He emphasises how the archive resists conceptualisation. *Arkhē*, the root of archive, at once connotes a *commencement* and a *command*. As the place where things commence it is a 'physical, historical, or ontological principle' and it is the place from where social order, law and authority might be given (Derrida 1997: 1). The archive, Derrida explains, is then potentially both an ontological and nomological principle. The archive is the privileged intersection of place and law – the topological and nomological. But the archive is a much more fraught concept, linked to the finitude of being, the limits of memory, and is not only about the past but also the future. Derrida emphasises that the archive is more of an 'impression' than a concept – it is *in-finite*, indefinite, at once closing down and opening to an outside (29).

The possibility of postcolonial sovereignty is homologous with the archive. Sovereignty is a problem of the 'limit' to the extent that courts or transitional political entities must articulate how a past 'event', such as the assertion of colonial sovereignty, can be delimited so that it can be grasped and disavowed. However, colonial sovereignty cannot be rendered entirely *finite* (closed down or bounded) in order for it to be fully departed from. The original colonial commandment has an *infinite* reach (always opening out) into a postcolonial juridico-political order. It is for this reason that postcolonial sovereignty needs to be regarded as *in-finite* (see Motha 2005). The notion of 'in-finite' sovereignty also neatly captures the spatial aspect of imperial sovereignty (the usurpation of territory and the creation of a delimited nation-state), and the temporal aspect of inaugurating 'postcolonial' law by preserving and disavowing this sovereign 'event'.

This in-finite character of postcolonial sovereignty can be observed in South Africa. The 'new' South Africa is by now famous the world over for a transformation from apartheid. But has the post-apartheid juridical order inaugurated a postcolony – that is, has South Africa been decolonised? In the South African setting there is a double-liberation at stake – from apartheid on the one hand, and from the cultural, social and economic consequences of a longer colonial domination on the other. There is also the question of whether sovereignty has been, and needs to be, 'returned' to the indigenous conquered people of South Africa before decolonisation can be achieved.

Among the key proponents of the view that South Africa is yet to be decolonised is Professor Mogobe Ramose, a philosopher at the University of South Africa. The process of decolonisation, in Ramose's view, is not concluded, and was not achieved through the elimination of apartheid and the guarantee of equality and civil rights in April 1994. While those who pushed a compromise in the early 1990s argued that they were averting civil war, Ramose's claim is that since colonisation South Africa has been 'practically in a state of war' (2007: 319–20). In his view it was gullible and misleading to think that apartheid was the fundamental problem. Freedom was reduced to the guarantee of fundamental rights and this was a mistake. The morality and political legitimacy of the colonial 'right of conquest' was left untouched. Ramose thus challenges the reasoning that asserted, from the Freedom Charter 1955 onwards, that 'South Africa belonged to all who lived in it.'

A post-conquest or decolonised South Africa, Ramose argues, must attend to the failure to recognise that the sovereignty of indigenous communities has been deprived through illegitimate war and usurpation. Abiding by community in African culture involves an ethical concern and obligation in relation to the three dimensions of the living, the living dead and the yet to be born. Thus the survival of customary kingship, and the memory of the heroes and heroines who fought against colonialism requires that parity – *horizontality* – be restored between the 'indigenous conquered peoples' and the coloniser. The 'reaffirmation' of such 'horizontal reasoning' is a necessary condition for a genuinely autochthonous constitution (Ramose 2007: 326).

The epistemic, cultural and philosophical manifestations of a lack of horizontality between coloniser and colonised are concrete. The lack of equilibrium and 'authentic liberation' is evidenced by the racial ideology that converted parliamentary supremacy to constitutional supremacy. Ramose (2007: 367) suggests that the move to constitutional supremacy rather than parliamentary supremacy ushered in by the new Constitution of 1996 involved fear of a black constituency. Parliamentary sovereignty – and the consequent threat of majoritarianism – was dealt with by the introduction of constitutional supremacy. Equality and civil rights would be guaranteed by the constitution – as would the ill-gotten gains of several centuries of colonial violence and usurpation. There was a fear that the putative 'black race' would have unanimity on all matters and thus threaten all 'other' interests if they were granted legislative or parliamentary supremacy. Rather than signalling the return of sovereignty to the colonised population, the terms of the transition from apartheid to post-apartheid are viewed by Ramose as yet another inscription of a colonial racial logic.

The subordinate status accorded to indigenous, Bantu or customary law in the Constitution of the Republic of South Africa is another example of a lack of parity between coloniser and colonised. For Ramose, the treatment of the Bantu philosophy of ubuntu[5], and the failure to accord it juridical and political parity in the Constitution is a sign of the lack of equilibrium:

Ubuntu [. . .] represents the epistemological paradigm that informs the cultural practices, including the law, of the Bantu-speaking peoples. Excluding it from the constitution is tantamount to denying the Bantu-speaking peoples a place in the constitutional dispensation of the country. The current Constitution is, therefore not the mirror of the legal ideas and institutions of the indigenous conquered peoples of South Africa. It follows then that a truly South African Constitution is yet to be born. On this reasoning, Act 108 of 1996 [the Constitution], has, perhaps inadvertently, set the stage for the struggle for a new constitutional order in South Africa. (Ramose 2006: 366)

Indeed, it seems clear from recent decisions of the Constitutional Court of South Africa that the early enthusiasm for drawing on ubuntu as a source of moral, ethical and political values is waning with the appointment of a new generation of judges. Increasingly, it is conventional judicial discourses of statutory construction, or Anglo-American judicial discourses and techniques that dominate.[6] This remains the case despite the fact that the subject matter of certain decisions – the implications of amnesty once granted to a person convicted of murder (*McBride*), and the procedure for granting pardons (*Albutt*) – presented the Constitutional Court with an opportunity to develop a postcolonial jurisprudence that takes seriously the need to decolonise the ethical and political languages and discourses of the law. What decolonisation requires is not the retrieval of an 'authentic past', but parity between the various conceptions of law of the conquered and the conqueror.

Bare Life and the Problem of the Political in South Africa

It is amidst the disputes just outlined concerning the new constitutional dispensation, the meaning and extent of postcolonial sovereignty, and tensions regarding the character of decolonisation that resort has been made to Agamben's notion of 'bare life' in South Africa. 'Bare life', as we will see shortly, has been deployed in the process of understanding and explaining tensions at the heart of sovereignty, law and political community. Resort to a 'form of life' such as 'bare life' has been made in the context of confronting a *crisis of the political*. The crisis of the political arises out of addressing the fundamental plurality of being beyond an essential basis for representing commonality. According to Johan van der Walt, 'apartheid was and is an exceptional example of representing the public instead of retrieving the public from its retreat from all representation' (van der Walt 2005: 10). That strained formulation expresses the conviction that plural existence should not be expressed through some essential basis of commonality. Apartheid, fascism of various kinds, or human existence reduced to labour are all ways of representing common existence through some essence.

The task of a renewed politics is then to retrieve the public or community from this 'retreat of the political' (see Lacoue-Labarthe and Nancy 1997). This crisis of the political is a key aspect, I argue below, for the proliferation of 'forms of life' in philosophical and juridical thinking. Before we move on to discuss that, it would be helpful to consider how 'bare life' was deployed in the process of attending to the crisis of the political in South Africa.

There is no shortage of accounts of how violent and disorderly the postcolony, and especially South Africa is. This excessive disorderliness is associated with kleptocratic and savage sovereignty throughout the global south (see Comaroff and Comaroff 2007). I have heard it remarked that it is because black South Africans exist in a condition of 'bare life' that crime is accompanied by extreme acts of violence in present-day South Africa. The ANC-led government is often accused of having a wrong-headed or incompetent approach to crime and violence.[7] Has the country literally and metaphorically 'gone to the dogs'? Such criticisms of the post-apartheid state go to the heart of the problem of archiving colonial sovereignty that I invoked at the outset. Is contemporary violence and disorderliness contingent on the brutalisations of colonialism and apartheid? Can such a question even be addressed in the register of tropes such as human/animal, political/bare life? What such accounts of violence and disorderliness seem to suggest is that once dehumanised or degraded by colonialism and apartheid, black people are unable to depart from regimes of normalised violence.

Johan van der Walt characterises the lives of black South Africans during apartheid by deploying the notion of 'bare life' or *homo sacer*:

> they [the majority of South Africans] remained expelled even when they continued physically to live in white South Africa. They had no civil rights to speak of and no freedom of movement. There were strict rules as to where they could go and when they could go there. And when they failed to observe these rules, their last remnants of *bios* (political life) turned into a matter of mere *zoē* (bare life or life as such). As the Sharpeville massacre and many subsequent killings would make quite clear, they could be killed for not observing the rules of apartheid without this killing constituting a crime. Black people who lived in South Africa had the status of Agamben's *homo sacer*. (Van der Walt 2005: 124)

Can it really be said that black people were rendered *homo sacer* by the extreme violence and degradation imposed by the apartheid regime? Black people during apartheid could be killed with impunity, in accordance with Agamben's enigmatic formulation in *Homo Sacer* that bare life can 'be killed without being sacrificed'– that is, that bare life ceases to figure in either sacred or profane modes of valuing or mediating life. My concern is with van der Walt's characterisation of the majority of South Africans as 'bare life' during apartheid – a designation I regard as spurious.

Let us assume that van der Walt intends that having 'the status of bare life' in the eyes of the colonial or apartheid state is distinct from actually being 'bare life' or *homo sacer*. However, one wonders what is gained by drawing lines between political and bare life, between human and animal, *bios* and *zoē* in the context of apartheid. There is a sense that the recognition of expulsion from the political is a precursor to 're-treating the political' – to attending to the problem of plurality in a post-apartheid order. But can the political or plurality be retrieved in this way? A host of other questions are also left unanswered. Have the majority of South Africans recovered their political life and agentive capacities? On what basis did this recovery take place? Was the abjectness of the status of bare life simply about formal rights of political citizenship or is much more at stake? If it is the case that humanity, equality or political life is recovered through the adoption of a sophisticated constitution, then the political is once again reduced to orders of representation and commonality.

If forms of life such as 'bare life' are to be deployed in the process of generating a post-apartheid theory of law, then these questions need to be addressed. Characterising black South Africans during apartheid as 'bare life' is far from helpful. It has the potential to deface the revolutionary struggles many South Africans engaged in against apartheid. Apartheid was toppled with the force of an eloquent, strategic, organised and sometimes violent will. This capacity to resist colonialism and apartheid goes to the heart of whether Europe's others are regarded as having the full capacity of selfhood – of being conscious beings of action, thought and invention – whatever the status accorded to them by their masters.

There is a problem of politics and the political that is being posed when the notion of 'bare life' is deployed to characterise life during apartheid. 'Forms of life' are a trope for the intersection between sovereignty, life and law. Why, then, has the re-treatment of the political taken place in South Africa and elsewhere through the deployment of 'forms of life' such as *homo sacer* or bare life? In the following sections I take up that question through a wider discussion of conceptualisations of 'forms of life' now circulating in philosophical and political discourse.

Forms of Life and the Crisis of the Political

Conflict and antagonism in postcommunist, post-colonial and post-conflict societies have come to be seen as a problem of the *political* as such. The intellectual currents that have informed attention on the political include: Arendt's work on plurality and concern to distinguish various modes of productive and political life; the left's revival of Schmittian decisionism and the friend/ enemy distinction as a useful critique of liberalism and delibera-tive democracy; and a largely poststructural tendency to imagine 'community' beyond communitarian essences after the totalitarian excesses of fascism and communism (Arendt 1958; Schmitt 1985; 1996; Mouffe 2000; Nancy 1991; Lacoue-Labarthe and Nancy 1997). The 'political' became a key focus of democratic theory at a moment when the autonomous liberal subject had been rendered illusory by social and political movements such as postcolonial-ism, feminism and critical race studies. Power also ceased to be treated as the over-determining action of a centralised sovereign or the state. Foucault explained how power was at once constituted and resisted within the body of the subject. The subject came to be regarded as individuated through biopolitical modes of power (see Foucault 2003; Butler 1997). The concept of the 'political' emerged in this context as the *space* in which a variety of sovereign antagonisms would play out.

Agamben's thought attempted to bring together Foucault's theorisation of subjection, Schmitt's thought on sovereignty, and Arendt's critique of rights and examination of the conditions of totalitarianism. According to Agamben, Foucault's attempts to de-emphasise the questions 'what legitimates power?' and 'what is the state?' removed the theoretical privileging of sovereignty but failed to explain the point of intersection between 'techniques of individualization' and 'totalizing procedures' (Agamben 1998: 6). Agamben's characterisation of the inclusive exclusion of 'aban-doned being' or 'bare life' from the political and juridical order did much to complicate the relationship between political-life (*bios*) and sovereignty. We were thus left with the concept of the 'political' as the central site where life was determined to be either mediated or unmediated by profane or divine law.

Political and ethical demands were made on the basis of a critical stance that tended to begin with charting the conditions of inclusion/exclusion from a realm of plural existence called the political. Cutting a long and interesting story short, if all normative orders were created through an exclusion of X-life from the relevant political community, then the task of critique and politics was to identify and respond to this constitutive abandonment of being. While some contented themselves with arguments for the strategic use of rights or a demand for the relevant kind of enfranchisement or recognition, at the heart of the treatment of the political as an ontological problem was the realisation that 'abandonment' and not some utopian notion of plurality was its fundamental condition. And abandoned being as the originary act of sovereignty left very little by way of a political programme that could escape this fundamental condition of a juridical and political order. Famously, by way of a new political horizon, Giorgio Agamben left us waiting, at the end of *Homo Sacer*, for the beautiful day of *zoē* to arrive. That is to say, *zoē* would need to become a form of life 'wholly exhausted in bare life and a bios that is only its own *zoē*' (Agamben 1998: 188). This new politics would require a shift, for Agamben, from 'form of life' to 'form-of-life'. This warrants further explanation.

The distinction Agamben draws between 'form of life' and 'form-of-life' is key in his thinking about sovereignty, law and politics. The former denotes the ostensible *facts* of human life which are often expressed through the separation of 'naked life' (*'nuda vita'* or 'bare life') from the various forms in which it is represented or identified – usually citizen or subject (Agamben 2000: 4). This abstract re-codification of life is what we find in a litany of social and juridical categories such as 'voter, worker, journalist, student, HIV positive, transvestite, porn star, elderly, parent, woman' and so forth (6–7). It is not that these categories are abstract as such. It is rather that political form and naked life are separated in the structure of representation of such categories. A 'form of life' is then a human life mediated by politics and political orders. Such a 'form of life' is politicised by submitting itself to a sovereign (as in the Hobbesian compact), or by being forcibly assimilated in states of exception or biopolitical modes of power. What Agamben is expressing through the notion 'form-of-life', on the other hand, is not simply facts of existence but the *possibilities* of life. With the aspiration of focusing on possibilities of life over facts, and gesturing towards a 'nonstatist politics', 'form-of-life' is 'a life for which living itself would be at stake in its own living' (9). As Agamben goes on to explain:

> Only if I am not always already and solely enacted, but rather delivered to a possibility and a power, only if living and intending and apprehending themselves are at stake each time in what I live and intend and apprehend – only if, in other words, there is thought – only then can a form of life become, in its own factness and thingness, *form-of-life*, in which it is never possible to isolate something like naked life. (Agamben 2000: 9, original emphasis)

'Form-of-life' and 'naked life' would not be distinguishable. This is what Agamben has in mind, when, at the closing stages of *Homo Sacer* he gestures towards a shift in conceptual paradigm which would lead to 'the constitution and installation of a form of life that is wholly exhausted in bare life and a *bios* that is only its own *zoē*' (Agamben 1998: 188).[8] In the passage cited above, Agamben refers to a 'thought' that would be a precursor to a 'form-of-life'. In relation to 'thought', Agamben says:

> Thought is form-of-life, life that cannot be segregated from its form; and anywhere the intimacy of this inseparable life appears, in the materiality of corporeal processes and of habitual ways of life no less than in theory, there and only there is there thought. And it is this thought, this form-of-life, that abandoning naked life to 'Man' and to the 'Citizen', who clothe it temporarily and represent it with their 'rights', must become the guiding concept and the unitary centre of the coming politics. (Agamben 2000: 11–12)

The kind of 'thought' that is at stake here is always a 'common' thought. Agamben does not intend this commonality in any communitarian way. Rather, it is the commonality that is inherent to the communicability of language: 'communication not of something in common but of communicability itself' (Agamben 2000: 10). The instance at which the potentiality of signification passes into the actuality of a signifier as the re-presentation of a 'thing itself' becomes an instance of the openness and possibility that only exists in and through *language*: 'The thing itself is not a thing; it is the very sayability, the very openness at issue in language, which in language, we always presuppose and forget, perhaps because it is at bottom its own oblivion and abandonment' (Agamben 1999: 35). Language is the presupposition of all appearance, institution and tradition:

> The presuppositional structure of language is the very structure of tradition; we presuppose, pass on, and thereby – according to the double sense of the word *traditio* – betray the thing itself in language, so that language can speak about something (*kata tinos*). The effacement of the thing itself is the sole foundation on which it is possible for something like a tradition to be constituted. (Agamben 1999: 35)

The constitution of the political, 'people', 'we civilised people who respect human rights', is the becoming actual of a potentiality which at bottom presupposes language.

What is expressed about 'form-of-life' through commonality, thought and communication is potentiality. The Aristotelian conception of potentiality and actuality presents the aporia of 'the presence of absence' (Agamben 1999: 178–9). Aristotle articulated this problematic in *De anima* as the question of why there is no 'sensation of the senses themselves'; 'in the absence of external objects, the senses do not give any sensation, although they contain fire, earth, water, and the other elements of which there is sensation' (Aristotle 1986: 94; cited in Agamben 1999: 178). Bearing in mind the unsustainable dichotomy between anima/animus,[9] what *animates* the 'potential' of the senses is the coming into contact with the principle of its own animation, its becoming or its passing into actuality. Although we know that sensation is the actualisation of the potential of the senses, the senses exist 'in the absence of sensation' (Agamben 1999: 178).

Agamben reposes this opposition of potentiality/actuality as the distinction between potentiality/impotentiality. 'Impotentiality' is 'potentiality' (the capacity to be something else) experienced as its own capacity to not be. Impotentiality is potentiality at the point of its privation. All potentiality must also be impotentiality. Potentiality must be experienced as the capacity to not be, to be its own lack. As Agamben puts it, the kind of potentiality that interests Aristotle is not the generic potential of a child to acquire knowledge. This is the potential to 'suffer an alteration' (Agamben 1999: 179). The 'potential' that does interest Aristotle, however, is the condition of already having something as a capacity, but then not bringing it to actuality. This is the capacity for a potentiality to maintain itself in its own privation (Agamben 1999: 179–80). The implications of this latter type of potentiality for a study of being, subject or form of life are considerable.

There are multiple figures and visions of politics that Agamben invokes through the notion of impotentiality. 'Whatever being', a figure that is developed in *The Coming Community*, and Herman Melville's scrivener in 'Bartleby' are among the key ones. Distinguishing potentiality from 'will', and impotentiality from 'necessity', Agamben argues that Bartleby's response, 'I would prefer not to', to a request from the man of the law, leaves the former dwelling obstinately in the 'abyss of potentiality' (Agamben 1999: 254). This refusal or withdrawal is a repudiation of sovereignty and violence as a means. However, Agamben treats this refusal as a thought rather than action – and as we will see, it is one of the reasons he has been accused of being quietist, fatalistic or utopian.

Amy Swiffen (2010: 174ff.) compares Agamben's and Žižek's approaches to the figure of Bartleby. Swiffen sums up a range of critiques levelled at Agamben well, and is thus worth quoting at length:

> Agamben's idea of a politics after sovereignty is premised on law freed from violence; however, when considered in light of the connection between law and language, the conclusion of his critique of sovereignty is that this nexus is immutable. There is no other form of law than sovereign law, which is always connected to violence. The concept of whatever being is generated through the abstract negation of this connection [. . .] If there is no form of law not connected to violence, it might be morally appealing to refuse political action that aims at creating a new law, but it might also be politically complacent, and even irresponsible. (Swiffen 2010: 177–8)

Agamben's thought on the conditions for the appearance of 'form-of-life' rests on a non-statist politics and a renunciation of violence as means. To the extent that law is inextricably tied to violence, it is renounced. That refusal of law is, as Swiffen suggests, complacent at a time when sovereign emergencies are multiplying. But it is a refusal that gestures towards a political stance that should not be ignored.

In the last part of this essay, I turn to consider whether *liminal beings* in the post-apartheid novel might provide another range of political possibilities, while preserving some of the qualities of impotentiality that Agamben has developed. Liminality is at once a strange and estranged concept. Many would dismiss it on the basis that its earlier iteration was in anthropological texts of an earlier time (see van Gennep 1960; and Turner 1967). I do not share this attitude. There is no need to confine the notion of liminality to the ethnographic setting of one of its earlier manifestations. I do not know of any 'pure' concepts, and when they are asserted the critic should be wary. Democracy, community, friendship, solidarity, love, rights, humanity, fraternity are just some of the regular political concepts that carry their own dangers and constitutive exclusions. It is precisely for that reason that existing concepts, including the ones just listed, need to be reinvigorated and given new content and possibilities. It is in that spirit that I seek to renew the notion of liminality (see also Motha 2010). To the extent that liminality signifies a space in-between – at once a place of refuge, invention, fluidity and movement along with the danger of being fixed in limbo – the concept can be productively deployed in the postcolonial setting.

In-finite Sovereignty and Liminality

When forms of life and the crisis of the political were examined above, I made the point that contemporary thinking, especially that charted by Agamben, had reached a point where the originary act of sovereignty left very little room to manoeuvre beyond the fundamental condition of juridical and political orders which are founded on the production of abandoned being. My contention here is that literature and other aesthetic forms can offer new insights in relation to this crisis of the political. Aspects of this crisis give rise to questions of commonality, the conditions of plurality and communicability. It is in responding to those challenges that I believe the post-apartheid novel, and especially van Niekerk's *Agaat*, can be instructive. There are possibilities (perhaps *thought* in Agamben's terms) specific to the form of the novel that enables the potentiality of its characters to at once manifest singularity and the problem of political representation. The novel expresses forms of life and being that cannot and should not be collapsed into any predetermined political programme or juridical model. The

liminal beings encountered in *Agaat* expose a problem of communication, and of originating political subjectivity and sociality.

If the novel is going to present a mode of thinking new forms
of life, what is the relationship between the imaginary and politics? There are two insights that drive my deployment of literary
figures. One is the centrality of literature for imagining resistant
beings and their political possibilities. The second is the need to
find concepts that are apposite for colonial and postcolonial settings, given how Agamben and other philosophers are seldom
attentive to that task. If a coming politics is to be marked by a
thought, communication and 'form-of-life' encountered in intimacy, corporeality and materiality, as Agamben has suggested,
where will this politics, and this being, be imagined? We have
seen how productive Melville's *Bartleby* has been for Agamben's
thought. The power of his refusal, the im-potentiality of his 'I
would prefer not to' without recourse to rights, objectives or legitimate ends shatters the instrumentality of a politics with essential
agents and pre-determined programmes. This refusal expresses
a form of resistance through a being, a liminal being, suspended
between possibility and actuality.

For a range of reasons elaborated above, especially to do with the
problem of archiving an in-finite colonial sovereignty, the notion
of *liminality* may prove to be a productive concept. Liminality, as
I have just suggested, bears the potential for holding in suspense,
being in-between, while at the same time conveying the possibility of movement – gesturing towards an opening and a traversal
to a place beyond. Colonial sovereignty is a command that must,
at the same time, be preserved and be departed from (it is *in-finite*
as I explained above). Liminality might then be the resistant or
emancipatory flipside of in-finite sovereignty. Liminality opens the
possibility of a non-sovereign subjectivity beyond orders of rights,
representation and associated forms of agency. Liminal beings
evade sovereign claims. They neither make them, nor succumb to
them. However, a liminal being would nonetheless sustain contact
between past and future. Such liminal beings are to be found in
South African post-apartheid literature.

In what follows, I take up the potentiality of liminal beings
through Marlene van Niekerk's novel, *Agaat*. This is an epic
novel traversing the era of apartheid from the early 1950s to the
new constitutional dispensation in 1994. The narrative centres
on two characters, Milla de Wet, a white woman who inherits a

farm called *Grootmoedersdrift*, and her coloured servant, Agaat. Each chapter of the novel is structured like a triptych – moving the reader in time from the present to the past, and through several narrative voices. There is the first-person voice of Milla who initially presents as a sovereign 'I'. But this ipseity is shattered by the narrative voice that speaks of Milla in the second person, and the poetic inscriptions of Milla's diary.

Perhaps the most obvious liminal space in the novel is Milla's death chamber. We first encounter Milla as she lies paralysed from the motor neurone condition, Charcot's disease. It is the time of transition to the 'new South Africa'. It is also a time of transition in Milla's farm. Milla is being cared for by Agaat, and unable to communicate other than by the movement of her eyelids. Each chapter moves us between Milla's death chamber and a narrative that stretches back to 1947 when Milla meets and marries Jak. The period covered by the novel is roughly that of the duration of apartheid. The narrative is then a co-emergence of Milla and Agaat as a product of colonialism and apartheid, but in the everyday intimacy of the home and the farm.

Milla's death chamber is also the space in which we encounter Agaat as the survivor and inheritor of the farm. We learn about Agaat's character, her unsurpassable skills as a farmer, as manager of labour and of the household, and as Milla's carer. Milla's and Agaat's fates have been intertwined, but with Milla's death a new regime of life will commence – the farm and household with Agaat as head. The space of Milla's death chamber is then a liminal space in which two beings co-emerge and a new order is inaugurated. It is this co-emergence of being, and the centrality of liminality for the process of decolonisation, that I wish to explore further.

There is of course the question of whose inner life the reader has access to in this novel – is it the white farmer Milla or is it also her servant, Agaat? And why are we even bothering with this particular colonial setting – the 'not quite white' farm? What are the implications of these questions for the relationship between literature and politics? A question is often posed about what is imagined and disseminated in literature, and by whom, in the context of post-apartheid South Africa. The regular objections include: literature is an elite form of art and expression; the most celebrated South African writers are white; why discuss a farm novel rather than a township novel? Why focus on the being and becoming of white characters when so many black South Africans live in abject conditions and make little or no appearance in literature? How are these objections to be addressed?

In one sense *Agaat* might be regarded as yet another farm novel written by an Afrikaner author. The farm novel (*plaasroman*) was a genre in which the colonial and apartheid conquest of territory was imagined and mythologised. A key myth of Afrikaner nationalism was of the Boer farmer – masculine, hardworking, Calvinist – resisting British colonial expansion and rule by driving his cattle and people over forbidding mountain ranges and making an inhospitable land productive. The fact that this independence from the British and conquest of territory was achieved through the dispossession and slaughter of the indigenous populations encountered by the Boers is seldom a feature of the archetypical farm novel.

It is in this respect that van Niekerk's *Agaat* is a profound reversal of the classic farm novel. One mundane but nonetheless significant feature of this is the close focus on farming techniques; on how the industrial and mechanised farming methods of Milla's husband Jak are observed to denude and destroy the land. Despite Jak's ambitions and pretensions, his strength and athleticism, and despite his violence against Milla and hostility to Agaat, his will and vision are broken and flawed. The careful attention to farming techniques in the novel – those of Milla and Agaat contrasted with that of Jak, is a powerful metaphor that displaces one of the founding myths of Afrikaner nationalism and apartheid. It places women, gendered relationships, the strategies of agricultural mass production, and a diverse range of farming practices at the centre of tensions in the South African farm. Most significantly, it is Agaat, the coloured maid, servant and worker who is at the heart of what unfolds between all other characters in the novel.

Agaat is found by Milla in 1953 as a neglected and sexually abused child who can barely speak. She has a malformed arm, possibly caused by an antenatal injury. She is first brought into Milla's home as a child – a substitute for the child that Milla and Jak have been unable to conceive. But when Milla later gives birth to her son Jakkie, Agaat is moved to the servant's room and is assiduously trained as a maid and farm worker. But Agaat's potential and powers surpass all Milla's training and designs. Agaat becomes the friend and confidante of Jakkie – closer to him than his parents would ever be. She observes the truth behind Milla's marriage – Jak's violence, Milla's contrivance and the suffering of beings without love.

The communication and communicability that Agamben sees as the key to a 'form-of-life' – 'communication not of something in common but of communicability itself' (Agamben 2000: 10) – is at the heart of Milla and Agaat *being-with* each other. The dying Milla can only communicate through blinking her eyelids to iterate the letters of the alphabet. Milla clings anxiously to language, to her mutual history with Agaat and to the potentiality of memory. Agaat reads the code. As Milla says (but only through Agaat's reading):

> It's going too slowly. I think too fast. I only get the odd word out. W·H·Y A·R·E Y·O·U O·N T· S·C·E·N·E S·O S·O·O·N A·T E·V·E·R·Y D·I·S·A·S·T·E·R W·O·N·D·E·R A·B·O·U·T Y·O·U·R T·R·U·E C·O·L·O·U·R·S S·I·C·K C·O·M·F·O·R·T·E·R F·I·R·E E·X·T·I·N·G·U·I·S·H·E·R S·L·I·M·E K·N·O·C·K·E·R D·I·S·T·R·U·S·T D·E·V·I·L. (van Niekerk 2006: 402)

It is only possible for Milla to communicate because of Agaat's reading of the movement of her eyelids. But what is communicated is a questioning of Agaat's motives. What is at stake here is not commonality between Milla and Agaat, then, but the space of a traversal in which the past is reinscribed and questioned. But this is also the space in which the present and future is invented through Milla and Agaat being so intimately with each other. As Milla approaches death, her life is recounted, reassessed, re-lived. In the process of this re-treatment and retrieval another Agaat and another Milla emerge. They are not fully known or formed subjects. There are other stories to be written, other narratives to be told. For now what is crucial is that Milla and Agaat have shared, are sharing, a world. The co-inscription of communication is at the origin of this world. And what is to come in the new order? What about Agaat's authoritarianism; what is the legacy of colonial discipline?

Conclusion

In the everyday recesses of farm, home, love, marriage and parenthood, van Niekerk has opened the possibility of a deep reflection on the corporeal and material conditions that constituted the violence of the apartheid order. *Agaat* delves into the intimate crevices of an apartheid-era home, and charts the co-dependence and co-emergence of a white Afrikaner woman and her coloured servant. Despite the commanding ambitions of farm owners, agricultural production was only possible because of servants and workers. This is a trite observation in any colonial context. What is crucial, however, is that it is not only the production of vast material disparities through the extraction of the surplus value of labour that marked the apartheid-era farm. The farm was the site for the fashioning of forms of life. Humans, animals, soil, grasses, insects, crafts, furniture, music, language and writing were produced within the farm. There is no life fully graspable or sayable to be found in *Agaat*. There is no absolute abandonment, bare life, or a life that can be fully apprehended. In *Agaat*, in writing, is a trace, a memory of co-origination. That co-origination of Milla and Agaat is a fundamental challenge for a nation-state, a 'people', that now grapple with what it means for coloniser and colonised to co-exist.

It is this problem of being-in-common that both Agamben and other theorists who think through various 'forms of life' grapple with. As we have observed in the discussion, considerable attention has been given to the persistence of sovereignty, and whether or not normative frameworks can expunge the violence at the heart of the production of forms of life. Through the notion of liminality I have attempted to counterpose a subject without sovereign origin or destination. Liminal beings are unformed, unsayable and defy regimes of recognition. While liminality is by no means the only way to re-imagine political subjectivity, it can be productive in the anti-colonial and postcolonial setting where in-finite sovereignty resists total closure of the past, and co-existing 'peoples' labour in the invention of a wholly new future.

References

Agamben, G. (1993), *Infancy and History: The Destruction of Experience*, trans. L. Heron. London and New York: Verso.

—(1998), *Homo Sacer: Sovereign Power and Bare Life*, trans. D. Heller-Roazen. Stanford: Stanford University Press.

—(1999), *Potentialities: Collected Essays in Philosophy*, edited by D. Heller-Roazen. Stanford: Stanford University Press.

—(2000), *Means Without End: Notes on Politics*, trans. V. Binetti and C. Casarino. Minnesota: University of Minnesota Press.

—(2005), *The Time That Remains: A Commentary on the Letter to the Romans*, trans. P. Dailey. Stanford: Stanford University Press.

—(2009), *The Signature of All Things: On Method*, trans. L. D'Isanto with K. Attell. New York: Zone Books.

Albutt v Centre for the Study of Violence and Reconciliation, CCT 54/09 (2010), Constitutional Court of South Africa, 23 February 2010.

Arendt, H. (1958), *The Human Condition*. Chicago: University of Chicago Press.

Aristotle (1986), '*De anima*', in *Aristotle in Twenty-Three Volumes, vol: 8; On the Soul, Parva Naturalia, On Breath*, trans. W. S. Hett. Cambridge, MA: Harvard University Press.

AZAPO v The President, CCT 17/96 (1996), Constitutional Court of South Africa, 25 July 1996.

Butler, J. (1997), *The Psychic Life of Power: Theories in Subjection*. Stanford: Stanford University Press.

—(2004), *Precarious Life: The Power of Mourning and Violence*. London: Verso.

—(2009), *Frames of War: When is Life Grievable?* London: Verso.

Comaroff, J. and J. Comaroff (2007), 'Law and Disorder in the Postcolony', *Social Anthropology*, 15: 133–52.

Derrida, J. (1997), *Archive Fever: A Freudian Impression*. Chicago: University of Chicago Press.

—(2002), 'The University Without Condition', in P. Kamuf (ed.), *Without Alibi*. Stanford: Stanford University Press, 202–37.

—(2009), *The Beast and the Sovereign, Vol. 1*. Chicago: University of Chicago Press.

Foucault, M. (2003), *Society Must Be Defended: Lectures at the College De France, 1975–1976*, trans. D. Macey. New York: Picador.

Klare, K. (1998), 'Legal Culture and Transformative Constitutionalism', *South African Journal of Human Rights*, 14: 146–88.

Lacoue-Labarthe, P. and J.-L. Nancy (1997), *Retreating the Political*. London: Routledge.

Madlingozi, T. (2007), 'Post-Apartheid Social Movements and the Quest for the Elusive "New" South Africa', *Journal of Law and Society I*, 34: 77–98.

Motha, S. (2005), 'The Failure of Postcolonial Sovereignty in Australia', *Australian Feminist Law Journal*, 22: 107–25.

—(2009a), 'Liberal Cults, Suicide Bombers, and other Theological Dilemmas', *Law, Culture and the Humanities*, 5: 228–46.

—(2009b), 'Archiving Colonial Sovereignty: From Ubuntu to a Jurisprudence of Sacrifice', *South African Public Law*, 24: 297–327.

—(2010), '"Begging to Be Black": Liminality and Critique in Post-Apartheid South Africa', *Theory, Culture and Society*, 27: 285–305.

Mouffe, C. (2000), *The Democratic Paradox*. London: Verso.

Nancy, J.-L. (1991), *The Inoperative Community*. Minnesota: University of Minnesota Press.

—(2007), *The Creation of the World or Globalization*. New York: State University of New York Press.

Patton, P. (2007), 'Agamben and Foucault on Biopower and Biopolitics', in M. Calarco and S. DeCaroli (eds), *Giorgio Agamben: Sovereignty and Life*. Stanford: Stanford University Press, 203–18.

Ramose, M. (2006), 'The King as Memory and Symbol of African Customary Law', in M. O. Hinz and H. Pateman (eds), *The Shade of New Leaves: Governance in Traditional Authority, A Southern African Perspective*. Berlin: Lit Verlag, 351–74.

—(2007), 'In Memoriam: Sovereignty in the "New" South Africa', *Griffith Law Review*, 16: 310–29.

Santner, E. (2007), *On Creaturely Life: Rilke, Benjamin, Sebald*. Chicago: University of Chicago Press.

Schmitt, C. (1985), *Political Theology: Four Chapters on the Concept of Sovereignty*. Chicago: University of Chicago Press.

—(1996), *The Concept of the Political*. Chicago: University of Chicago Press.

Swiffen, A. (2010), 'Giorgio Agamben: Thought Between Two Revolutions', in C. Barbour and G. Pavlich (eds), *After Sovereignty: On the Question of Political Beginnings*. Abingdon: Routledge, 166–79.

The Citizen v McBride, CCT 23/10 (2011), Constitutional Court of South Africa, 8 April 2011.

The State v Makwanyane, CCT 3/94 (1994), Constitutional Court of South Africa, 6 June 1995.

Turner, V. (1967), *The Forest of Symbols: Aspects of Ndembu Ritual*. Ithaca, NY: Cornell University Press.

van der Walt, J. (2005), *Law and Sacrifice: Towards a Post-Apartheid Theory of Law*. London: Birkbeck Law Press.

van Gennep, A. (1960), *The Rites of Passage*. Chicago: University of Chicago Press.

van Niekerk, M. (2006), *Agaat*. Cape Town: Jonathan Ball.

Notes

I am grateful for the very generous and helpful comments on drafts by the editors of this volume, and for many conversations with Karin van Marle, Sarah Wood, Tshepo Madlingozi, Peter Fitzpatrick and Helen Carr.

1. Agamben himself has given close attention to time, especially messianic time, and the philosophy of history with reference to Walter Benjamin's and Michel Foucault's work. See generally Agamben 1993; 2005; 2009.

2. Countless references can be supplied to illustrate this tendency within Agamben's work; these will do: 'The structure of the exception delineated in the first part of this book appears from this perspective to be consubstantial with Western politics' (1998: 7), and later 'this ancient meaning of the term sacer presents us with the enigma of a figure of the sacred that, before or beyond the religious, constitutes the first paradigm of the political realm of the West' (9). While the grammarian focus on classical Greek and Roman sources might explain some of the desire to confine claims to something called the 'West', my suggestion is that Agamben gives no attention to the work done by his deployment of this trope.

3. Also see Derrida (2009) for an elaborate critique of Agamben's misreading of Foucault. I am grateful to Peter Fitzpatrick for this reference.

4. See section 37 of the Constitution of the Republic of South Africa, which puts in place elaborate safeguards regarding the declaration of states of emergency – the subject of so much attention when it comes to the political and juridical significance of Agamben's thought.

5. Justice Mokgoro explained ubuntu in the following way in *The State v Makwanyane* (1994), which prohibited the application of the death penalty in South Africa: 'Generally, *ubuntu* translates as *humaneness*. In its most fundamental sense, it translates as *personhood* and *morality*. Metaphorically, it expresses itself in *umuntu ngumuntu ngabantu*, describing the significance of group solidarity on survival issues so central to the survival of communities. While it envelops the key values of group solidarity, compassion, respect, human dignity, conformity to basic norms and collective unity, in its fundamental sense it denotes humanity and morality. Its spirit emphasises respect for human dignity, marking a shift from confrontation to conciliation. In South Africa *ubuntu* has become a notion with particular resonance in the building of a democracy', at paras 307–8.

6. See *The Citizen v McBride* (2011); and *Albutt v Centre for the Study of Violence and Reconciliation* (2010). These recent cases might be compared to the early post-apartheid judgments such as *AZAPO v The President* (1996); and *The State v Makwanyane* (1994).

7. For instance, this was the implication when President Mbeke was criticised by *The Citizen* newspaper for writing in support of a con-

victed murderer who had been granted amnesty and had applied to be commissioner of police. See *The Citizen v McBride*.

8. For a discussion and critique of this 'conceptual revolution', see Paul Patton (2007: 218).

9. 'anima' (air breath, life, mind, soul – associated with the feminine); 'animus' (actuating feeling, animating spirit, usually hostile and associated with the masculine), *The New Shorter Oxford English Dictionary*.

III. Biopolitics and Bare Life

7

Encountering Bare Life in Italian Libya and Colonial Amnesia in Agamben

David Atkinson

For all his admirable and clear-eyed engagements with totalitarianism and its biopolitical interventions, and for all his persistent efforts to address 'the camp' and the haunting presence of the Holocaust in twentieth-century European thinking, it is curious that Giorgio Agamben largely elides colonial contexts in his writing. This is all the more perplexing as the applications of surveillance, oppression and, in extremis, violence directed at those with differently racialised bodies characterise totalitarianisms and their camps, but also many colonial regimes at various times and places. Indeed, colonial contexts surely produced the sites and occasions where the conceptual frames of bare life and states of exception that Agamben explores were planned, articulated and realised most starkly. Therefore, this chapter adopts two foci to explore the conundrum of Agamben's absent colonial consciousness.

The first focus outlines how Agamben's conceptual frames help us to comprehend the nature of the Italian colonial record in Cyrenaica (in modern Libya) – and particularly the genocide of its nomadic and semi-nomadic peoples in a system of concentration camps in the early 1930s. The experience of these camps echoes closely Agamben's extended discussions of the camp as the 'nomos of the modern': the site where the logic of Western exception and biopolitics are most fully exposed (Mills 2008: 83). Yet in contrast to Agamben's preoccupation with Nazi Death camps, my focus illustrates how bare life was produced and states of exception realised in the concentration camps created in Italian Cyrenaica in the inter-war period. As such, it explores the purchase of Agamben's theories in illuminating how bodies were dehumanised, excluded and persecuted in colonial contexts where latent and actualised violence were so readily applied as part of governance.

The second focus is more speculative, but I offer it within the context of this collection's wider discussions of Agamben's ambivalences towards the colonial and its consequences. This half of the chapter speculates upon why Agamben does not consider examples from the Italian colonial experience, nor even mention them, in his publications. It suggests that Agamben was, perhaps unwittingly, subject to a wider and wilful amnesia that works to forget the Italian colonial record. This conscious neglect of the colonial past stretches through academia to popular cultures. At its most problematic, it promulgates the myth of the *Italiani brava gente* – of the Italians as 'good' and 'decent' colonisers and, by implication, this myth excuses their colonial record. Recent scholarship has emphasised that the ways in which these notions are still articulated within and beyond Italy remain deeply problematic, but their durability is evidence of the colonial amnesia that still swirls around swathes of Italian society and, it appears, aspects of Agamben's work also.

States of Exception in Italian Cyrenaica

The first sections of this chapter outline how Agamben's notions of states of exception and *homo sacer* find purchase in attempts to understand the Italian colonial persecution of nomadic and semi-nomadic Cyrenaican society in the early 1930s. My focus on Cyrenaica is deliberate. The state of Libya was only created formally in 1934, and the episodes I consider took place before this date in the then Italian colony of Cyrenaica – the eastern coastal region of modern Libya. Rather than address the whole of Libya (and read the region in our contemporary Western, state-centric terms), we should try to recover the scale on which the Cyrenaicans understood and struggled over this region, and we should recognise that in 1911 the Italians encountered a land with a range of distinctive regions and tribal territorialities (Ahmida 1994; 2005). The production of the modern state of 'Libya' and its imposition on top of these regions was another form of colonial appropriation. Further, the focus on a region rather than state may allow this more grounded study to contribute in two additional ways. First, it augments our understandings of how colonialism functioned in different times and places: it textures and nuances our wider comprehension of the colonial past and, perhaps, how it bleeds into the present. Second, it also contributes another case study that explores the potential of Agamben's ideas to illuminate how bodies are persecuted, dehumanised and excluded by the application of sovereign power in colonial contexts.

Agamben's theories are particularly useful for my chosen example of early 1930s Cyrenaica (now part of modern Libya) because of his focus on the biopolitics of twentieth-century totalitarianism and the ways in which state power was exercised through the policing and regulation of colonial bodies. Here I briefly note the process whereby Cyrenaican nomadic and semi-nomadic Bedouin were surveilled, controlled spatially and increasingly abjected as they were steadily reduced to the status of bare life by the regime's colonial discourse and its practical actions. They were gradually excluded from the rights of Italian colonial society (insofar as limited rights existed for colonial subjects) and eventually forced to exist within a string of sixteen concentration camps that housed them for, by some accounts, up to five years until the organised resistance was broken (Ahmida 2006). I spend more time on this episode to demonstrate how these *homines sacri* were denied rights and dignity, but nevertheless remained subject to the colonial state's surveillance, regulation and persecution in the material states of exception constituted by these camps. Here then, is another episode when 'deviant' individuals were excluded from society – although in this instance these relations were amplified further by the essentialising category of race that was so central to the constitution of colonised and colonising subjectivities under colonialism. These distinctions also found spatial articulation in the divisions of racialised bodies across and through the multiple and variegated spaces of colonial society – and especially in this case, through what we might call the *spaces* of exception in the Italian concentrations camps in North Africa. To outline this history we first have to engage the little-known histories of Italian colonialism.

Remembering Italian Colonialism

Despite the inter-disciplinary flurry of interest in all things imperial, colonial and post-colonial in recent years, even amongst Italianists and historians of Italian Fascism the histories of Italian colonialism were seldom told until relatively recently (Ben-Ghiat and Fuller 2005a; De Donno 2006; Labanca 2002). And although the Italians' use of poison gas and machine guns against a poorly armed population in their 1935–6 invasion and conquest of Abyssinia are routinely mentioned in general histories (mainly because this episode undermined the League of Nations), for the main this late-colonial war and its aftermath shares the general neglect of Italian colonialism in the academy. And yet through the first half of the twentieth century the Italian state expanded its colonial territories exponentially. In 1900 Rome controlled Somaliland and Eritrea; by 1914 the empire stretched to the Dodecanese islands and the North African coastal regions of Cyrenaica and Tripolitania; by 1940 Italian possessions included Abyssinia and the North African colonies had been integrated along with the desert interior, into a new colony that from 1934 was constituted as Italian 'Libia'. In 1941 the imperial project continued with invasions of Albania and Greece – although these interventions, along with the wider Italian war effort, ended in defeat and, as a consequence, the loss of the colonial empire. This sudden collapse tends to mask how persistently the Italian state had pursued its imperial ambitions in the Mediterranean and North and East Africa. And although this pursuit wavered at different times and, to varying degrees, it was negotiated separately in each different spatial and temporal context, this project spanned both the Liberal regimes that preceded the Great War and Mussolini's later Fascism as the Italian state sought its 'place in the sun' (Palumbo 2003a).

In addition, this process marked Italian society as well as its colonial domains. Although we are now more sensitive to the local negotiations of empire (Stoler 2002), the Eurocentric modernisation theories of nineteenth- and twentieth-century European colonialism assumed that political change and transformation flowed one way through colonial relationships: from the 'modern', 'rational' West to the 'timeless', 'unchanging' colonised Other. By contrast, Stoler (2009) argues that these traditional statist historiographies and models of modernity remain too blunt for tracing the complex and fine-grained circuits of people, knowledge, ideas and communication that actually constituted the colonial world at regional and local scales. Rather, metropole and colony constituted one another. Therefore, the making of a self-consciously *modern* Italian colonial empire was a key part of Fascist Italian ambitions to render the nation a modern, technical state that could bear comparison with other industrialised European powers (Gentile 1994). Indeed, so significant was this process for Italy that

Ben-Ghiat and Fuller argue that constructing a modern empire was simultaneously a fundamental tenet of Fascist identity, key to the regime's attempts to remake the state and Italian citizens, and finally, central to attempts to assert Italy amidst the other great powers (Ben-Ghiat and Fuller 2005b: 2). Fuller adds that modernity and colonialism were also seen as being mutually constitutive: the Italians needed colonial territory to *be* modern, while the business of forging an empire would unify Italians (Fuller 2007). Here, according to the regime, modernising and (in the terms of the day) 'civilising' Africa was also a national project of renewal at home. It follows that, if colonialism and modernity were seen as entwined by inter-war Italians, it is perhaps less surprising that the colonies became laboratories for modern planning (Fuller 2007; McLaren 2006), biopolitical population management (Horn 1994; Ipsen 1996) and the most contemporary forms of warfare (Ben-Ghiat and Fuller 2005b). If he had addressed Italian colonialism, Agamben would probably add 'the camp' to this list, as it was, to his thinking, 'the political space of modernity itself' (Agamben 1998: 174).

The Conquest and *Reconquista* of Cyrenaica: The Biopolitics of Colonialism

The Italians gained possession of the two separate Ottoman provinces of Tripolitania and Cyrenaica in the aftermath of the Italian–Turkish war of 1911–12 when diplomats representing European states met to divide African territories. The Italians swiftly pushed their military presence further inland, but these advances were lost due to a revolt from some of the tribes from the interior, and Italian involvement in the First World War from 1915 which occupied Rome's political and military elites (Cresti 2011). The Italian presence in Cyrenaica and Tripolitania therefore remained marginal, and after the 1918 armistice Italy descended into chaos as the Liberal government failed to address the aftermath of the conflict and promised land and electoral reform. The left and right mobilised to take advantage of the political crisis as the state slipped towards civil war. Amidst all this, the colonies were largely ignored and left to organise themselves.

In Cyrenaica, the Italians had agreed to share power with local tribes under the terms of the Acroma accords (1913). In part this reflected the distinct regional identity of Cyrenaica where the distances and deserts that separated it from neighbouring regions had engendered a history of political and economic autonomy throughout the centuries of distant Ottoman rule (Ahmida 2005). Therefore, while the colonial authorities controlled the cities of Cyrene, Benghazi and the coastal strip, the inland plateau and the Saharan interior was divided amongst a mosaic of established tribal territories that were transcended, in turn, by a regional layer of political governance provided by the Sanusi religious fraternity (Santarelli et al. 1986). The Sanusi were an Islamic order founded in 1843 that encouraged simple, austere Islamic observance (Peters 1990). They had based themselves in Cyrenaica because of its relative isolation, but had subsequently spread rapidly across the Sahara and along the Egyptian coast into the Arabian peninsular (Cresti 2011). Their network of lodges, called *zawiyas*, eventually totalled forty-nine and served as places of education, religious teaching and poor-relief (Del Boca 2005). They were also centres of banking, administration and commerce: taxing and regulating trans-Saharan trade, including slaves until the 1930s (Wright 1988). In essence, the Sanusi were the secular, political authority in the Saharan interior and their pan-Islamic, anti-colonial sentiments were one of the reasons that Cyrenaica managed to resist the Italian *reconquista* for ten years.

The tensions inherent to this power sharing became more problematic after the Fascist government of Mussolini was established in October 1922. For a regime that increasingly promoted Italy's international prestige and developed an increasingly aggressive foreign policy, it was inevitable that Cyrenaica and the Fezzan (the interior Saharan region of modern Libya) would also be subjected to Italian 'pacification'. In the spring of 1923, the Italians abandoned the Acroma accords unilaterally: they attacked the Sanusi camps and captured half of their regular troops. In turn, and particularly given this volte-face by their former partners, some (but not all) of the Sanusi elite, and many of the nomadic and semi-nomadic Bedouin of the region were unwilling to surrender their authority over the interior. A bitter and bloody conflict ensued until 1932.

After the initial skirmishes when the better-armed and equipped Italians inflicted heavy defeats on the resistance, the Sanusi leadership and the Bedouin who constituted the bulk of the resistance turned to guerrilla warfare. This relied upon their greater mobility, speed, and familiarity with Cyrenaica's geography and landscapes.

Forming small, roaming fighting bands called *muhafiziya*, the resistance exploited their understanding of the region to attack and harass the Italians in ever-changing locations before dissolving into the relative anonymity of the nomadic and semi-nomadic tribes of the coastal strip and interior to avoid detection and to replenish with food, supplies and recruits (Atkinson 1999; Rochat 1973). The resistance thus offered no clear targets to the Italians and simultaneously undermined Italian notions of 'pacified' territory by operating between the coast and the interior in areas that the Italians believed they had already 'conquered'. The *muhafiziya* relied upon the crucial assistance of so-called *sottomessi* communities that had already 'submitted' nominally to Italian forces, but continued to supply the resistance (Cresti 2011). In response to this guerrilla campaign the Italians increased their own mobility and also, in late 1923, started to attack the more permanent Sanusi *zawiyas* and, more indiscriminately, the camps of the wider Bedouin communities. This widened the conflict to Cyrenaicans not directly involved in the armed struggle such as women, children and the old (Del Boca 1991; Rochat 1973). At the same time, the rights of the Bedouin were slowly rescinded: access to education and the rights to any employment beyond simple labouring were restricted (Ahmida 2006: 180). As Agamben (2005: 132) notes, a 1926 Fascist law withdrew citizenship from Italians who had proved 'unworthy' during the First World War; elsewhere in Europe citizenship also became contingent rather than automatic. Given this, the gradual exclusion of Cyrenaicans from the limited rights of colonial citizenship was not surprising.

Through the mid and late 1920s the Italian authorities adopted more explicitly spatial strategies in their attempts to materialise their conceptions of controlled, pacified territory, but they complemented these initiatives with more precise biopolitical interventions. These measures rendered Cyrenaica an increasingly martial, disciplined landscape. The Bedouin's horses were confiscated, and their mobility and communications with other parts of the region were restricted. Nomadic and semi-nomadic groups were forced to camp in designated areas around Italian bases where they were subject to constant surveillance and sudden inspection. Even tribes that were not overtly involved with the resistance and the 'pacified' *sottomessi* were subject to Italian spatial regulations and constraints (Rochat 1973; Santarelli et al. 1986). These strictures were designed to curb the flows of reinforcements, supplies and information to the resistance, and any sign of complicity with the *muhafiziya* drew harsh punishments (Santarelli et al. 1986). Bedouin bodies and lives had become a key focus of the Italian campaign.

Perhaps inevitably these privations meant that this deepening struggle was not supported unanimously by the Cyrenaican people. The Sanusi leadership was fractured at times, and the increasingly difficult situation of the *sottomessi* was worsened in many cases by the 'taxation' of the *muhafiziya* who raised 'religious dues' and requisitioned supplies from the 'pacified' population, sometimes by force (Santarelli et al. 1986). The colonial authorities armed some *sottomessi* to encourage resistance to these enforced subsidies, yet many of these weapons found their way to resistance fighters – as the *sottomessi* resented the Italians still more than *muhafiziya* 'taxation' (Del Boca 1988). But while these policies failed to hinder the resistance and quell its wider support, they also further undermined European conceptions of militant 'rebels' and 'pacified' civilian populations and, I suspect, prompted the Italians to incorporate still more biopolitical strategies into their wider campaign.

With time, therefore, the Italians accelerated their persecution of the Cyrenaican people as they increasingly saw *all* the nomadic and semi-nomadic population as implicated in the resistance. The regime appointed General Rodolfo Graziani to defeat the rebellion by whatever means. Graziani was an experienced desert campaigner and the commander who had reconquered Tripolitania and the adjacent Saharan interior from 1922 onwards. His appointment signalled an increased hostility within both Italian colonial discourse and colonial practice towards the resistance and towards nomadism more generally (Atkinson 1999; 2007). Such prejudice and the desire to discipline and sedentarise nomads were standard elements of European 'high modernism' at home and in colonies (Bauman 1989; Scott 1985). In Cyrenaica, however, Italian anxieties about nomadism, and particularly its undisciplined nature and unpredictable movement (as perceived by Europeans), saw Italian colonial discourse portray the Bedouin increasingly as 'uncivilised', 'disorderly' and 'backwards'. Graziani especially emphasised what he saw as their innate, anti-modern deviance in his accounts of the colonial war (Graziani 1932; 1937). The Bedouin resistance and their supporters were, it seemed to Graziani, beyond comprehension and, by extension, beyond rational regulation and order (Atkinson 2007).

In turn, Graziani styled his military campaign as a 'war without quarter' and he marshalled the fearsome technologies of modern warfare against these enemies. In the interior the *muhafiziya* were harried still more by mechanised Italian forces and aircraft. Sanusi lodges were closed and desert wells poisoned as Graziani sought to crush *muhafiziya* mobility completely (Del Boca 1991; Rochat 1973). Cross-border caravans from Egypt were a significant source of resistance supplies and to strangle these, Graziani ordered the construction of a 282-kilometre-long barbed-wire fence that ran from the Mediterranean coast southwards along the Egyptian frontier (Santarelli et al. 1986). Equipped with the latest military technology and patrolled by aircraft, the fence materialised the arbitrary boundary between British and Italian colonial domains that followed a 'scientific' degree of longitude. In practice it carved through indigenous conceptions of traditional tribal territories and imposed European notions of fixed and impassable boundaries onto the desert landscape. These modern technologies of warfare halted many supplies to the *muhafiziya* and their military campaign waned – although they still managed 250 attacks upon Italian forces in 1931 (Ahmida 1994).

The Camps, Bare Life and Exception

The wider Cyrenaican population were an additional, and more vulnerable, target for this new Italian strategy and they too were targeted to restrict sources of refuge, anonymity and supplies for the resistance (Santarelli et al. 1986). In an attempt to control the *sottomessi* completely the sixteen concentration camps were established along the coast and towards the interior in January 1930 (Cresti 2011). Built at a cost of 13 million lire, they were designed to contain almost the entire population of over 100,000 people and their 600,000 livestock (Ottolenghi 1997; Salerno 1979; Walstron 1997). In apologist discourse after the conflict, the camps were said to provide local peoples with their first taste of Western medical supplies and provisions (Pisenti et al. 1956). However, this strategy was evidently a blunt measure to restrict supplies to the *muhafiziya* and to constrain the people spatially: as they were forcibly marched to these camps – for an arduous 657 miles in one instance (Ahmida 2006: 183) – the Bedouin became subject to European territorialities and controlled, bounded space. To enable surveillance, they were made to camp in regular, ordered lines with uniform spaces between tents – in stark contrast to their traditional conceptions of group encampments and movement across territory. Bedouin found outside the camp without permits were punished harshly and their herds were confiscated (Del Boca 1988). Many of the imprisoned were subject to forced acculturation, and some Bedouin were forcibly enlisted into the Italian military (Labanca 2005). Spatial restriction and surveillance thus encroached into Bedouin lives. At more intimate, bodily realms, the nomads were also subjected to strategies that targeted their health while restricting their rights, dignity and identity within these material spaces of exception.

Within the camps this focus on dehumanising the Bedouin, in Agamben's terms reducing them to bare life, continued. Conditions were lethal. The food supplied by the Italians was rationed, but the Bedouins' herds were only permitted to graze within a given distance of the camps. The livestock that were central to the nomadic culture and economy were destroyed by these measures – with between 80–95 per cent of cattle, sheep and goats dying by 1934 (Ahmida 2006: 183; Guerri 1998). The collapse of their food supplies caused famine in some areas. The consequent shift from a traditional diet of meat and milk to the limited, tinned rations provided by the Italians also impacted upon the health of the Bedouin. Italian medical provision was minimal and even in areas that avoided mass starvation, many Bedouin suffered from malnutrition and its connected diseases. Exacerbating this, basic hygiene provision was poor and typhus and other diseases were endemic. Leaving the camps was restricted and controlled by permits, and inmates were also forced to undertake labour for the Italians – building further barbed-wire fences and coastal road that would enable the Italian military to mobilise more quickly. All these factors proved lethal: the lower estimates attribute 35,000 fatalities to the camps, others estimates rise to 70,000 (Ahmida 2006: 183; Labanca 2005: 32). When other deaths in the conflict, in forced deportations, and through disease and starvation are added to those who were forced into exile, the total Cyrenaican population declined from 225,000 in 1928 to 142,000 in 1941 (Segrè 1987). For some, this qualifies as genocide (Del Boca 1988; Salerno 1979; Santarelli et al. 1986).

Although few Cyrenaican voices recorded this struggle formally

– not least as illiteracy was high amongst the nomads – traces of the oral cultures and poetry of the Bedouin were collected by the Libyan Studies Centre in Tripoli (Jerary 2005). Some were published in English by Ahmida, who also undertook interviews with camp survivors (Ahmida 1994; 2005; 2006). In her work on the oral histories of Italian colonialism in East Africa, Taddia (2005) points out that such research can unsettle over-arching categories of postcolonial analysis: her work retrieved positive memories of the Italian period and uncovered collaboration with the 'oppressors', for instance. Such dissonance muddies the simple and neater narratives that insist on a clear, univocal subaltern voice (Stoler 2009). Nevertheless, this work on oral histories was crucial for capturing at least some Cyrenaican memories of the camps. These voices recall the indignities of displacement, exile and internment, of being forced to salute the Italian officers and flags, and to witness executions, and recounted the routine verbal and physical abuse. The degrading conditions in the camps are captured by recollections of shame at how their clothing was reduced to rags in confinement. Shame, a phenomenon Agamben engages frequently in his discussions of Auschwitz (Vogt 2005), also echoes through the poetry retrieved by Ahmida (2005) which included stanzas such as:

> I have no illness except the suppression of hardship and disease,
> worry over horses . . .
> and work for meagre wages as the whips cry out lashing.
> What a wretched life,
> And when they're done with men, they turn on the women.
> (Ahmida 2005: 49–50)

Finally, one interviewee recalled how, to avoid starvation 'Many of us in the Aguila camp ate grass, ice and insects; others searched for grain in animals' dung to stay alive' (Ahmida 2006: 186). These Bedouin voices offer overdue and alternative perspectives on the camps; they also describe the shame, degradation and suffering of the colonised who, while existing in this state of bare life, are deemed of no importance to the colonisers.

The resistance finally collapsed once their inspirational leader Omar Al-Mukhtar was captured and executed in September 1931. The Italians declared the 'rebellion' defeated in January 1932 (Santarelli et al. 1986) and the surviving nomadic population was slowly released from confinement. They remained subject to elements of the state of exception, however, with Italian surveillance and restrictions upon their mobility and where they could camp still shaping their lives (Cresti 2011). Simultaneously, Italy's colonial project in the region gathered pace. The territories of the Cyrenaican interior were mapped and surveyed, with the populations also subject to ethnographic surveys and eugenic measurement (Atkinson 2003). This rendered the territory knowable to Italian imaginations and, through scientific method, established the now-submitted population as different and Other. Finally, the imposition of new Italian settler landscapes was inaugurated on Italy's new 'Fourth Shore' from the mid 1930s. The Bedouin were denied access to some of their traditional territories and were left the lands deemed too poor for the settlers who were shipped into the new Cyrenaica (Cresti 1996; 2011; Del Boca 1991; Ipsen 1996; Pelligrini and Bertinelli 1994; Segrè 1974). Still marked as dangerous and deviant, the Bedouin were mired at the edges of 'civilised' colonial society.

Applying Agamben

There was an established history of violence from Italians towards colonial subjects, and more locally, a history of deportations from the North African colonies in the initial occupation from 1911 (Labanca 2005). Labanca points out that these precedents helped to foreground the violence of the 1930s and camps that were, in his words, 'unusually brutal' even by the standards of European colonialism (27). Indeed, this systematic assault upon bodies and lifestyles was premeditated. According to Graziani, writing to Foreign Minister De Bono in Rome before the Cyrenaicans were marched into captivity:

> The camps are nearly completely finalised and should ensure the elimination of the collaboration of the *sottomessi* with the rebels. [These people] can prepare for a future as a more docile population, and one adapted to labouring, so that they will be of relevance and use in the new territories to which they will be transferred. [Their] losing the habits of nomadism and acquiring those that are correct and present in settled populations, are necessarily grounds for the establishment and development of the programme for the pacification and colonial exploitation of Cyrenaica. (Santarelli et al. 1986: 80)

This process clearly targeted Bedouin bodies, mobility and life-styles and, when their resistance continued, Bedouin lives too.

It seems to me that Agamben's theories illuminate the enormity of this genocide usefully. Here was a clear instance of biopolitical warfare increasingly focused on nomads who found themselves dehumanised and stripped of their rights as part of a process intended to diminish their resistance. This process eventually led to the camps: pure spaces of exception materialised behind barbed wire where the lack of dignity and rights, plus the fatalities from violence, hunger and disease, rendered the Cyrenaicans *homo sacer* existing beyond 'civilisation'. In *State of Exception* Agamben insists that:

> modern totalitarianism can be defined as the establishment, by means of the state of exception, of a legal civil war that allows for the physical elimination not only of political adversaries but of entire categories of citizens who for some reason cannot be integrated into the political system. (Agamben 2005: 2)

I argue that we can identify such states of exception in inter-war Cyrenaica.

In addition, we can note how other aspects of Agamben's theories mesh closely with our understandings of the nature of modern European imperialism and its production of colonial space. One of Agamben's wider points is that camps and their dehumanising purpose are not aberrations, but actually reveal the foundations and logic of Western juridico-political structures. His relentless use of Auschwitz as a limit case has attracted critique for its vague historical precision, its attempt at a transhistorical 'apocalyptic significance' (LaCapra 2007: 135), and as an 'extreme and absurd' case that offers a 'distorted history' and the prospect of nihilism rather than any optimism (Laclau 2007: 22). In the case of the Italian camps, we might not make as many over-arching claims as Agamben, but it does help us to conceptualise them as not being anomalous, exceptional sites produced beyond normal civilisation. Rather, just as the Holocaust emerged from the structures of modern society (Bauman 1989), these camps were also a product of the more routine exceptionalism of modern governance. Agamben emphasises (when he does dip into history in a more sustained manner), that states of exception were created routinely in inter-war Europe – with Italy, he continues, serving as 'a juridico-political laboratory' for this process (Agamben 2005: 16). Given Ebner's (2011) claims that 'ordinary violence' marked daily life under Fascism on the mainland (although Ebner also says little about the colonial context), it is no surprise that such institutionalised violence was articulated still more across the colonial territories – especially as it was in the colonial realm where Europeans deemed themselves superior to local populations.

Equally, if the colony and metropole are mutually entwined, and if the business of possessing colonial territory and having an imperial profile internationally was a key marker of modernity for the Italian state, then the camps can also be seen as crucial elements in this self-conscious constitution of Italy as a modern, early twentieth-century imperial state. Again, rather than being abnormal and atypical, these camps were an essential, strategic element of the Italian state's modernity and its wider, international reach. As Agamben explains briefly:

> This space devoid of law seems, for some reason, to be so essential to the juridical order that it must seek in every way to assure itself a relation with it [. . .] On the one hand, the juridical void at issue in the state of exception seems absolutely un-thinkable for the law; on the other, this unthinkable thing nevertheless has a decisive strategic relevance for the juridical order and must not be allowed to slip away at any cost. (Agamben 2005: 51)

This same point is made by Gregory (2004) in his discussion of the Abu Ghraib prison complex outside Baghdad and its intrinsic connections to the wider US campaigns against its enemies. He asks us to recognise that rather than being exceptional, Abu Ghraib is enfolded into our Western selves and our colonial histories. The camps in Cyrenaica are likewise hard-wired into Italy's colonial past, but were also significant to the development of Italian state mechanisms. The possession of colonial territories – complete with spaces of exception – allowed Italy to be internationally significant. The camps therefore performed this additional role in the constitution of the modern Italian juridico-political structures, but by ignoring these histories Agamben neglects their significance.

Forgetting Empire

The colonial episode is central to the post-colonial identity of modern Libya. According to Ahmida, 'The agony suffered in the camps along with the enduring loss of dignity and autonomy has left deep psychological scars on Libya's national memory' (Ahmida 2006: 183). By contrast, in Italy these histories attract little of the notoriety they deserved; indeed, the colonial record remains a fleeting, elusive aspect of Italian memory. The final section of this chapter outlines Italy's widespread neglect of its colonial past and speculates tentatively that this may partially explain why, in turn, Agamben tends to neglect colonialism in his writing. At minimum, the broader silences surrounding colonialism in Italy may have made this topic appear less compelling to Agamben. In addition, the general absence of this theme from much academic, political and popular debate means that Agamben will have felt little obligation to incorporate the colonial (as might be the case in some other countries). Thus, at one level his Italian context made it easier for Agamben to elide the colonial.

More recently, however, elsewhere there *were* pockets of academic and public debate upon colonialism that Agamben must have been aware of – but he nevertheless continued to bypass this theme. This neglect is perplexing for various reasons – not least because of his personal biography as an Italian intellectual with leftist sympathies, but also because of how elsewhere he variegates his focus on totalitarianisms and the histories of states of exception. Of course, his colonial silence may simply be due to the Eurocentrism of much of the Western philosophical debates Agamben is embedded within, but in order to contribute to this collection's wider discussion of Agamben's non-encounter with colonialism, I will outline how the often unspoken histories of Italian colonialism may have constituted the background for his silence on the wider business of colonialism.

The Italian empire was collapsing when Agamben was born. According to the few scholars working in the area, the 'repression' or 'displacement' of the memory of Italian colonialism began swiftly afterwards (Del Boca 2003; 2005; Labanca 2005; Taddia 2005). This widespread selective amnesia was embedded in Italy's difficult post-war contexts. In part, this forgetting was a reaction to the fall of Fascism and its corrosive impacts: the social dislocation and trauma of recent warfare in Italy, and an economy with chronic problems meant that for some there was little time for colonial guilt and memories. Also, Foot argues that the 'failure to take responsibility for the occupations and crimes of and crimes in Africa, Yugoslavia, Greece, France and Albania was also part of an international pact of forgetting' (Foot 2009: 79). That said, other aspects of the recent war surfaced regularly in Italian social memory: the Italian Resistance, for example, was celebrated – especially by the left – as a founding moment of the post-Fascist republic (Cooke 2011).

The colonial amnesia persisted, however, and reached such a problematic state that some of the leading scholars of Italian colonialism have felt compelled to make stark claims about the situation. In 2005 Del Boca complained that Italian schoolchildren still had no suitable textbooks on the topic, and Taddia argued that consequently, recent generations did not even realise that Italy once possessed an empire (Del Boca 2005; Taddia 2005). In sum Del Boca stated bluntly that 'In Italian culture there has been and continues to be an almost total repression of colonialism and its crimes, and genocides' (Del Boca 2005: 195). This was, he argued, evidence of a wider and 'more underhanded campaign of mystification and disinformation that aims to protect a romantic and mythical vision of [Italian] colonial history' (197). This conscious forgetting stymied the development of genuine postcolonial debate in Italy and the decolonisation of national identity (Palumbo 2003b). At its most pernicious it also sustained the myth of the *Italiani brava gente* (the Italians as a good people). This obstinate, essentialising belief suggests the Italians, in contrast to other nations, were relatively benign and popular colonial masters (Del Boca 1992; Doumanis 1997). The myth allows Italians to regard themselves as a 'lesser evil' than their imperial peers (Ben-Ghiat 2004) and helps to reproduce the widespread lack of serious debate about colonialism, and, at worst, allows the denial of these histories (Del Boca 2003).

Popular myths about the colonial record were exacerbated because very few academics broached these histories. The first critical academic accounts of Italy's colonial record emerged only in the 1970s thanks to isolated left-leaning historians such as Giorgio Rochat (1973) and Angelo Del Boca (1988; see also De Donno 2006; Malgeri 1970). Their efforts were nevertheless undermined in part by wider academic traditions in which the ethnocentric and state-centred historiographies of most scholars of international fascism tended to ignore the colonies and focus solely on the actions of fascist regimes in Europe. The colonies and metropole were held apart artificially in such analyses – again eliding much attention to colonial contexts (Ahmida 1994; Ben-Ghiat and Fuller 2005a). The peripheral role of the colonies in much contemporary work on Italian Fascism suggests that some academics still reproduce this problematic and artificial separation.

Italy's colonial record and a nascent postcolonial debate eventually began to emerge more regularly in the 1990s. In 1996 the Italian government finally admitted the use of asphyxiating gas in the 1935–6 Abyssinian campaign (Del Boca 1996). This prompted a national debate, as did the 2002 repatriation of the ancient obelisk of Axum, which had been taken from Abyssinia in 1935 and re-erected as part of the Fascist re-planning of Rome (Del Boca 2003). As a leftish academic and commentator in late twentieth-century Italy, Agamben will surely have been aware of these emerging debates about Italian colonialism, its troubled record and its torturous aftermath. Further, it was in these years that he was increasingly questioning issues of power, authority and their application through societies (Mills 2008). Finally, Agamben has shown increasing interest in issues of memory in more recent writing (Agamben 2009a; 2009b). And yet still he says virtually nothing about colonialism, despite his otherwise bold and pioneering work in fraught and challenging fields that plenty of writers avoid (Atkinson 2011).

This silence on the colonial does not mean that Agamben avoids the wider problematic phenomena in the period. Indeed, at times he is careful to distinguish between 'totalitarianism' and 'Fascism' rather than conflate these categories with Nazism. Likewise, he sometimes nuances discussions of exception, exclusion and bare life by noting the various forms of fascism that scarred the twentieth century. In the introduction to *Homo Sacer*, for example, he chides Foucault for eliding 'the exemplary places of modern biopolitics: the concentration camp and the structure of the great totalitarian states of the twentieth century' (Agamben 1998: 4). He then disaggregates Nazism and Fascism when noting how they 'transformed the decision on bare life into the supreme political principle' (Agamben 1998: 10). In particular it is surprising that his focus on camps, and Auschwitz as the archetypal space of exception, did not prompt some thinking on colonial ambitions, violence and terror. For the Holocaust and Nazi expansionism can be seen as a systematic and particularly devastating form of colonialism. The conquest of adjacent territories, the unification of the imagined German Volk within these expanded borders, and the gradual exclusion and eventual extermination of those deemed extraneous to these domains, was colonialism writ large (Jan van Pelt and Dwork 1996). As mentioned above, as the modern machinery that enabled this process, the camps were not the aberrations it is easier to imagine, but were part of a wider imperial-colonial project. Here again, the colonial is avoided – despite Agamben's concerns leading him towards this theme.

Of course, Agamben is not alone in exploring Auschwitz and the dark heart of twentieth-century Europe as limit cases that expose the nature of the human condition under extreme duress. As 'the fundamental biopolitical paradigm of the West' (Agamben 2005: 181), this camp serves his purposes well. But just as historian Mark Mazower rarely strays beyond Europe while considering the sobering issues of twentieth-century Europe as a 'Dark Continent' (Mazower 1998), Agamben likewise ignores the reach of European influences beyond Europe and the convulsions colonialism visited on other regions.

Conclusion

In many respects Agamben is a distinctive writer who, to my mind, betrays clear traces of his situated positionalities. As his interpreters often note, Agamben is steeped in classical philosophy and thinking. For one, his work is 'more akin to the classical learned figures of the Italian Renaissance – schooled in various fields of study, including aesthetics, religion, politics, law and ethics' (Mills 2008: 1). This erudition reflects the persistence of classical learning in Italian school curricula of the mid-twentieth century. Further, Mills also comments on Agamben's ways of writing and constructing arguments: noting the iterative, refracted nature of his arguments that lacks the linear arguments and the 'straightforward incremental or systematic trajectory' that she and other anglophone writers anticipate (Mills 2008: 2; LaCapra 2007; Vogt 2005). Again, this *rhetorical* way of arguing and constructing points is more typical of Italian academia; here again Agamben can be situated in his contexts.

At the same time, Agamben escapes the colonial past of Italy in common with his broader disinterest in the colonial and postcolonial. He is not obliged to address Italian colonialism, of course, but I have tried to outline how this elision may have been easier because such moves were common in Italian academic, political and popular debates for much of the post-war period (although this is changing more recently). Although this context might help explain why it was easy for Agamben to disregard colonialism, it does not explain why he does. Indeed, given the criticism he attracts for what some regard as his indiscriminate selection of examples and brief case studies (Mills 2008; Norris 2005), colonialism and its ready biopolitical governance would seem a theme of clear potential for him. Further, in Cyrenaica Italian colonialism produced the kind of concentration camps that materialised his theories. Agamben, however, leaves these histories untouched.

References

Agamben, G. (1998), *Homo Sacer: Sovereign Power and Bare Life*, trans. D. Heller-Roazen. Stanford: Stanford University Press.
—(2005), *State of Exception*, trans. K. Attell. Chicago: University of Chicago Press.
—(2009a), 'What is the Contemporary?', in *What is an Apparatus? And Other Essays*, trans. D. Kishik and S. Pedatella. Stanford: Stanford University Press, 39–54.
—(2009b), 'Philosophical Archaeology', in *The Signature of All Things: On Method*, trans. L. D'Isanto with K. Attell. New York: Zone Books, 81–115.
Ahmida, A. (1994), *The Making of Modern Libya. State Formation, Colonization, and Resistance, 1830–1932*. Albany: State University of New York Press.
—(2005), *Forgotten Voices: Power and Agency in Colonial and Postcolonial Libya*. London: Routledge.
—(2006), 'When the Subaltern Speak: Memory of Genocide in Colonial Libya 1929 to 1933', *Italian Studies*, 61: 175–90.
Atkinson, D. (1999), 'Nomadic Strategies and Colonial Governance: Domination and Resistance in Cyrenaica, 1923–1932', in J. Sharp, P. Routledge, C. Philo and R. Paddison (eds), *The Entanglements of Power: Geographies of Domination/Resistance*. London: Routledge, 93–121.
—(2003), 'Geographical Knowledge and Scientific Survey in the Construction of Italian Libya', *Modern Italy*, 8(1): 9–29.
—(2007), 'Embodied Resistance, Italian Anxieties, and the Place of

the Nomad in Colonial Cyrenaica', in C. Ross and L. Polezzi (eds), *In Corpore: Bodies in Post-Unification Italy*. Madison, NJ: Farleigh Dickinson University Press, 56–79.

—(2011), 'Remembering Nazi Intellectuals', in S. Legg (ed.), *Sovereignty, Spatiality and Carl Schmitt: Geographies of the Nomos*. London: Routledge, 201–10.

Bauman, Z. (1989), *Modernity and The Holocaust*. Ithaca, NY: Cornell University Press.

Ben-Ghiat, R. (2004), 'A Lesser Evil? Italian Fascism in the Totalitarian Equation', in H. Dubiel and G. Motzkin (eds), *The Lesser Evil: Moral Approaches to Genocide*. New York: Routledge, 137–53.

—and M. Fuller (eds) (2005a), *Italian Colonialism*. New York: Palgrave Macmillan.

—and M. Fuller (2005b), 'Introduction', in R. Ben-Ghiat and M. Fuller (eds), *Italian Colonialism*. New York: Palgrave Macmillan, 1–12.

Cooke, P. (2011), *The Legacy of the Italian Resistance*. London: Palgrave Macmillan

Cresti, F. (1996), *Oasi di Italianità: la Libia della colonizzazione agraria tra fascismo, guerre e indipendenza (1935–1956)*. Turin: Società Editrice Internazionale.

—(2011), *Non desiderare la terra d'altri: La colonizzazione italiana in Libia*. Rome: Carocci Editore.

De Donno, F. (2006), 'Recent Work on Italian Colonialism: Review Article', *Italian Studies*, 61: 262–8.

Del Boca, A. (1988), *Gli Italiani in Libia. Dal fascismo a Gheddafi*. Milan: Mondadori.

—(1991), *Guerra Italiane in Libia e in Etiopia. Studi Militari 1921–1939*. Treviso: Pagus.

—(1992), *L'Africa nella coscienza degli italiani*. Rome-Bari: Laterza.

—(1996), *I Gas di Mussolini. Il Fascismo e la Guerra d'Etiopia*. Rome: Riuniti Editore.

—(2003), 'The Myths, Suppressions, Denials, and Defaults of Italian Colonialism', in P. Palumbo (ed.), *A Place in the Sun; Africa in Italian Colonial Culture from Post-Unification to the Present*. London: University of California Press, 17–36.

—(2005), 'The Obligations of Italy Toward Libya', in R. Ben-Ghiat and M. Fuller (eds), *Italian Colonialism*. New York: Palgrave Macmillan, 195–202.

Doumanis, N. (1997), *Myth and Memory in the Mediterranean: Remembering Fascism's Empire*. London: Palgrave Macmillan.

Ebner, M. (2011), *Ordinary Violence in Mussolini's Italy*. Cambridge: Cambridge University Press.

Foot, J. (2009), *Italy's Divided Memory*. London: Palgrave Macmillan.

Fuller, M. (2007), *Moderns Abroad: Architecture, Cities and Italian Imperialism*. London, Routledge.

Gentile, E. (1994), 'The Conquest of Modernity: From Modernist Nationalism to Fascism', *Modernism/modernity*, 1: 55–87.

Graziani, R. (1932), *Cyrenaica Pacificata*. Milan: Mondadori.

—(1937), *Pace Romana in Libia*. Milan: Mondadori.

Gregory, D. (2004), 'The Angel of Iraq', *Environment and Planning D: Society and Space*, 22: 317–24.

Guerri, G. B. (1998), *Italo Balbo*. Milan: Mondadori.

Horn, D. (1994), *Social Bodies: Science, Reproduction, and Italian Modernity*. Princeton: Princeton University Press.

Ipsen, C. (1996), *Dictating Demography. The Problem of Population in Fascist Italy*. Cambridge: Cambridge University Press.

Jan van Pelt, R. and D. Dwork (1996), *Auschwitz: 1270 to the Present*. New York: W. W. Norton.

Jerary, M. (2005), 'Damages Caused by the Italian Fascist Colonization of Libya', in R. Ben-Ghiat and M. Fuller (eds), *Italian Colonialism*. New York: Palgrave Macmillan, 203–8.

Labanca, N. (2002), *Oltremare: Storia dell'espansione coloniale Italiana*. Bologna: Il Mulino.

—(2005), 'Italian Colonial Internment', in R. Ben-Ghiat and M. Fuller (eds), *Italian Colonialism*, New York: Palgrave Macmillan, 27–36.

LaCapra, D. (2007), 'Approaching Limit Events: Siting Agamben', in M. Calarco and S. DeCaroli (eds), *Georgio Agamben: Sovereignty and Life*. Stanford: Stanford University Press, 126–62.

Laclau, E. (2007), 'Bare Life or Social Indeterminancy?', in M. Calarco and S. DeCaroli (eds), *Georgio Agamben: Sovereignty and Life*. Stanford: Stanford University Press, 11–22.

Malgeri, F. (1970), *La Guerra Libica*. Rome: Edizioni di Storia e Letteratura.

Mazower, M. (1998), *Dark Continent: Europe's Twentieth Century*. London: Penguin.

McLaren, B. (2006), *Architecture and Tourism in Italian Colonial Libya: An Ambivalent Modernism*. Seattle: University of Washington Press.

Mills, C. (2008), *The Philosophy of Agamben*. Montreal: McGill-Queen's University Press.

Norris, A. (ed.) (2005), *Politics, Metaphysics, and Death: Essays on Giorgio Agamben's* Homo Sacer. Durham: Duke University Press.

Ottolenghi, G. (1997), *Gli Italiani e il Colonialismo. I Campi di Detenzione Italiani in Africa*. Milan: Sugarco.

Palumbo, P. (2003a), *A Place in the Sun: Africa in Italian Colonial Culture from Post-Unification to the Present*. London: University of California Press.

—(2003b), 'Introduction: Italian Colonial Cultures', in P. Palumbo (ed.), *A Place in the Sun: Africa in Italian Colonial Culture from Post-Unification to the Present*. London: University of California Press, 1–14.

Pelligrini, V. and A. Bertinelli (1994), *Per la storia dell'amministrazione coloniale Italiana*. Milan: Giuffrè.

Peters, E. (1990), *The Bedouin of Cyrenaica. Studies in Personal and Corporate Power*. Cambridge: Cambridge University Press.

Pisenti, P., A. Sardi, E. Canevari, M. Bocca, M. Belfiori, L. Villari, P. Pascal and V. Teodorani (1956), *Graziani*. Rome: Revista Romana.

Rochat, G. (1973), 'La repressione della resistenza araba in Cirenaica nel 1930–31, nei documenti dell'archivio Graziani', *Il Movimento Di Liberazione in Italia*, 110: 3–39.

Salerno, E. (1979), *Genocidio in Libia*. Milan: Sugarco.

Santarelli, E., G. Rochat, R. Rainero and L. Goglia (1986), *Omar Al-Mukhtar. The Italian Reconquest of Libya*, trans. J. Gilbert. London: Darf.

Scott, J. C. (1985), *Weapons of the Weak: Everyday Forms of Peasant Resistance*. London: Yale University Press.

Segrè, C. G. (1974), *Fourth Shore: The Italian Colonization of Libya*. Chicago: University of Chicago Press.

—(1987), *Italo Balbo: A Fascist Life*. London: University of California Press.

Stoler, A. L. (2002), *Carnal Knowledge and Imperial Power: Race and the Intimate in Colonial Rule*. London: University of California Press.

—(2009), *Along the Archival Grain: Epistemic Anxieties and Colonial Common Sense*. Oxford: Princeton University Press.

Taddia, I. (2005), 'Italian Memories/African Memories of Colonialism', in R. Ben-Ghiat and M. Fuller (eds), *Italian Colonialism*. New York: Palgrave Macmillan, 209–19.

Vogt, E. (2005), 'S/Citing the Camp', in A. Norris (ed.), *Politics, Metaphysics, and Death: Essays on Giorgio Agamben's* Homo Sacer. Durham: Duke University Press, 74–106.

Walstron, J. (1997), 'History and Memory of the Italian Concentration Camps', *Historical Journal*, 40: 169–83.

Wright, J. (1988), 'Outside Perceptions of the Sanussi', *The Maghreb Review*, 13: 63–9.

Note

I would like to thank Simone Bignall for very useful and thoughtful editorial comments. The translation is mine. Where possible I have used English-language references for this English-language collection.

8

Abandoning Gaza

Ariella Azoulay and Adi Ophir

The creation of the 'Gaza Strip' as a separate territorial unit was the product of conquests of large parts of Palestine by Jewish forces in 1948 and the declaration of the State of Israel in a territory that included lands allocated to the Palestinian State according to the UN Partition Plan. Since then, the Gaza Strip has had a special status in the Israeli political and military discourse. Even before its occupation in 1967, the Strip had been exceptional, an appendage, a wasps' nest – both a threat and a burden. In 1948 Israel conquered neighbouring areas in the Negev and (temporarily) in the northern Sinai Peninsula, along with other territories that were meant to be part of the Palestinian State, but did not attack the Gaza Strip. The Rhodes Armistice agreements, signed in March 1949 between the State of Israel and Egypt, approved Egyptian rule in the Strip. Gaza became a haven for Palestinians who were expelled from the territories conquered by Jewish forces and were interred in hastily constructed refugee camps.

During this time, Egypt controlled the Strip without annexing it. It ruled Gaza as a close, separate colony; it was reluctant to assume full governing responsibilities and did little to alleviate the harsh economic conditions that resulted when the Strip was excised from the rest of Palestine in 1948. At the same time, until the Sinai War in 1956, Egypt supported the Palestinian armed struggle against Israel, which was launched from the Strip. This made the area subject to repeated Israeli offensives – described as 'retaliations' – and helped Israel justify its conquest of the Sinai Peninsula in November 1956. This conquest took place – after some hesitation – only at the last stage of the Sinai War, after the main Egyptian force in Sinai had been destroyed. Soon after, when it was forced by the US and the USSR to withdraw from the Sinai Peninsula, Israel tried to keep its grip on the Strip in order to prevent the return of the Egyptian army to Gaza. Hoping to convince the superpowers to agree to its rule in Gaza, Israel stated that it was ready to consider sharing power with the UN and would naturalise some of the Strip's inhabitants, also offering to resettle within Israel an unspecified number of refugees (Tobi 2001). Israel was forced to withdraw from Gaza, but a special concern for Gaza's refugees, both as a 'security threat' and as a 'humanitarian problem', has persisted ever since, making the Gaza Strip exceptional in more than one way.

Unruly and Unwanted

When war broke out in 1967, Dayan had reservations about occupying the Strip because the density of the refugee camps and the spirit of resistance there had grown alarming. Ground forces entered the Strip only on the second day of the fighting and apparently against his judgement. Upon its second conquest by Israeli forces in June 1967, about 60 per cent of the Strip's inhabitants were refugees of the 1948 war[1] and their descendants. Most lived in the refugee camps and did not relinquish their demand to return to their villages of origin. A caricature published in an Israeli newspaper upon the conquest of Gaza portrayed the refugees as people trapped inside a football, with Egyptian, Syrian and Jordanian feet kicking it to and fro. The caricature is an apt expression of the common attitude these nations shared towards Palestine: on the one hand, clearly no one wanted to bear this burden; while on the other, there was no indication that Israel bore any responsibility for the creation of the 'refugee problem', nor any obligation to deal with it.

The Occupation in 1967 did not change Israel's refusal to take any special responsibility for the Palestinian refugees it had created in 1948. But soon after the war ended, and throughout the first two decades of the Occupation, Israel acted – in the West Bank as well as in Gaza – as a colonial power that assumed governmental responsibilities for the population under its control. Even then, the over-populated Gaza Strip was perceived as a special problem, and calls to somehow get rid of this piece of territory (instead of strengthening the grip over it) were frequently heard from across the political spectrum (see Haas 2000). When Labour came to power following the 1992 elections, Israel's desire to be rid of responsibility for Gaza achieved a respectable political guise under the plan 'Gaza first', which the Minister of Foreign Affairs at the time, Shimon Peres, was eager to promote. Peres proposed using the partial transfer of governing authority to the Palestinians in Gaza 'to run their own show' as a means to change direction in the Israeli–Palestinian conflict, setting a new horizon for the political process.

Israel's shirking of responsibility for administering the life of Palestinians was significantly facilitated by the Oslo Accords (1993). The withdrawal of the army from most of the populated area of the Strip and the transfer of certain governmental responsibilities to the quasi-autonomous government of the Palestinian Authority (PA) were seen by many as a great advantage for Israel. Indeed, when Yasser Arafat entered the Strip with his armed militias in July 1994, the Israeli interest in the Strip and its inhabitants was quick to evaporate: 'Gaza after the 1994 retreat was considered dead news. We sang "Goodbye, Gaza" and built a tight separation fence around it. It no longer interested us. Let them all perish in there' (Eldar 2005: 125).

This change in the Israeli attitude to Gaza was made concrete mere days after the signing of the Oslo Accords, even before the 'peace celebrations' had died down. The ruling apparatus imposed a long-term closure on the Gaza Strip, turning it into a separate, sealed unit, disconnecting thousands of workers from their sources of livelihood inside 'Israel proper' while shirking all responsibility for finding them alternative employment. Furthermore, the movement of goods and raw materials was hindered by border crossings, deterring potential investors (Eldar 2005: 116).[2] As Sara Roy (1995) meticulously details, the Gaza Strip was made subject to a process of economic 'de-development'. Within a few years, the Strip – already a relatively poor and highly crowded area that managed, however, to sustain itself in spite of the economic degeneration process imposed upon it by its occupying rulers – became a humanitarian case, the responsibility for which was relegated to others.

Most of the contact Israelis had with Palestinians inside the Strip was at this time reduced to the realm of security, including the safe movement of Israelis to and from the settlements, whose expansion had never ceased. All other contact took place at the crossings, control of which was now ever more tightened. Plans to build a port in Gaza rapidly evaporated; the Dahaniya airport promised in the Oslo Accords was only briefly functional; the safe passage between the Gaza Strip and the West Bank started operation in October 1999 and ceased after a mere nine months (Gisha 2006). All the while, military presence on the ground persisted along the Gaza Strip's main roads and outer borders, dissecting the Strip into four regions – respective of the settlements and their connecting bypass roads – that could be easily separated from one another. A part of the military hold on the Strip, however, was already carried out in the sea and in the air.

During the Oslo period there were, of course, other aspects to the new form of control in Gaza. The Strip had previously been a nearly continuous region, singularly populated by Palestinians and controlled by the PA within the constraints set by the Accords. The PA was authorised to administer most facets of everyday life and a considerable part of the economic activity, as well as economic, legal and administrative planning within the region. Various economic initiatives emerged under the auspices of different international organisations, and through the mediation of Israeli officials and entrepreneurs new housing projects, hotels and public institutions were built and new sources of employment were created inside the Gaza Strip – courtesy of the disproportionate expansion of the PA's civil and military government apparatuses.

However, the Israeli decision to go on controlling Gaza as a prison, both separating and abandoning it, sabotaged investment in its economic development and continuously worsened its economic situation (see Roy 2007). When Israel's civil and military colonial presence in the Gaza Strip ended, the Strip's division into four separate area cells ended as well. Instead, new dividing lines appeared, at first within close range of the fence surrounding Gaza, and later deep in the heart of the Strip.[3] The withdrawal of the controlling apparatus from Gaza Strip and the dismantling of the Jewish settlements there created a new situation, unprecedented since the onset of the Occupation: on one side of the border between the Gaza Strip and Israel lived Israeli citizens; on its other side, Palestinian non-citizens. The exclusion of the latter from the Israeli political system has been presented ever since as if it had always-already been a fact of political life in the region. The Sharon government declared that with the dismantling of the settlements and the withdrawal of army forces from the Gaza Strip, the Occupation there had come to an end and Israel no longer bore any responsibility for this territory and its inhabitants. This has been reaffirmed by several rulings of the

High Court of Justice, rejecting petitions from NGOs and Gaza Strip inhabitants demanding that the state provide the means for Palestinians to receive 'welfare controlled by Israel', for example by opening Gaza's border crossings for import and export, and by giving permission for Gazans to visit relatives or study in the West Bank or to enter Israel for medical treatment unavailable in the Gaza Strip. Relying on (and interpreting) both Israeli and international law, the Court ruled that the State of Israel owes Gazans nothing but minimal humanitarian aid, which in actuality means nothing more than allowing international organisations to send necessary supplies. Both the government and the High Court ignore the obvious fact that 'ending the Occupation has not ended Israel's effective control of the Gaza Strip and its surroundings' (Gisha 2007). Disregarding the claim by Gisha (the Legal Centre for Freedom of Movement) that Israel effectively controls the Strip and is answerable to the Hague Regulations and the Fourth Geneva Convention, the High Court of Justice ruled in two separate cases that the disengagement and the Israeli government's promise to do 'everything in its power to prevent a humanitarian crisis in the Gaza Strip' has rendered the issue 'theoretical, without any practical outcome' (High Court of Justice 2007a; 2007b).

The Court thereby accepted the government's position and ruled that responsibility for Gaza borne by the government of Israel can be reduced to its duty to prevent humanitarian disaster. By doing so, the Court ignored the fact that the condition of Palestinians in the Gaza Strip is a direct consequence of their imprisonment within the giant pen that Israel has erected for them (with Egypt's cooperation), and in fact the Court effectively excluded the Palestinians from its field of vision. For the High Court of Justice, the inhabitants of the Gaza Strip are no longer subjects of the Israeli sovereign. The Court has failed to recognise that, precisely for this reason, the Gazans are non-subjects of the Israeli state. Their elected, semi-autonomous government is incapable either of forming a state or of running it, but this statelessness is precisely the form and effect of their relation to a certain state – Israel – that has deprived them of their own statehood and does everything it can to keep them abandoned, forsaken between a suspended war and a suspended catastrophe. The condition under which Palestinians live and die, love and work, raise children and pray to God is determined, to an extent unprecedented in the contemporary world, by a series of quite simple acts of state. The 'disengagement' constituted the Gaza Strip as a no-man's-land, where the entire population has become a client of humanitarian agencies. The Strip is excepted from Israeli law and out of range of the Israeli sovereign responsibility, but completely within its rule and control, effectively preventing the emergence of any other power that could assume the responsibility of a sovereign government. The Palestinians in Gaza are the abandoned people of the Israeli regime.

In fact, abandonment has been an official Israeli policy in Gaza since the beginning of the second Intifada. The Palestinian individual, no longer perceived as a subject with an identity who must be subjugated but also cared for, remained tagged as a client of humanitarian aid, a hunted person, a name on an elimination list, a dot upon the radar screen or a spot on the monitor inside a military pilot's cockpit. The Israeli regime, having shirked its duties towards some of its subjects, did not relinquish the sovereign's ultimate right: the authority to take life. Even before the disengagement, the Gaza Strip contained 1.5 million exceptions to the rule, people living liminally – on the threshold of the law as well as on the brink of catastrophe. In response to Palestinian armed resistance during the Al Aqsa Intifada, Israel adopted the policy of targeted killings,[4] the majority of which were carried out in the Gaza Strip. These assassinations by decree take place according to changing military regulations, when persons suspected of 'terrorist activity' are targeted from helicopters and unmanned aerial vehicles, which often kill many others who happen to be near the target. Lives are forsaken, by virtue of who one is thought to be a suspect by Israel security forces, or whom one happens to associate with or even merely pass by in the street. The densely populated area makes everyone vulnerable. Combined with the siege, the rationing of basic supplies, and liberalisation of regulations for opening fire, the new policy has turned each and every inhabitant of the Strip into *homo sacer*, in the sense that Agamben gives this term. The Palestinian inhabitant of the Strip is a person who has been placed under the sovereign ban, because the sovereign who is still authorised to kill him is no longer obliged to protect him. Such a person has become fair game: killing or hurting him is permissible and goes unpunished; those involved in injuring him enjoy impunity; and finally, his self-sacrifice is not recognised as such, by the sovereign at least, and his death can assume no transcendent value (Agamben 1998).

Derek Gregory (2004) has already proposed a systematic use of Agamben's notions of sovereignty, exception and abandonment for analysing control of the Occupied Territories since the outbreak of the Al Aqsa Intifada, and others have followed him (for example, Lentin 2004; Tawil-Souri 2011; Hanafi 2010; Azoulay and Ophir 2004). In what follows we shall propose a series of observations on the situation in the Gaza Strip that makes use of Agamben's conceptual grid, yet expose its limitations in dealing with the complexity of one ongoing, but quite unusual case of colonisation in which pushing the colonised to the brink of catastrophe has become more than a means of governance; it has become the mode in which they are ruled.

Two Reservations

Our first reservation concerning the use of the Agambenian concept of *homo sacer* in the context of the Palestinian Occupied Territories concerns the implied passivity of the forsaken Palestinian. Clearly, as a policy, abandonment is a response to active, persistent and often painful Palestinian resistance, not a reflection of its passivity. Nowhere is this clearer than in the context of the way Palestinians handle the deaths of their people who have been lost in the struggle against Israel. The Israeli sovereign state has never controlled Palestinian representation of death and sacrifice. By withdrawing from the densely populated areas in the Strip, the camps and the town, Israel suffered a certain weakening of its grip over the way Palestinians farewell their dead. For as long as the ruling apparatus administered the Palestinians' lives, it was able to intervene violently and extensively in the management of Palestinians' regard of their dead, and it did this from the very beginning of the Occupation by setting the dates of funerals, violently dispersing funeral and memorial processions, and maintaining displays of 'withheld violence' in the very space where funerals took place.[5] This insistence on administrating Palestinian death decreased and nearly ceased with the Oslo Accords when Israel relinquished control of Palestinian daily life.

The Palestinians, for their part, turned their dead into sacred victims and self-sacrifice into a lethal mode of operation. Every casualty was declared a *shaheed* (witness) who not only sacrificed his own life for a noble cause but also, through his own death, bore witness to the conditions of his abandonment. This does not

suffice, of course, to change the politics of abandonment characteristic of the Israeli sovereign in Palestine. But it does emphasise
how 'abandonment' means different things to either side, resulting
in different kinds of strategies. For the Israeli ruling power, the
Palestinians are indeed abandoned and rendered entirely vulnerable, *homines sacri*; for the Palestinians, the abandoned who have
died become *shaheeds* and through their death actively sanctify
their common struggle. The mass funerals, mourning tents and
memorial ceremonies have always been sites of resistance; but
when Israel withdrew its full control following the Oslo Accords,
the Palestinians were able to manage their own representations of
death and their leave-taking from the dead, and through a celebration of death, turn abandoned life into sanctified life.

Our second reservation is more serious and concerns not only
the use of the Agamben's model of *homo sacer* to theorise the
situation in Israel–Palestine but also the limit of his concept of
exception. Certainly, Agamben's analysis of the sovereign exception helps us identify abandonment as the present form of colonial
domination in the Occupied Territories. Specifically, the withdrawal of Israeli military forces from the Gaza Strip, together
with the administrative apparatus dealing with civilian population
(little or malfunctioning though it was), has turned the Strip into
a zone of exception where biopolitical control of life has been delegated by the state to humanitarian organisations, while the state
itself exercises violence that has little or no relation to the law. In
the Gaza Strip it is certainly true that 'humanitarian organisations
[. . .] can only grasp human life in the figure of bare and sacred
life, and therefore, despite themselves, maintain a secret solidarity
with the very power they ought to fight' (Agamben 1998: 133).
However, in this case the solidarity is not secret, as we shall show
below, but a professed rule of the game for both state authorities
and humanitarian activists.

This, however, is not so much due to the naivety and limited
power of the humanitarian organisations, but rather due to the
humanitarianisation of the state on the one hand, and the systematic integration of humanitarian agencies of various kinds in
the government of the Strip on the other. The withdrawal of the
law and other Israeli state formations from the Strip at the time
of the 'disengagement' was combined with the closure of the area,
which often turned into a fully imposed siege. This combination
has made humanitarian intervention both possible and necessary.

But we note that it is this intervention and not the application of the law that is potentially and occasionally suspended by sovereign decisions. Israel has announced that its rule in the Gaza Strip was terminated, and so from the point of view of the Israeli legal system (represented by the government and accepted by the court), Israeli law no longer applies in the Strip; it has not been suspended but abolished altogether. The area has been declared ex-territorial. However, the occasional suspension of humanitarian assistance – on which the Palestinians rely for their very subsistence[6] – brings Gaza back into the realm of Israeli rule and restores the fundamental relation of inclusive exclusion between the sovereign and the exception. Gaza is the area in which Israel can create famine, even starve people to death, but refrains from doing so. The postponement of a wholesale regime-made disaster and the maintenance of a chronic, 'low-profile' one, is the way the Gaza Strip is contained within the sphere of Israeli rule. This includes, as we shall see below, a rule of law, at least as far as the operations of the Israeli army and security apparatus are concerned.

On the Brink of Catastrophe

The Gaza Strip was fenced in with barbed wire as part of the Oslo Accords. When the second Intifada broke out in October 2000, the closure gradually became a fully fledged siege and economic de-development rapidly deteriorated into a 'humanitarian crisis' that permanently threatens to plunge into the abyss of a 'humanitarian catastrophe'. After the disengagement in August 2005, ground control inside the Strip was replaced by full peripheral ground control, accompanied by control of the air and the sea (see Weizman 2007: 238–9), as well as occasional ground incursions into the Strip and airborne attacks. Gaza was enclosed, pen-like, with rare entry and exit permitted only to a few individuals and altogether prohibited over long stretches of time because the crossings often are closed. Passage to Egypt, too, while not under official Israeli control, is indirectly subject to full Israeli monitoring.[7] Territorial waters around the Gaza Strip are fully controlled by the Israeli Air Force. Remote controlled monitoring and surveillance enable ongoing control, both comprehensive and localised, throughout the area and of every single individual moving within it.

This monitoring is based on census data which Israel has been withholding in spite of having been committed in 1995 as part of the Oslo Accords to transfer this information to the Palestinians: Israel did not register hundreds of Gazans who had relocated to the West Bank and were then forced to move back to Gaza (see B'Tselem 2007a). The fence continues to contain the Gaza Strip within the Israeli 'customs shell', so that all goods imported to the Strip through Israeli-controlled terminals can be taxed. This fence has not eliminated the connection of the Strip to the Israeli power grid and telecommunications networks working from inside Israel. Gaza cannot sustain itself without the ongoing supply of electrical power, fuel, food and raw materials that reaches it through Israel. A severe shortage of various medical services that before the disengagement brought hundreds of Gazans into Israel for medical treatment even now remains unsolved (Eldar 2007). Containers with goods that do not qualify as urgent humanitarian aid according to Israeli authorities' standards pile up on the Israeli side. Farm produce imported by the Gaza Strip decomposes at the crossings because of long delays, while Gazan produce rots on the other side of the fence, inflicting heavy financial losses on merchants. The Gaza Strip has remained under full siege since the abduction of Israeli corporal Gilad Shalit by Palestinian combatants in 2006. Every once in a while it is bombed from the sea and from the air and raided by special troops, whether in response to the scattered rockets fired on neighbouring Israeli villages and towns or, allegedly, due to efforts to pre-empt such attacks. Every once in a while individuals suspected as 'terrorists' are targeted and killed from the air.

Under these circumstances, the threat of catastrophe is not the result of military activity or of the economic policy of a 'strong state', nor is it a consequence of the fiascos of a 'weak state', one that is deteriorating, surrendering to the violence of paramilitary groups; it is rather the result of the *withdrawal of a part* of the ruling apparatuses of a strong state – Israel – from a defined territory kept under strict closure. The administration of justice, law enforcement and welfare has been withdrawn. The closure of the Strip and – until the time of the disengagement – its spatial fragmentation have prevented Palestinian governing bodies from effectively replacing the withdrawn governing apparatuses by looking after the population abandoned by the Israeli ruling apparatus. Hence, the need to *prevent* catastrophe (without removing its causes) has become an essential component in the structure of Israel's control of the Strip.

In 2003, following more than two years of Palestinian uprising and Israeli oppression, Jean Ziegler, special envoy of the
UN Secretary General, stated plainly: 'the OPT are on the verge
of humanitarian catastrophe.'[8] He also claimed that the Israeli
authorities 'acknowledged that there is a humanitarian crisis in
the Territories. They did not contest the statistics indicating a rise
in the extent of malnutrition and poverty among Palestinians'
(Ziegler 2003: 3–4). Although Israel has continually obstructed
the work of organisations such as UNRWA, Oxfam, US AID or
the International Red Cross, who provide aid to the Territories,
it has remained officially and practically committed to preventing
the Territories from crossing this dangerous threshold. 'There will
be no hunger in Palestine,' members of the control apparatus have
repeatedly insisted, and they made sure that 'cases of local want
would not turn into outright starvation'.[9] To curb malnutrition,
UNRWA officials added iron to the flour they provided, and by
means of a simple food supplement kept the Palestinian population from crossing the threshold of malnourishment, without
moving it further away.[10]

The ruling apparatus quickly adopted the humanitarian discourse
and institutionalised its ties with the humanitarian organisations.
Thus, Lieutenant Colonel Orli Malka, Chief of Foreign Relations
and International Organisations at COGAT (Coordinator of
Government Activities in the Territories) remarked: 'In the order
of operation, among the targets cited for operational attack and
the men wanted for elimination or capture, appears the following
article relating to the humanitarian realm!' (in Azoulay 2003). The
ruling power acknowledges the possibility that its military actions
generate a humanitarian crisis, it is aware of the catastrophic
implications of the regimentation of movement, and is prepared to
monitor the humanitarian crisis, equipping itself with the means
of surveillance, point of view and conceptualising language of the
humanitarian organisations, as it controls the adaptation of data
to the changing threshold of the crisis that requires intervention:
'Israel will prepare itself to provide humanitarian needs [. . .] No,
there will be no hunger. But this policy is extremely clear. There
will be no hunger in the Territories, no way' (Lt. Col. Malka, in
Azoulay 2003).[11]

In June 2007 the hostility between the Hamas government,
elected in January of that year, and the PLO that lost the election
deteriorated into violent clashes between the two parties. The PLO

tightened its control in the West Bank while the Hamas government in the Strip disconnected itself from the Palestinian Authority and dismantled the Fatah apparatus in Gaza. Israel's response, backed by its main allies, the US and many European states, was to boycott the Hamas government and impose a siege on the Strip. Ever since, Israel has invested much effort in counteracting the Hamas government's operations, reducing its capacity to a minimum. Any service provision beyond the most basic humanitarian aid has been consistently sabotaged. In September 2007 the Israeli government asked the defence forces, the Ministry of Foreign Affairs and juridical bodies to prepare a plan 'that would address all military and civilian aspects of impacting the services provided by Israel to the Gaza Strip' (Harel and Ravid 2007). As part of this economic rationalisation, the Israeli army was asked to propose a 'price tag' for the launching of Qassam rockets and mortar shells. In October the cabinet decided to disconnect areas around the fence from the power grid during the evening hours. Several days later, however, the prime minister announced that the cutting of power would not lead to a humanitarian crisis (Harel and Yissakharof 2007).

At the end of October 2007 the government legal adviser intervened and forbade the army to cut off power or fuel supply to the Gaza Strip (Mizrahi 2007); however, he did not rule out rationing their supply: the judicial arm and the military disputed the rationing of vital services, not Israel's actual right to turn the supply of these services into a means of control, monitoring and collective punishment. Two weeks later an arrangement was reached and the legal adviser agreed in principle to a new plan by the defence apparatus, aimed at restricting the power supply to the Gaza Strip. According to the plan, the principle of 'blackout Gaza' is changed. Instead of blacking out neighbourhoods or parts of the Strip for foreseen periods of time, the entire power supply would be reduced and limited through 'current pacers' installed upon all power lines in the region. These power limiters would enable Israel to provide the Strip with less electricity per day, but the responsibility for

> distributing the reduced amount of power will lie with the consumers, namely the Gaza authorities [. . .] Increased consumption of electricity would bring about power-cuts and short circuits – and Gazans will have to make do with less [. . .] This will ensure the continued power supply for humanitarian needs and the Hamas government

will no longer be able to blame Israel for power cuts at a hospital, for example. (Kaspit 2007)

The initial brutality of the policy decision proposed by the Ministry of Defence was restrained by the Ministry of Justice, with the result being a more finely honed tool for creating humanitarian disaster in Gaza and monitoring its limits. As in the administration of food supply to the West Bank through 'back to back' installations introduced at the beginning of the Second Intifada,[12] so too 'current pacers' are the tool that generates disaster while at the same time limiting it, meting it out to the 'proper degree'. The legal instruction given to the Ministry of Defence had a clear, dual purpose. On the one hand, the instruction turned the disaster threshold into a means of governance. One could, then, always claim that the threshold had not been crossed, that minimum conditions for Palestinian existence have not been impacted, and so forth. On the other hand, the decision pushed the responsibility for 'impacting life' itself over to the Palestinians, making them full partners in the creation of want and the onset of disaster conditions.

Gradually, since the disengagement from Gaza, there emerged a sophisticated mechanism for the creation of controlled scarcity in the Strip. Documents relating to the Gaza closure policy released by the Israeli Defence Ministry reveal a series of rules controlling and blocking transfer of goods into the Gaza Strip, and formulas for calculating the amount of commodities allowed into the Strip.[13] These rules and formulas have guided the ruling apparatus since the disengagement (in August 2005) until the end of May 2010, when Israel succumbed to international pressure. This pressure has mounted in response to the deadly attack by the navy on a Turkish flotilla that tried to break the siege on Gaza. The documents reveal a policy whose mission was

> monitoring basic products out of the variety entering the Gaza Strip, including basic food products, fuel, controlling the amount of those products, detecting shortages, surpluses and establishing warning lines, addressing problems that arise as a result, providing current information and real-time warning to decision-makers. (Gisha 2010)

According to the documents, the state approved 'a policy of deliberate reduction' for basic goods in the Gaza Strip. The state set a 'lower warning line' to give advance warning of expected short-ages in a particular item, but at the same time approved ignoring that warning, if the good in question was subject to a policy of 'deliberate reduction'. Moreover, the state set an 'upper red line', above which even basic humanitarian items could be blocked, even if they were in demand (Gisha 2010).

As Gisha clearly states, the creation of scarcity has little to do with 'security reasons', of course. The decision whether to permit or prohibit an item is largely based on 'the public perception of the product' and 'whether it is viewed as a luxury'. In other words, goods characterised as 'luxury' items – such as choco-late and paper – would be banned. The procedures determine that the list of permitted goods 'will not be released to those not specified!!', which means that merchants in Gaza could not know what they were permitted to purchase (Gisha 2010). But the most important aspect of the policy in the context of our argument is that the Defence Ministry created a series of formulas to compute product inventory. The calculations are presumed to allow the Coordinator of Government Activities in the Territories (COGAT) to measure what is called the 'breathing span'. By dividing the inventory in the Strip by the pre-defined daily consumption needs of residents, the formula calculates the number of days it takes for residents of Gaza to exhaust their 'breathing span' and run out of basic products.

Israeli control of Gaza's gates[14] and the near-total isolation of the Strip from the rest of the world has enabled the ruling appa-ratus to set the unemployment rate in the Gaza Strip, as well as the income levels, production possibilities, modes and rate of distributing food and medication by international organisations, and to establish the level of malnutrition.[15] In the present era of global economy, the actual isolation of a very densely populated area from its entire surroundings over an extended period of time amounts to creating disaster conditions inside the isolated area and obstructing efforts to cope with disaster as it happens. By monitoring the entry and exit gates, Israel is capable of setting the patterns for the disaster's expansion and intensity. This kind of governance through catastrophisation is a new component in a new economy of violence (see Ophir 2010). Closure of the Strip, economic strangulation and the destruction of civil infrastructures greatly exacerbate the impact upon every single person wounded or killed, every demolished home, every damaged public building.

These, in turn, escalate economic deterioration and the ability to maintain normal life activity of any kind.

Excluded, surrounded and isolated, the existence of the Strip's inhabitants has been reduced in the eyes of the ruling power to the mere presence of mouths to be fed with the barest minimum (see B'Tselem 2005).[16] Everyone is aware of the fact that opening the gates to human movement and goods is a humanitarian matter, and it is brought up as a humanitarian problem in every round of meetings and following every violent attack. Even when the gates are closed, on days when violence rises and tensions mount, closure is perceived as temporary and after several days, or weeks at the most, the transfer of humanitarian aid is renewed, and sometimes exit permits are even granted to the ailing and the wounded who need medical treatment outside the Strip. Punitive actions such as severance from the electrical power grid or fuel supply are taken in a measured, calculated manner, in an effort to impact for the sake of exerting pressure but also to halt just in time a dramatic deterioration of the humanitarian situation.[17] By closing the gates of the Strip and disconnecting its electricity supply, the ruling power could, if it wanted, create famine within days or weeks. But so far it has been made clear that such severe measures are not included in Israel's repertoire. Israel is ready to approach the threshold of catastrophe in a controlled manner, but not to cross it.

Clearly, the threshold of catastrophe has never been a fixed line. Since the 1970s the humanitarian conditions considered unbearable and the interventions considered permissible have undergone significant erosion. During the First Intifada the line threatened to be crossed with every local curfew that lasted over a week, but this hardly ever resulted in exceptional humanitarian intervention. In 2007, after long weeks of closure and fragmentation into separate 'area cells' impacting the fabric of life of hundreds of thousands, this situation had become the rule, and the extensive humanitarian activity of numerous local and international organisations had created a new routine of life. Prior to the Oslo process hardly any non-governmental organisations shared the burden of responsibility with the Israeli government for the population in the Territories, except for UNRWA, which provided mainly for the refugee camp inhabitants and only 10 per cent of its budget was allotted to supply food directly to the needy. In 2007 about ten organisations were providing food in the Occupied Territories, with UNRWA handling over one half of the population in the Gaza Strip where thousands of families live outside the refugee camps; 54 per cent of its budget was then dedicated to direct aid for the needy (UNRWA 2007). Catastrophe – actual and extensive disaster – is in the air, more concrete than ever, and the Israeli control apparatus, UN agencies and the non-governmental organisations collaborate in acting on their commitment not to allow this threat to materialise, thus keeping the humanitarian indicators below the threshold.

The occasional 'humanitarian gestures' which the Israeli government is willing to make within the ritual of negotiations towards the political negotiations, or in response to the Palestinian internal struggle, remain essentially symbolic. When concrete, they are a part of the measures that would be taken in any case to avoid crossing the threshold of catastrophe. When violence escalates the catastrophisation process, the Israeli administration takes special caution to prevent disaster as soon as the threshold appears to have been crossed. This occurred, for example, during the short civil war in which Hamas took over the Gaza Strip and distanced forces loyal to Fatah in June 2007. When the crisis broke out, most of the humanitarian organisations active in the Strip published emergency reports that predicted full closure of the Gaza Strip and calculated how long the available basic food supplies, fuel and medicine would last (OCHA 2007a). However, a few days after violence erupted, Israel allowed supply trucks to enter the Strip, carrying provisions from UNRWA, the UN World Food Programme and the International Red Cross, and vaccines supplied by UNICEF. These were successfully delivered in spite of the fact that these organisations had to coordinate the delivery with the boycotted Hamas government. Starvation was prevented, but the Strip remained under siege, and goods not included in the humanitarian basket remained stuck in Israel. Additional damage was done to the sinking Palestinian economy that became all the more dependent upon international aid, as well as on the willingness of the Israeli government to open a 'humanitarian safety valve' in the wall surrounding the Gaza Strip.[18]

The 'disengagement' has changed the status and significance of Palestinian civilians in the Strip. They are now not only objects of attack, manipulation and domination; their suffering has become an asset at stake for the rival parties. The ability to calculate, demonstrate and predict this suffering has acquired strategic significance. Through the combined and orchestrated use of siege, violent attacks and humanitarian practices, catastrophisation has become a major means of ruling the Gazans. Once the threshold of catastrophe has been more or less established, the scope for abandoning the population in a designated area is identified and can be used perspicaciously as a means of control. One can estimate in advance for how long the terminals may remain closed and the supply of food, water, fuel, electricity and medications may be cut.

A space has thus been designated in which the suffering of the population becomes a legitimate instrument. Measuring and calculating calories and hospital beds, clean water and fuel becomes crucial for the instrumentalisation of human suffering and its integration in the war machine. Humanitarian knowledge, expertise and practices have been directly and indirectly incorporated into the military apparatus, and humanitarianism has become a branch of the military.

This new constellation became plainly evident during the massive Israeli assault on the Strip ('Operation Cast Lead') that started in the last days of December 2008, following weeks of rocket attacks. The assault lasted three weeks; about 1,400 people were killed and more than 11,000 housing units and 1,500 shops, factories and public administration buildings were destroyed or damaged.[19] The gap between the lives lost and the houses destroyed is telling: 1,400 lives to 11,000 housing units. This ratio – about eight houses for every person killed – calls for an explanation, especially in view of the population density in the Strip. Contrary to what first meets the eye, what explains the pattern of destruction and killing in Gaza is the kind of care Israeli soldiers took to reduce civilian casualties on the one hand, and the surgical precision with which most houses were destroyed, bulldozed, shelled from the air or exploded by ground forces on the other. This does not mean that more care could not have been exercised, even by military standards and accepting the military point of view. Reports of brutality, negligence and indifference to Palestinian life abound, especially with regard to the conduct of the rank and file.[20] However, when considering the planning of specific operations, the tactics employed and the kinds of weapon used in these operations, and the role of the 'embedded lawyers' in approving and restraining operations, it becomes clear that the army's policy was to spread destruction while keeping the number of 'non-combatants' killed as low as possible, in conformity with international humanitarian law – as this has been interpreted by the state's legal experts (see Weizman 2009). 'We did not wish to kill Palestinians, we wanted to hit them in their pockets', said a military strategist in a closed meeting that convened to discuss the Goldstone report at Tel Aviv University.[21]

These words do not exhaust the motives behind the ferocity of the Israeli exercise of force at the time, but they certainly represent the rationality of the ruling apparatus. Hitting Palestinians in their pockets means impoverishing them further, adding scarcity to an already defunct economy. In most cases, the aim of the extensive use of violence was not death but destruction, whereby violence has turned into an instrument of catastrophisation constrained by certain legal provisions. Thus, warning people – usually through a cell-phone announcement – minutes before hitting a house has become common practice. It has achieved two things at once: respect for what the Israeli legal experts conceive as legal use of force by the military; coupled with immense destruction of the Palestinian urban space, its infrastructure and built environment, which does not, however, create immediate and dramatic change in the measureable variables that determine the threshold of humanitarian emergency. Since food shortage and supply, as well as sanitary conditions, had been bad for a long time before the attack, the destruction of thousands of overly crowded houses and their replacement with temporary tents and the creation of new traumatised public spaces as a result of the massive destruction amplify the need for humanitarian aid. Humanitarian aid has long replaced labour and commerce in Gaza, but the destruction inflicted on the Strip in January 2009 was precise action of the kind that keeps life on the brink of catastrophe, without crossing the red lines of the humanitarian charts and without giving rise to new emergency claims.

Going back to Agamben's model of the exception, we should note the clear difference between emergency and exception in the case of the Gaza Strip: the exceptional status of Gaza for the Israeli sovereign does not lie in the suspension of the law but in the suspension of humanitarian provisions that threatens to bring about – but indefinitely suspends – the creation of 'a real humanitarian emergency'. After the abolishment of the law and the official declaration that Israel's rule in the Strip has terminated, the administration of catastrophe is the mode of implementing and maintaining the exception, of including the excluded, and of abandoning the governed.

Referring to an apparent lacuna in the state of exception (conceived as 'a state of necessity'), Agamben writes:

> The lacuna is not within the law [*la legge*], but concerns its relation to reality, the very possibility of its application. It is as if the juridical order [*il diritto*] contained an essential fracture between the position of the norm and its application, which in extreme situations, can be filled only by means of the state of exception, that is, by creating a zone in which application is suspended, but that law [*la legge*], as such, remains in force. (Agamben 2005: 31)

Clearly, in our case, this structure has been entirely inverted. Looking at the Israeli sovereign, it is clear that what remains in force is not the law but the authorisation to use force beyond the realm where the law applies, and to use it in order to create a fracture in the biopolitical (humanitarian) order (from which the law has been excepted), and not the juridical one. The aim of this act is to suspend the provision of essential means of subsistence, so that the threat of catastrophe, though suspended, remains in force. If there is a law whose suspension is relevant in this situation, it is not the law of the Israeli sovereign, but the law of nations, the international humanitarian law and its major conventions, which are constantly invoked here by all protagonists, Israeli judges and lawyers included, with no sovereign moment in sight.

References

Agamben, G. (1998), *Homo Sacer: Sovereign Power and Bare Life*, trans. D. Heller-Roazen. Stanford: Stanford University Press.

—(2005), *State of Exception*, trans. K. Attell. Chicago: University of Chicago Press.

Algazi, Y. (1974), *Father, What Did you Do when they Demolished Nader's House?* Published by the author: Tel Aviv.

Al-Haq Independent Palestinian Human Rights Organisation (2009), 'Operation Cast Lead': A Statistical Analysis, August, available at http://www.alhaq.org/pdfs/gaza-operation-cast-Lead-statistical-analy sis%20.pdf, accessed 22 September 2011.

Azoulay, A. (2003), *The Food Chain*, documentary film, available at http://cargocollective.com/AriellaAzoulay/filter/Films#1164266/The-Food-Chain, accessed 22 September 2011.

— and Ophir, A. (2004), 'The Israeli Ruling Apparatus in the Palestinian

Occupied Territories', paper presented at the conference on *The Politics of Humanitarianism in the Occupied Territories*, Van Leer Jerusalem Institute, 20–1 April.

— and Ophir, A. (2012), *This Regime which is not One: Democracy and Occupation between the Sea and the River (1967 –)*. Stanford: Stanford University Press. [Published in Hebrew in 2008, Tel Aviv: Resling.]

Bertini, C. (2002), *Personal Humanitarian Envoy of the Secretary-General Mission Report 11–19 August*, available at http://www.domino.un.org//bertini_rept.htm, last accessed November 2007.

B'Tselem (2005), *Gaza Prison*, report, March, available at http://www.btselem.org/Download/200503_Gaza_Prison_English.doc, accessed 22 September 2011.

—(2007a), *The Gaza Strip: One Big Prison*, report, May, available at http://www.btselem.org/sites/default/files/publication/200705_gaza_insert_eng.pdf, accessed 22 September 2011.

—(2007b), *Rafah Crossing*, report, available at http://www.btselem.org/gaza_strip/rafah_crossing last accessed 29 September 2011.

—(2009), *Press Releases*, September, available at http://www.btselem.org/english/press_releases/20090909.asp, accessed 22 September 2011.

Coordinating Council of the Palestinian Private Sector PSCC (2007), *Private Sector Perspective to Cope with the Current Economic Crisis in the Gaza Strip*, report, available at http://www.paltrade.org/en/publications/EN_Private_Sector_Perspective_to_Cope_with_the_Current_Economic_Crisis_in_the_Gaza_Strip.pdf, accessed 22 September 2011.

Dugard, J. (2004), 'Statement by Mr. John Dugard, Special Rapporteur on the Situation of Human Rights in the Palestinian Territories Occupied by Israel since 1967', submitted to the General Assembly of the United Nations, New York, 28 October, available at http://www.cjpme.ca/documents/Dugard-Statement-2004.pdf, accessed 22 September 2011.

Eldar, A. (2007), '40% of Gazans' Requests to Get Medical Treatment in Israel Have Been Declined', *Haaretz*, 7 September, available at http://www.haaretz.co.il/hasite/spages/901993.html, accessed 22 September 2011.

Eldar, S. (2005), *Gaza to Death [A'aza K-Mavet]*. Tel Aviv: Yediot Achronot.

Feldman, Y. (2010), 'Red Lines: Rationing Food to Besieged Gaza', *Mitaam*, 22: 132–43.

Gisha (2006), 'Disengagement Danger: Israeli Attempts to Separate Gaza from the West Bank', briefing paper, February, available at http://www.

gisha.org/UserFiles/File/publications_english/Disengagement%20 Danger%206%20feb%2006.pdf, accessed 22 September 2011.

—(2007), 'Disengaged Occupiers: The Legal Status of Gaza', report, January, available at http://www.gisha.org/UserFiles/File/publica tions_english/Publications%20and%20Reports_English/Executive Summary.pdf, accessed 22 September 2011.

—(2010), 'Due to Gisha's Petition: Israel Reveals Documents Related to the Gaza Closure Poligy, 21 October, available at http://www.gisha. org/item.asp?lang_id=en&p_id=517, accessed 28 September 2011.

Gregory, D. (2004), *The Colonial Present: Afghanistan, Palestine, Iraq*. Malden, MA: Blackwell.

Haas, A. (2000), *Drinking the Sea of Gaza: Days and Nights in a Land under Siege*, trans. E. Wesley and M. Kaufman-Lacusta. New York: Holt.

Hanafi, S. (2010), 'Governance, Governmentality, and the State of Exception in the Palestinian Refugee Camps in Lebanon', *Journal of Refugee Studies*, 23(2): 134–59.

Harel, A. and B. Ravid (2007), *Haaretz*, 6 September, available at http:// news.walla.co.il/?w=/21/1165656, accessed 22 September 2011.

Harel, A. and A. Yissakharof (2007), *Haaretz*, 26 October, available at http://www.haaretz.co.il/hasite/pages/ShArtPE.jhtml?itemNo=91737, accessed 22 September 2011.

High Court of Justice (2007a), *The Association for Civil Rights in Israel v the Ministry of Defense*, 5841/06

High Court of Justice (2007b), *Hamdan v Southern Commander General*, 11120/05

International Development Committee of the British House of Commons (2004), *Development, Assistance, and the Occupied Palestinian Territories*, available at http://www.publications.parliament.uk/pa/ cm200304/cmelect/cmintdev/230/230.pdf, last accessed November 2007.

Kaspit, B. (2007), *Maariv NRG*, 15 November, available at http:// www.nrg.co.il/online/1/ART1/659/418.html, accessed 22 September 2011.

Lentin, R. (2004), '"No Woman's Law Will Rot This State": The Israeli Racial State and Feminist Resistance', *Sociological Research Online*, 9(3), available at http://www.socresonline.org.uk/9/3/lentin.html last accessed 29 September 2011.

Mizrahi, S. (2007), *Maariv NRG*, 29 October, available at http://www. nrg.co.il/online/1/ART1/652/552, accessed 22 September 2011.

OCHA (2005–6), 'Access and Movements', The United Nations Office of Coordination of Humanitarian Affairs, occupied Palestinian territories, *The Humanitarian Monitor*, periodical reports 2005–6, available at http://www.ochaopt.org/reports.aspx?id=105&page=4, accessed 22 September 2011.

OCHA (2007a), 'Gaza Crisis', The United Nations Office of Coordination of Humanitarian Affairs, occupied Palestinian territories, *The Humanitarian Monitor*, June 2007, available at http://www.ochaopt.org/gazacrisis.aspx?id=1000, accessed 22 September 2011.

OCHA (2007b), 'Access and Movements', The United Nations Office of Coordination of Humanitarian Affairs, occupied Palestinian territories, *The Humanitarian Monitor*, periodical Reports 2006–7, available at http://www.ochaopt.org/reports.aspx?id=105&page=3, accessed 22 September 2011.

Ophir, A. (2010), 'The Politics of Catastrophization', in D. Fassin and M. Pandolfi (eds), *Contemporary States of Emergency: The Politics of Military and Humanitarian Intervention*. New York: Zone Books, 59–88.

Oxfam (2007), 'Poverty in Palestine: The Human Cost of the Financial Boycott', briefing note, April, available at http://www.oxfam.org/en/policy/bn070413_palestinian_aid_boycott last accessed 29 September 2011.

—(2008), 'The Gaza Strip: A Humanitarian Implosion', March 2008, available at http://www.oxfam.org.uk/resources/policy/conflict_disasters/gaza_implosion.html, accessed 22 September 2011.

—(2009), 'Gaza Humanitarian Crisis', available at http://www.oxfam.org.uk/oxfam_in_action/emergencies/gaza_crisis.html, accessed 22 September 2011.

Roy, S. (1995), *The Gaza Strip: The Political Economy of De-Development*. Washington, DC: Institute for Palestine Studies.

—(2007), *Failing Peace: Gaza and the Palestinian-Israeli Conflict*. London: Pluto.

Tawil-Souri, H. (2011), 'Qalandia Checkpoint as Space and Nonplace', *Space and Culture*, 14(1): 4–26.

Tobi, Y. (2001), 'Israel's Policy with Respect of the Gaza Strip and its Refugees, November 1956–March 1957', *Jama'a*, 7: 9–53.

United Nations Relief and Work Agency (UNRWA) (2007), 'Emergency Appeal', available at http://www.un.org/unrwa/publications/pubs07/EA_en.pdf, accessed 22 September 2011.

Weizman, E. (2007), *Hollow Land: Israel's Architecture of Occupation*. London: Verso.

—(2009), 'Lawfare in Gaza: Legislative Attack', *Open Democracy*, 1

March, available at http://www.opendemocracy.net/article/legislative-attack, accessed 22 September 2011.

Ziegler, J. (2003), 'Economic, Social AND Cultural Rights: The Right to Food', *[unofficial] Report by the Special Rapporteur*, (Advanced Edited Copy). Geneva: United Nations.

Notes

A fuller version of this text will appear in Azoulay and Ophir (2012).

1. The estimated number is 200,000, mostly from the southern coastal plain, including 3,000 who were transferred from Mag'dal in a special operation in 1950 after the end of the war.
2. Foreign investors who sought cheap labour in the Gaza Strip cleared out as soon as they realised that 'conditions of passage might make their investment unprofitable'(Eldar 2005: 116).
3. When firing was renewed after the disengagement, the army declared areas near the fence out of bounds for Palestinians, as 'no-man's-land', and when the Qassam fire was resumed, the army marked a new line, very close to residential buildings in neighbourhoods of the Northern Gaza Strip, into which the army began to fire artillery, openly aiming to hinder Qassam launching groups from moving freely. In spring and summer 2007 a new area of some kilometres inside the Strip was marked, where the army's initial combat activity was resumed, and violence often erupts depending on intelligence about the organisation or the presence of 'armed insurgents'.
4. These assassinations by decree take place when persons presumably identified as suspected of 'terrorist activity' are targeted from helicopters and UAV, often killing many others who happen to be near the target.
5. Israel used to interfere with non-violent funerals and memorial ceremonies from the beginning of the Occupation. Funerals and memorial processions have served as a pretext for arrests and interrogations ever since the onset of the Occupation (see Algazi 1974).
6. This suspension, and the resumption of a fully imposed siege, remains an inherent potentiality for the Israeli sovereign even after Rafah crossings were opened by Egyptian authorities in June 2011, at the time this chapter was submitted to the editors.
7. Until its final closure in June 2007, the Rafah crossing operated by force of an agreement stipulating the presence of EU and PA inspectors (who could reach Rafah only through the Kerem Shalom

crossing, which is under full Israeli control). 'Control room' allowed Israel to prevent the opening of the crossing. See Gisha (2007).

8. Similar figures and formulations documenting the humanitarian disaster in the Gaza Strip appeared in numerous reports of various international organisations as well as on behalf of foreign governments and parliaments. The multiplicity of such reports is noteworthy; the Occupied Palestinian Territories are certainly one of the most thoroughly documented disaster areas in the world. See for example Bertini (2002); Dugard (2004); International Development Committee (2004).

9. Colonel Orli Malka and Lieutenant Colonel Itzik Gorevitch, interviewed by Ariella Azoulay in her documentary film, *The Food Chain* (2003).

10. Comment by UNRWA General Director, Richard Cook, interviewed by Ariella Azoulay in her documentary film, *The Food Chain* (2003).

11. These utterances characterise the attitude towards Palestinians since the First Intifada. In his book Shlomi Eldar cites David Maimon, Commissioner of the Prison Service, who in 1987 said to Hisham Abd Al Razeq, elected spokesman by his fellow inmates at Nafha prison: 'If I could deny you the air you breathe and still keep you alive, I would do it' (Eldar 2005: 54).

12. A few large parking lots were prepared next to several border crossings as well as checkpoints in the heart of the West Bank, where a truck loaded with goods arriving from Israel and an empty truck that will carry the same cargo inside the Palestinian territory are parked back to back. The cargo is transferred from one vehicle to the other under close scrutiny of the defence forces. Only goods that are delivered in this manner may legally enter the West Bank. See Azoulay (2003).

13. The existence of that mechanism has been suspected for a long time. See Feldman (2010).

14. Prior to the Second Intifada, 1,700 trucks a day crossed the Karni terminal. At the later stages of that Intifada, about 350 trucks a day got through: 'This lifeline supplies only a quantity that could keep Gaza alive. No more, no less' (Eldar 2005: 123). After the disengagement the crossing was closed nearly half the time, and even on days when it was opened, no more than 150–200 trucks a day got through, as 400 trucks were actually set as the minimum for Gaza not to starve. See B'Tselem 2007a; Gisha 2007; OCHA 2005–6. On the nature of Israeli control of the crossings, including the one at Rafah, see Eldar 2005: chapters 5, 6; on the control of the crossings

prior to the disengagement see B'Tselem 2005; on the control of the crossings following the disengagement, see B'Tselem 2007b and OHCA 2007b.

15. On disaster conditions in the Gaza Strip see, for example, periodic situation reports by United Nations OCHA and the periodic reports by Oxfam (for example, 2008; 2009). On the implications of the economic boycott on the humanitarian situation in the Gaza Strip see Oxfam (2007).

16. We prefer the term 'holding-pen' to 'prison' because it emphasises the biopolitical aspect of the siege. In prison even non-citizens enjoy a minimum of rights.

17. The bombing of Gaza's power station that had supplied 43 per cent of the city's electricity paralysed Gaza and immediately impacted the supply of fuel and water, as well as medical and sanitation systems. Major Najar, deputy chief of the municipal water service of the Gaza shore, explained: 'If we do not get more fuel in the next few days, we face catastrophe' (Gisha 2007: 37). Such a warning is part of the dynamics of catastrophisation in the Occupied Territories, and calls for local intervention until next time.

18. In 2006 income per capita in the Gaza Strip was 2.1 dollars a day (after a drastic decline to 150 dollars per year, it rose in 2009 to 1,000 dollars a year). Nearly two-thirds of the population now depend on food handouts. According to reports of the Palestinian Center of Commerce and the Palestinian Industrialists Union of 12 July 2007, during the first month of Hamas being in power, over 1,300 containers with imports on their way to the Strip were held in storerooms in Israel. The general loss as a result of suspending delivery of these goods has been estimated at 16 million dollars. See the report by the Coordinating Council of the Palestinian Private Sector PSCC (2007).

19. B'Tselem estimates that Israeli security forces killed 1,387 Palestinians during the course of the three-week operation. Of these, 773 did not take part in the hostilities, including 320 minors, 109 women over the age of 18 and 248 Palestinian police officers, most of whom were killed in aerial bombings of police stations on the first day of the operation (B'Tselem 2009). According to the Palestinian Human Rights organisation Al-Haq (2009), the number of people killed was 1,409. Al-Haq's report counts 11,154 housing units, 211 industrial premises, 703 shops and 700 public buildings which were completely destroyed or severely damaged.

20. See a collection of reports from Israeli human rights groups at http://

gazaeng.blogspot.com, accessed 22 September 2011, and the report by B'Tselem (2009).
21. Adi Ophir's personal testimony.

9

Colonial Histories: Biopolitics and Shantytowns in the Buenos Aires Metropolitan Area

Silvia Grinberg

> The separation of politics and humanitarianism that we are witnessing today is the extreme phase of the separation of the rights of man from the rights of the citizen.
>
> (Agamben 1998: 169)

In this chapter, I set out to share some reflections formulated in the process of a research project that I have been working on since 2004.[1] The project addresses issues raised by experiences of biopolitical control in contexts of extreme urban poverty. The research considers neo-colonial aspects of the operation of governmentality (Foucault 2006), in terms of the experiences of people living in locations usually called shantytowns, in the Buenos Aires Metropolitan Area (Argentina). Ever since the shantytown's inception in the colonial era, the operation of the sovereign exception has been crucial to maintaining the conditions in which the daily life of the population of shantytowns unfolds. It is important to point out that this analysis revolves around the understanding that daily life in territories marked by environmental decay (Davies 2007) is characterised by the kind of 'abandonment' Agamben associates with the sovereign exception, rather than by the extra-judicial status of these territories as such. In these urban spaces, access to water, electricity, a sewage system, trash collection and so forth is exceptional, and yet this reality has become such a normalised phenomenon that it is perceived as unremarkable. Images of extreme poverty have incomprehensibly become a 'natural' part of our socialscape. Just as Walter Benjamin (2001) foresaw, such realities have become the rule to which we have grown accustomed and before which we are often dumbfounded. In this chapter, however, I draw inspiration from Hannah Arendt (2010), who cautions against allowing such experiences to become thought of as mundane and commonplace.

Along with Agamben, I attempt to comprehend the absolute and total normalcy of the exception, which characterises the socio-political nature of the shantytowns. More specifically, I argue that Agamben's thinking sheds light on the extra-judicial status of those urban spaces that have been 'abandoned' by the State and, though densely populated, are not recognised on official maps. Nonetheless, and though it may seem paradoxical, the State makes itself felt in these areas in many ways. Thus, in the words of Agamben, the fact that the state of exception has become the rule 'not only appears increasingly as a technique of government rather than an exceptional measure, but it also lets its own nature as the constitutive paradigm of the judicial order come to light' (Agamben 2005: 6).

By cultivating an understanding of the mechanisms of control played out in modern biopolitics, the work of Agamben has offered an explanatory framework for thinking about Benjamin's maxim according to which the exception has become the rule. While neither of these thinkers focused their attention directly upon colonial power, and nor did they draw explicit critical attention to the pockets of urban poverty that we seem to have grown accustomed to in the twenty-first century, in this chapter I draw from Agamben's work in order to argue that such urban spaces are possible precisely because they are located at the very site of the sovereign exception.

The research[2] informing this chapter interrogates the technologies mobilised for governing populations (Rose 1999; Dean 1999) in these urban spaces. Thus, in keeping with Agamben's question (2001) concerning 'the camp', and how it operates to make sovereign power possible, the question I ask here is: 'what are shantytowns?' This question, along with Agamben's work on biopolitical control, provides a framework for thinking about the mechanisms and principles of governmentality that were enabled by the consolidation of shantytowns in the twenty-first century. Agamben offers conceptual tools for theorising the link between violence and rights as part and parcel of sovereignty, a link according to which the state of exception is defined:

> The sovereign power is this very impossibility of distinguishing between outside and inside, nature and exception [. . .] What happened

and is still happening before our eyes is that the 'juridically empty' space of the state of exception [. . .] has transgressed its spatiotemporal boundaries and now, overflowing outside them, is starting to coincide with the normal order, in which everything again becomes possible [. . .] One of the paradoxes of the state of exception lies in the fact that in the state of exception, it is impossible to distinguish transgression of the law from execution of the law, such that what violates a rule and what conforms to it coincide without any remainder. (1998: 38, 57)

The judicial status of these urban spaces in Buenos Aires can be characterised as 'empty' in this way. Indeed, the State is present in these territories precisely through the operation of the 'state of exception'. Agamben discusses the notion of the 'state of exception' in relation to those places that, despite the fact that law is suspended within their confines, perform an essential role in maintaining and legitimating sovereignty. The situation of a 'state of exception' is clearly evident in de facto governments or in concentration camps. Here, though, I refer to a *sui generis* suspension of the norm, whereby extreme urban poverty is produced and reproduced in shantytowns every day by means of a very complex network of actions. Of course, shantytowns are not concentration or refugee camps; their inhabitants are not prevented from coming and going, or from working. But they live on the symbolic borders of the nation, occupying an ambivalent 'inside/outside' citizenship status. Indeed, this occupation of 'border space' is what characterises the territories of the shantytowns and the subjects that inhabit them. The notion of exception offers a way of understanding the complex dynamics of these processes of 'inclusive exclusion,' which frame the living conditions of approximately 20 per cent of the population of Buenos Aires.

Here, I aim to draw out the historical links with colonialism that have been the formative basis of these contemporary spaces of exception in Argentina. The urban territories traced and demarked during the colonial period were indelibly impressed by the colonial experience and, like mnemonic traces, they can still be perceived in the urban territory of the Buenos Aires Metropolitan Area. In this framework, the notion of territory takes on a specific meaning: it is understood as

the intersection of different lines of force in the context of a situation, without thereby falling into the error of ethnomethodology for which

social relations are based only on interaction between individuals. A
situation objectively defined by social forces that bear unequal legiti-
macies [. . .] (Ortiz 2000: 64)

The spaces where shantytowns have grown exponentially in
recent decades were also the spaces where, in the sixteenth
century, the native Querandí, Guaraní and Quilmes peoples were
rounded up. The territory of the urban shantytown takes the form
of imbricated strata, heterogeneous layers of historical experiences of oppression, that infuse the space and inflect the forms of
'belonging' that are possible within it. In the words of De Certeau
(1984):

> The place is a palimpsest. Scientific analysis knows only its most recent
> *text*; and even then the latter is for science no more than the result of
> its *epistemological decisions*, its criteria and its goals. Why should it
> then be surprising that operations conceived in relation to this recon-
> stitution have a 'fictive' character and owe their success less to their
> perspicacity than to their power of breaking down the complexion of
> these interrelations between disparate forces and times? (De Certeau
> 1984: 202)

This chapter seeks to consider how colonialism informed the
constitution of sovereignty in ways that are rearticulated in the
continuing contemporary production of these urban spaces. As a
result, since colonial times, these urban spaces have existed in a
permanent state of suspension of legal normalcy.

The Creation of the Sovereign Exception: From the Colony to the Colonised

Two realities, separated by 400 years, intersect in the territory of
the Buenos Aires Metropolitan Area around the basin of the Río
de la Plata. This region is known for many things, but perhaps
mostly for tango. It is also marked by the scarcity of references to
its development as a colony, and especially by the lack of reference to those who inhabited this space before the arrival of the
Europeans. Indeed, unlike much of Latin America, in the Río
de la Plata region it is very difficult to find contemporary traces
of the native peoples, and signs of their colonial domination are
now perceptible only in the absence of these peoples. Despite laws

protecting Indians, the Spanish conquest in the Río de la Plata, as opposed to much of Latin America, was characterised by rapid transculturation and/or extermination of the original population. Indeed, the modern invisibility of the native people does not mean that they never lived here or that conquest and colonisation never happened. The markings of conquest must be sought elsewhere.

One of the first research tasks was to attempt to get an overview of the history of the territory where, at present, more than 2 million people are estimated to live in different shantytowns.[3] We learned that this history goes back to colonial times. The Spanish Crown first reached the Río de la Plata region in the sixteenth century, founding what is now the city of Buenos Aires. The project, then, was carried out in areas that, in the sixteenth century, constituted the limit of the territory, that is, the areas that colonial authority chose not to enter. Now, these same areas serve as a boundary of the shantytowns.

Colonisation of the Río de la Plata responded to a number of different geopolitical and economic factors linked to the domination of territories to the east of the Tordesillas line,[4] as well as the need for an autonomous route to the Atlantic (Vera de Saporiti 1999). One of the first tasks faced by the colonial power was to organise the colonised space. The territories themselves were demarcated by the colonial authority, and many of those sixteenth-century roads are still found in the city. Among many other streets, the Spanish coloniser Juan de Garay developed what is now called Márquez Avenue. This is an avenue that runs through the periphery of the City of Buenos Aires. The zone on the outskirts of the city has one of the highest poverty rates in Argentina as well as the highest population density. One of the particularities of this area of the city is that the river water is relatively shallow, which made it an attractive site for colonial development: it was ideal for building roads that provided internal communication, making this a nexus of the territory. Thus, in the late sixteenth century the main routes that continue to connect the city to the rest of the country were first drawn. Indeed, some of them are now the sites of major highways. One of the routes drawn in early colonial times was 'the bread route', now Márquez Avenue; it currently marks the border between those who are inside and those who are outside the shantytown area. From there to the Río las Conchas (now the Reconquista River) was swampland that once, years before it was filled with waste, provided a protective shield against flooding. According to Morello (1974), it was in these gorges and grasslands, whose mud absorbed men, that the Indians would hide from the colonial authority. These lands also constituted a strategic location from which to loot the merchandise that the colonial power would take to the port.

It was therefore in these territories that 'the struggle over the inner border' began (Morello 1974). This struggle arose because, within the territorialised space of the colony, colonial power was also exercised by dividing up the Indians, who were assigned as labour to colonial masters, according to what was called the *encomienda* system. This was the judicial figure by which the Spanish colony dealt with the native peoples in what became Latin America. The system provided a means to organise labour and develop a labouring class. Thus, in return for the services rendered to the Crown in 'the Indies', the king gave the Spanish subject (the coloniser or *encomendero*) compensation in the form of labour. In exchange, the Spanish subject was expected to 'take care' of the Indians, both materially and spiritually, by educating them in the Christian faith. In the context provided by this system in the years after conquest, it is possible to trace parallel processes in the Río de la Plata region that afford an understanding of some of the marks, as well as the absences, left upon the colony in this part of South America, which was characterised by rapid transculturation and the extermination of native peoples.

An ambivalent colonial policy towards the native peoples emerged because, despite the laws that protected the Indians by prohibiting the usurpation of lands, Juan de Garay divided up terrains such that deeds were granted to colonisers. The territory that we are dealing with is a vast area around the Río las Conchas which flows into the Río de la Plata. Thus, this area clearly demonstrates not only the urban grid that Garay drew but also the type of connection that the colony established with the native peoples.[5] The border of the small farms in what is now Suárez[6] was the 'road on the way to the city of Santa Fe', currently Márquez Avenue. On one side lay those small farms and on the other the marshlands, where Guaraní, Querandí and Araucano Indians would hide from colonial authority (Moreira 2006). Starting from this origin, then, this zone – which is currently called the Reconquista River region – became a place for colonised individuals to escape to and yet, simultaneously, a place where they could potentially be cornered. The colonial authority did not enter this marshy area because their horses would sink, so it was a good place to hide. At the same time, the colonised could not get out of the area or, rather, if they did, they could be trapped by the colonial authority.

Nonetheless, as a local historian points out, 'the first colonizers brought over very few women and that led to a war over women [. . .] the Spanish began to steal women from the Indians which gave rise to an olive-skinned, half-Indian and half-European gaucho population' (Morello 1974). And the descendants of that mixed gaucho population constitute the majority of the inhabitants of the shantytowns; they are the descendants of the native peoples and the contemporary evidence of their elimination as 'peoples' during the colonial period. So these olive-skinned individuals, the descendants of those mixed-race gauchos,[7] are the ones who now inhabit the shantytowns, located on the same lands where the Querandí, Guaraní and Araucano peoples once hid from the Spanish. Indeed, that darker population is still the 'other' of normal Argentinian society; an object of suspicion and disrepute (Bhabha 2002; Seri 2009).

After independence and the creation of the Argentine State, the logic of control that had been established by the conquering Spanish power was passed down to the land-holding bourgeoisie. As Seri points out, 'State violence was geared towards the elimination of the "domestic fronts" of native peoples and regional *caudillos*[8] and, after the arrival of waves of immigrants at the end of the 19th century, of radical syndicalists and revolutionaries' (Seri 2009: 668). Thus, in the process by which the nation-state was taking shape, there was already a low level of differentiation between the military and the police forces. Operative fictions such as Sarmiento's formulation of 'civilisation or barbarism'[9] contributed to legitimising violence as necessary to the construction of an identity and a common national destiny. In the nineteenth century, this violence took shape as the massacre of thousands of Indians in what was called the Conquest of the Desert.[10] In the continuation of the battles over inner borders that had begun during the colonial period, that massacre would not be carried out by the colonial power but by the incipient Argentine State.

While the continuity may be ambiguous, in many ways those first years of colonisation established a framework of control based on a politics of exclusion, thus enabling elements of the contemporary logic of governmentality, as well as the judicial status of exception that still defines these urban spaces. The Spanish did not venture into these terrains, and what happened in the space from 'the bread route' to the river was not their concern. Once an Indian left that area, though, he could be killed without that act being considered a homicide. As I will discuss below, 400 years later the same logic of control still governs the relationship between the 'inside' and the 'outside' of the shantytown.

Shantytowns: The Normalised Exception

In the city of Buenos Aires, the shantytowns emerged as such in the early twentieth century. In those years when the process of industrialisation was at its peak, shantytowns were a stopover point for the thousands of workers who came to the city from rural settings or small towns in the outlying provinces. These people stayed in the shantytowns only temporarily; once they had found jobs, they invariably moved out of the shantytowns and into working-class neighbourhoods. Many of these neighbourhoods were constructed by the State. Shantytowns were thus a port of entry for individual participation in industrial capitalism. However, the nature of shantytowns has changed over time. In the twenty-first century, shantytowns are no longer stopover locations that individuals inhabit in transit to proper destinations and permanent modes of habitation. At the current time, two or three generations of people have been born in them. In fact, since the late 1970s, shantytowns have been inhabited by those individuals who have been systematically excluded from the formal employment market.[11] We are witnessing a historical reversal of the twentieth-century migratory movement associated with an industrialising workforce: if those who arrived in the early twentieth century stayed in shantytowns while looking for work, often in factories, the inhabitants of these areas in the twenty-first century are people who have been fired from factories.

From the twenty-first century, the shantytowns have been inhabited by a population that, in my view, reformulates the biopolitical fracture that, as Agamben points out (1998), has been in effect since the French Revolution. This is a fracture by which the presence of the people 'becomes an embarrassing presence, and poverty and *exclusion* appear for the first time as an intolerable *scandal*' (Agamben 2000: 32–3, my emphasis). Extreme poverty in the twenty-first century has become the norm rather than the exception. In the words of Agamben:

the exception is what cannot be included in the whole of which it is a
member and cannot be a member of the whole in which it is always
already included. What emerges in this limit figure is the radical crisis
of every possibility of clearly distinguishing between membership and
inclusion, between what is outside and what is inside, between exception and rule. (Agamben 1998: 25)

The shantytown comprises a population that had been banned and
'delivered over to its own separateness and, at the same time, consigned to the mercy of the one who abandons it – at once excluded
and included, removed and at the same time captured' (Agamben
1998: 110).

What is it that defines these urban spaces as shantytowns? It
clearly is not only the fact of poverty, which is generally evident
in large cities. In fact, the shantytown is characterised by the
illegal status of the occupation of its territory; historically, those
individuals who arrived and lived in these makeshift neighbourhoods built their houses on terrain that did not (and does not)
belong to them. Accordingly, shantytowns are differentiated from
planned settlements. As Oszlak (1991) explains, a settlement is the
legitimate occupation of an uninhabited area parcelled in keeping
with the adjacent neighbourhoods. By contrast, 'occupation' is
the word used to describe the illegitimate taking of a terrain by
a group of individuals who arrive in an unplanned or unsolicited
way, and claim spaces on which they stealthily proceed to build
their houses. The first construction is erected very quickly, usually
in less than a day. As a result of the initial 'occupation', sidewalks
are constructed in an ad hoc manner, and square blocks and
parcels of land are carved out. In settlements, the community designates space for the construction of a school or a first aid centre,
as well as a soccer field or plaza. The construction of the neighbourhood's infrastructure is thereby collective. In shantytowns,
the mechanism of occupation is individualised. Each family group
arrives on its own and builds a house as best it can. There is no
urban organisation within the shantytown; there are no streets,
just passageways. If one is not familiar with the neighbourhood,
it is hard not to get lost. Nor are there spaces planned for group
use; schools and first aid centres appear, if they appear at all, a
good deal after the initial occupation has taken place. From this
perspective, then, shantytowns are uncertain terrains, disturbing
spaces of indifference characterised by an absolute indistinction of

fact and law (Agamben 1998). And, just as during colonial times the coloniser defined the legal terms of occupation, today the Argentine State defines the legality (or otherwise) of the occupation of these terrains, both implicitly, by imposing norms of social inclusion, and explicitly, by evicting inhabitants. By means of this process, a situation of abandonment and a twofold precariousness is constructed, resulting from the fact of living in a state of exception, and from the specific material conditions of life in the shantytowns.

All facets of life are difficult in these neighbourhoods: inhabitants share a common lack of access to electricity, clean water, trash collection or even food. The inhabitants must demand access to utilities that are usually provided to citizens as a normal matter of procedure. These demands are seldom met. And even when their demands are satisfied, supply continues to be highly precarious. None of the services that arrive in the shantytowns are considered something that people should receive, simply by virtue of being citizens. Running water is a clear example of this. The publicly held company that distributes potable water to the whole city of San Martín did not include the shantytown in its water distribution regime in a deliberate and organised way; instead, the company left unsealed a pipe that historically runs through what is today the main artery of the shantytown. On the basis of that pipe, the neighbours organised a very complex network that now brings water to houses via hoses. This has given rise to countless problems of supply and on a daily basis puts at risk the health of the population, since these garden hoses do not comply with minimal environmental health standards (Curutchet et al. 2010). After the neighbours tirelessly struggled with this situation and made ongoing demands for improvement of the water supply, which nonetheless remain unheard, a precarious water distribution network was established by means of a wholly informal process. The lack of access to utilities, then, constitutes a clear example of the effects of a state of exception, according to which the Argentine State can fail to attend to the welfare of the inhabitants of the shantytown, who must therefore live outside of the law, excluded from normal social processes and provisions. The State, by means of inaction, allows access to services, but it neither constructs nor takes responsibility for those services. It has abandoned all responsibility for these services to the shantytowns.

The shantytown exists as a space that is not authorised by law but 'permitted' to operate as an exception to the rule of 'normal' civil life. Indeed, the State's function in these spaces is precisely to allow a suspension of the law to take place. For instance, the city government is the body that must ensure that open-air trash dumps (that are in violation of all health regulations and pose a risk to the community) are not used by the public in a manner that contradicts normal civil health protections. Nonetheless, unabash-edly affirming the state of exception that reigns in the shantytown, the mayor of San Martín told the community leader of the shanty-town, the man who oversees the clandestine trash dump:

> keep at it, but above the [trash] mound; I want you to keep an eye on everything that falls off the truck; make sure nothing toxic or polluting falls off because that will get me in trouble; it should be neutral trash [. . . the mayor told me] to generate my own salary because he cannot pay me if I work for him, 'I can't pay you a salary,' he said, 'but I know that wherever I go you are organising people for me; you are doing a good job but I can't get you a municipal job with a salary,' he said. (Shammah 2009: 133–4)

Trash is one of the main sources of income in these urban spaces (Grinberg 2010). The inhabitants of the areas where CEAMSE[12] operates go to the *quema* ('burning', the name that has been given to these dumps because trash was once burned there) to look for food, mostly expired supermarket produce. They also rummage for metal, cardboard and other material that they can then sell. As a result, the mayor 'permits' without authorising those who work for him to generate that income by creating a clandestine trash dump. The State itself, then, both creates the norm and explicitly suspends the existing legislation in the exceptional space of the shantytown. And, as Agamben points out, 'The exception does not subtract itself from the rule; rather, the rule, suspending itself, gives rise to the exception and, maintaining itself in relation to the exception, first constitutes itself as a rule' (Agamben 1998: 18). This state of affairs holds subjects captive 'within the outside'; in daily life, situations like the one at the trash dump are erratically 'authorised' in the sense that they are 'permitted', but they may at any moment be recognised to be 'unauthorised' because normally 'illegal', and so banned.

Something similar happens with the occupation of the lands. In the city we are discussing, there is a 'reurbanisation' plan that entails the eradication of the shantytowns.[13] Indeed, the fact that the State can decide to eradicate the shantytowns indicates their very condition as exception. Thus, the vulnerability and violence that living in exception entails is not only illustrated by the particularities of living in decaying contexts of extreme urban poverty with no access to utilities and so forth, but also by the fact that even when people build homes, and decorate and improve them year after year, they can be evicted at any moment. This is clear in the comments of one resident, who refers to a housing complex being built by the State as part of the reurbanisation plan:

> D: The other day, they came by here to ask us who wanted to move over there. The woman who lives across the street said she didn't because she has a handicapped son, and the woman at the corner didn't want to either. I wasn't around, but I don't want to either.
> I: And why don't you want to move?
> D: What for? Have you seen them? They are a bunch of tall buildings across from Fuerte Apache![14] Take a look at my home. There is no way I am leaving here. I built this place myself. When I bought it, it was a trash dump.
> I: It was a trash dump?
> D: Yes, pigs were kept here, so imagine everything there was. I gradually filled it in and built it up.
> I: And you bought the lot of land?
> D: Yes, though the papers were not in order. I know that, but I bought it anyway because they told me this area was going to improve, so I 'bought' here. (Interview with a fifty-year-old woman)

In this interview, then, the woman makes reference to a deed that she knows to have no legal validity for which she, nonetheless, paid. Despite this, and the fact that she has lived in this space for over twenty years, she is well aware that she could be evicted at any moment. Indeed, that is one of her main concerns, and a concern of many other residents of the area. And it is that very state of legal suspension and exception (buying an invalid deed for a property from which one could be evicted at any moment) that generates the greatest vulnerability for residents of this area. It entails being constantly exposed to the threat and violence that abandonment brings.

Thus, despite the millions of people who live in these urban spaces and the ad hoc emergence of the public schools, welfare

plans, first aid centres and countless non-governmental organisations that operate within their confines, a politics of exception
determines the form that life takes in these areas. The distinctive trait of shantytowns, then, is their operation according to
Agamben's maxim: what marks these areas is not, ultimately, their
illegality but the fact of their formal abandonment: everything that
happens in these spaces takes place according to the logic of the
exception. As Agamben explains, while conventionally the 'state
of exception' is formally declared by the State in emergency situations so as to enable an extraordinary suspension of the law in
order to enable the normalisation of the situation, in the case of
the shantytowns the suspension of legal rights is a normal condition of life. There is no 'state of emergency' here; just a permanent
situation of exception. This is where the words of Agamben take
on special significance. As he says:

> Every attempt to rethink the *political space* of the *West* must begin
> with the clear awareness that we no longer know anything of the
> classical distinction between *zoē and bios, between private life and
> political existence, between man as a simple living being at home in
> the house and man's political existence in the city*. (Agamben 1998:
> 188, my emphasis)

This lack of distinction between *zoē* and *bios* becomes most
apparent when doing fieldwork in these neighbourhoods. One
expects to find a space where the State is absent, but one soon real-
ises that the State's effects are everywhere sharply felt. However,
the State does not make itself felt in these spaces in the same way
that it does outside of them. The State is present in the shantytowns in the form of the sovereign exception; it renders the exception the norm. Like a government without government (Dean
1999), the shantytown is the most ordinary expression of the
sovereign violence of abandonment.

The *Homo Sacer*

Thus far, I have discussed the spatialised characteristics of power
relations that were forged during the colonial period and that continue into the present. Although Agamben's work does not address
the colonial context or the ways in which sovereignty differentiates populations according to race and ethnicity (Butler 2006),

whether in colonial times or in the present, the figure of the *homo sacer* can be useful in describing the relationship between the coloniser and the colonised, as well as the positions of the subjects that currently inhabit shantytowns. In theorising the *homo sacer*, Agamben refers to the figure created by Roman law to refer to those who, by means of a double exception, are positioned simultaneously outside and inside the normative juridical structures of public life. The *homo sacer*'s life cannot be sacrificed, yet killing him does not constitute an act of homicide. Later in this text, in relation to Arendt's analysis of declarations of rights, Agamben insists there is a need to capture the biopolitical significance of those rights, identifying modern biopolitics as specifically characterised by its occupation of the threshold between inside and outside of the realm of politics. He writes:

> And when natural life is wholly included in the polis – and this much has, by now, already happened – these thresholds pass, as we will see, beyond the dark boundaries separating life from death in order to identify a new living dead man, a new sacred man. (Agamben 1998: 131)

As we have seen, the conquest of the Río de la Plata region took a very specific form that was marked by exception, both in terms of the logic of the occupation of the territories and the norm of the royal *encomienda* system. The current traces of this colonial arrangement consist of a group of subjects whose expulsion from the formal economy has simultaneously ostracised them from the broader political community, expulsed by the power of events. In the words of one local resident, 'I lived in Munro because I didn't make enough even to cover rent, and there are five of us.' These, then, are subjects who, due to political, social and economic events, have been left to lead lives that, in terms of the functioning of the system, are superfluous; their humanity makes them 'sacred' and non-sacrificial, yet they are able to be abandoned. In the analytic circumstances of the shantytown, Agamben's emphasis on 'homicide' must be replaced by the more general idea of dramatically decayed living conditions that result in the reduced mortality of the inhabitants. In other cases, however, just as when the colonial authority pursued native peoples to the swamplands and trapped them there to hide or die, the central idea of a semi-sanctioned 'killing without committing homicide' continues to be operative.

This now often characterises the relationship between those who live in the shantytowns and the police apparatus that disciplines them. While in the normal course of events the police – like the conqueror of distant times – stay at the edges of the shantytown, in certain situations[15] they come in armed and ready to put down unrest. When that happens, there are frequent instances of trigger-happy violence; people are killed and the police go untried and unpunished. While often acknowledged as 'police brutality', these incidents simply occur with impunity; no explanation or motive is given, or, when there is a motive, it never comes anywhere near justifying the resulting deaths.

To walk through the shantytown is to walk through intersecting streets or passageways, which often are less than a metre wide. Since they are made of dirt, when it rains people often cannot leave their homes, which often only consist of nooks from which other passageways emerge. If you are not from the shantytown, it is easy to get lost in these ramshackle passages. Tall poles holding up power lines rest on other poles about to fall over. Open drainage pipes with hoses distribute the water to the houses; these are the same channels into which the sewers drain. The deeper one goes into the neighbourhood, the lower the terrain becomes. It is built upon landfill, where trash is dumped every day.[16] These are the same lands where, in the sixteenth century, the native peoples walked and hid. These days, the position of the subjects in this area is not much different. In terms of real-estate interests, this is a degraded terrain (Davies 2007); it is a hiding place for many urban tribes. The sixteenth-century marshlands have become an 'ecological belt', a euphemism for a rubbish dump, with its terrain filled time and again with the city's trash. The conquerors did not enter into these swamps, and now the police authority rarely does; instead, they park their vehicles on the border between the inside and outside of the shantytown, which they carefully monitor. And, the same possibility of killing without committing homicide that once characterised the relationship with the native peoples is operative in relation to the inhabitants of the shantytown.

Just as the native peoples were often formally unrecognised in colonial times, the vast majority of the young people who live in the shantytowns either do not have the identity cards given to all citizens of Argentina, or else they get them very late. Thus, the school enrols students without any documentation that proves their birth or their personhood before the State. In terms of civil existence and citizenship, they are not recognised; they are 'no names'. Given the lack of documentation and since it is mandatory to be six years old to start first grade, it is common for parents to present dental certificates as proof of age.[17]

This situation echoes that described by Arendt:

> The paradox involved in the loss of human rights is that such loss coincides with the instant when a person becomes a human being in general – without a profession, without a citizenship, without an opinion, without a deed by which to identify himself. (Arendt 1958: 302)

And that is what happens to many who live in shantytowns. Left to their own devices, not only without jobs but without any prospect of ever getting a job, the supernumerary (Castel 1997), the *shantytowners*, are the *homines sacri* of the twenty-first century. Like the *homo sacer*, the people in shantytowns are abandoned to manage their own survival, not only because they are in an exceptional situation but also because if they want to keep living they must assume the responsibility for that exceptionality, which has become the rule. If industrial capitalism describes a society in which subjects are inscribed in terms of their work life and their individual rights, in this chapter we have tackled the forms of subjectification facing those who have been expelled from factories and have drifted into the exceptional political space of the shantytown.

Conclusion

This chapter has discussed the ways that, since colonial times, the constitution of the Argentine State has been marked by the logic of exception. In the Río de la Plata region, unlike other regions of Latin America, the historical legacy of colonisation is not overtly identified with those who are the acknowledged descendants of dispossessed native peoples, but remains discernible in the population that now inhabits the shantytowns. It is in this context that I have been able to begin to grasp the process of colonisation that established the logic of exception and the resulting abandonment of this population.

One of the questions that quickly comes to mind when one is close to shantytowns is whether everything that happens in them, from their founding to their daily functioning, occurs in processes that take place outside the law. Through Agamben, we have attempted to develop another response, one that looks to biopolitics, rather than legality, to understand the dynamics that characterise these densely populated spaces where the presence of the State is felt every day but in the form of the sovereign exception. Indeed, this sovereign exception goes back to how colonisation was enacted in the Río de la Plata region where, unlike other regions of Latin America, it entailed constant exception from the royal norm that prohibited both the usurpation of lands and the extermination of populations. We have here attempted to show how those dynamics from that period endure in the present logic and living conditions of the shantytowns.

Thus, when we walk through these areas, we are not walking though excluded territories or urban spaces that exist in a state of illegality and/or at the margin of the State. Instead, we walk through spaces that constitute a key part of sovereignty. This, as Agamben points out, is precisely the paradox of the state of exception by which it becomes very difficult to distinguish between transgressing the law and executing it. Indeed, it is at the heart of the State where they coincide perfectly. It is the very bareness of *life* in these spaces that perplexes us. It is a question of a reality too open, of ways of inhabiting a territory that brings the historical conditions of colonised existence back into present time; indeed, that territory itself constitutes, as the Uruguayan writer Eduardo Galeano calls it, the open veins of a Latin America that does not stop bleeding (1980). In the Río de la Plata region, in the city of Buenos Aires, the specificity of this reality lies in the fact that since the times of conquest these spaces have been defined as spaces of exception: the shantytowns lie on the territory in which native peoples once were trapped.

In governing the liminal population (Foucault 2006; 2007), the central concern is to avoid placing the system at risk (Grinberg 2007). In this context, precarious life at the border, in the shanty-town, does not make news. As the history of the twentieth century has demonstrated in other contexts: 'The world found nothing sacred in the *abstract* nakedness of *being human*' (Arendt 1958: 299, my emphasis). Indeed, for those who live in that nakedness, 'not the loss of specific rights but the loss of a community willing and able to guarantee any rights whatsoever has been the calamity that has befallen ever increasing numbers of people' (297). Just as for the Spanish conqueror the Indian was not a concern until he left the swamp, in present times the shantytowns make the news when robberies and violence take place outside its confines. This is when the *shantytowner* becomes dangerous; a dark man – the olive-skinned gaucho – who, by virtue of his unruly or deviant status in relation to the norm, becomes the suspected perpetrator of crime, and only then becomes newsworthy.

In conclusion, it is likely that one of the basic lessons provided by reading these complex realities through Agamben's paradigms is the possibility of understanding that we are not faced with extreme questions, exceptional cases, but rather with situations where the exception has become the norm and it is this normalisation that contains the most dangerous aspect of these realities: when they become ordinary, normalised forms of exception, they exist as part of an unremarkable landscape and, at that very moment, we cease to be astonished. What takes place, then, is radical acceptance. In this context, poverty becomes spectacle for television programmes that show fights, crimes and other misfortunes that place life in shantytowns on the border and renders it insignificant and banal. That happens, as Agamben perceived years before his studies into biopolitics, at the very moment that the ordinary becomes extreme, when 'modern man makes his way home in the evening wearied by a jumble of events [. . .] none of them will have become experience' (Agamben 2001: 14).

References

Agamben, G. (1998), *Homo Sacer: Sovereign Power and Bare Life*, trans. D. Heller-Roazen. Stanford: Stanford University Press.

—(2000), *Means Without End: Notes on Politics*, trans. V. Binetti and C. Casarino. Minnesota: University of Minnesota Press.

—(2001), *Infancy and History: The Destruction of Experience*, trans. L. Heron. London and New York: Verso.

—(2005), *State of Exception*, trans. K. Attell. Chicago: University of Chicago Press.

Arendt, H. (1958), *The Origins of Totalitarianism*. San Diego: Harvest.

—(2010), *Lo que Quiero es Comprender. Sobre mi Vida y mi Obra*, trans. M. Abella and J. L. López de Lizaga. Madrid: Editorial Trotta.

Benjamin, W. (2001), *Iluminaciones IV: Para una Crítica de la Violencia y Otros Ensayos*, trans. R. Blatt. Madrid: Ediciones Taurus.

Bhabha, H. (2002), *El Lugar de la Cultura*, trans. C. Aira. Buenos Aires: Manantial.

Butler, J. (2006), *Vidas Precarias: El Poder del Pueblo y la Violencia*, trans. F. Rodriguez. Buenos Aires: Paidós.

Castel, R. (1997), *La Metamorfosis de la Cuestión Social: Una Crónica del Salariado*. Barcelona, Mexico and Buenos Aires: Paidós.

Curutchet, G., S. Grinberg and R. Gutiérrez (2010), 'Entre la Vida en el Barrio y la Potencia del Zanjón. Condiciones, Fatalismos y Posibilidades de la Remediación Ambiental', in *Actas del Sexto Encuentro del International Center for Earth Sciences, E-ICES 6*. Mendoza: International Center for Earth Sciences, 20–1.

Davies, M. (2007), *Planeta de Ciudades Miseria*, trans. J. M. Amoroto Salido. Madrid: Foca.

Dean, M. (1999), *Governmentality: Power and Rule in Modern Society*. London: Sage Publications.

De Certeau, M. (1984), *The Practice of Everyday Life*, trans. S. Rendall. Berkeley: University of California Press.

Defensoría del Pueblo (2007), *Informe especial de la cuenca del río Reconquista*. Buenos Aires: Oficina Defensoría del Pueblo.

Foucault, M. (2006), *Seguridad, Territorio y Población*, trans. H. Pons. Buenos Aires: Fondo de Cultura Económica.

—(2007), *Nacimiento de la Biopolítica*, trans. H. Pons. Buenos Aires: Fondo de Cultura Económica.

Galeano, E. (1980), *Las Venas Abiertas de América Latina*. Mexico: Siglo XXI.

Grinberg, S. (2007), 'Pedagogical Risk and Governmentality: Shanty Towns in Argentina in the 21st Century', *SCARR*, April, available at http://www.kent.ac.uk/scarr/events/Grinberg-%20(2).pdf, accessed 23 September 2011.

—(2009), 'Políticas y Territorios de Escolarización en Contextos de Extrema Pobreza Urbana', *Revista Archivos de Ciencias de la Educación* (4ª época, Argentina UNLP), 3(3): 81–99.

—(2010), 'Schooling and Desiring Production in Contexts of Extreme Urban Poverty: Everyday Banality in a Documentary by Students: Between the Trivial and the Extreme', *Gender and Education*, 22(6): 663–77.

Moreira, O. (2006), *Buscando en Viejas Máscaras el Rostro de la Novedad: Continuidades y Rupturas en los Modos de Disciplinamiento Explicitados por Michel Foucault*, MA Thesis, EHU-UNSAM, Argentina.

Morello, A. (1974), *Reseña Histórica de la Ciudad y el Partido de Gral. San Martín*, Buenos Aires: Ediciones Testimonio.

Ortiz, R. (2000), *Modernidad y Espacio: Benjamin en Paris*. Bogotá: Grupo Editorial Norma.

Oszlak, O. (1991), *Merecer la Ciudad: Los Pobres y el Derecho al Espacio Urbano*. Buenos Aires: CEDES/ Hvmanitas.

Rose, N. (1999), *Powers of Freedom: Reframing Political Thought*. Cambridge: Cambridge University Press.

Seri, G. (2009), 'Metáforas Policiales, Elisiones y Calidad de la Democracia en Argentina y Uruguay', *Revista SAAP*, 3(3): 663–94.

Shammah, C. (2009), *El Circuito Informal de la Basura*. Buenos Aires: Editorial Espacios.

Vera De Saporiti, A. (1999), 'Estructura Social de Buenos Aires y su Relación con el Espacio Colonial (1580–1617)', *Historia Crítica*, December: 49–64.

Williams, R. (2000), *Palabras Clave: Un Vocabulario de la Cultura y la Sociedad*, trans. H. Pons. Buenos Aires: Ediciones Nueva Visión.

Notes

1. I have been able to carry out my research thanks to the following subsidies: 'La escuela en la periferia metropolitana: escolarización, pobreza y degradación ambiental en José León Suárez (Buenos Aires Metropolitan Area)', CONICET 2010–12; 'Dispositivos pedagógicos y producción de subjetividad en emplazamientos urbano/marginales. Un estudio en caso en la Enseñanza Secundaria Básica del Partido de Gral. San Martín'; PICT 2005–9, Proy. No. 33413, Agencia Nacional de Promoción Científica y Tecnológica, Argentina y Secretaría de Ciencia y Técnica, UNSAM SC06/079, 2004–8.

2. Briefly, this research uses an ethnographic perspective based mainly on observation and interviews in order to register the interactions between subjects in the context of neighbourhood life. Following Williams (2000), this research aims to capture an understanding of lived culture, against the backdrop of institutions, formations and the experiences of subjects. It makes use of De Certeau's (1984) approach to ways of operating that occur, take shape and are produced in the everyday life of territories; that is, in the everyday life of subjects, neighbourhoods and institutions. While schools are the privileged site of much of this research, due to limitations of space in this text I have chosen to focus my analysis on the neighbourhood territory.

3. Despite attempts to collect census data in order to arrive at a precise figure for the size of the population that lives in these neighbourhoods, the numbers are always approximate.

4. The Treaty of Tordesillas was an agreement signed in 1494 by the kings of Castile and Aragon and the king of Portugal. It established a division of the conquered territories, and the annexation of the New World by means of a dividing line in the Atlantic Ocean and the adjacent lands. The treaty was signed to avoid conflicts between the Spanish and Portuguese Crowns interested in controlling seas and lands.

5. See the Special Report on the Río Reconquista Basin (Defensoría del Pueblo 2007).

6. Suárez is the name of the area where the shantytowns discussed here are located.

7. Very pejoratively, in colloquial language these people are often called 'black heads', a term that refers to a set of cultural, and even criminal, stereotypes. The figure of the 'black head' stands in contrast to the blue-eyed white man who, in regions like Latin America, defines the ideal European man, the agent of progress and civilisation.

8. The term *caudillo* refers to a certain type of leader mostly associated with the nineteenth century. *Caudillos* were usually men with military backgrounds who promised the inhabitants of a region benefits in exchange for loyalty and commitment. Their power was based on the support of major fractions of the masses. In Latin America, *caudillismo* as a social and political phenomenon exercised great influence on the logics by which political parties were constituted in the twentieth century.

9. The opposition between civilisation and barbarism characterised colonial justifications for the construction of the nation-state. The former was linked to Europe and the latter to both the native peoples and their *gaucho* descendants.

10. The Conquest of the Desert was a military campaign waged by the Argentine State against the Mapuche and Tehuelche peoples for the purpose of exercising real dominion over the Pampa region and Patagonia. The State claimed that it had inherited those lands from the Spanish Crown, though they were controlled until that time by different Indian tribes. The Conquest of the Desert is used to refer not only to the campaign waged by Roca in 1879, but also to earlier campaigns carried out against those peoples by the Spanish colonisers and Argentine national and provincial governments.

11. These descriptions and the others that appear in the text are based on interviews and conversations with residents of the shantytowns and those who live nearby. Due to considerations of space we have not provided transcriptions of the interviews.

12. CEAMSE is a solid urban waste management company that uses a sanitation landfill system and implements reduction, minimalisation and recycling policies for waste from the Buenos Aires Metropolitan Area. CEAMSE charges city governments and/or private companies for receiving waste. Across from the CEAMSE dump are the shantytowns. In some areas, 'clandestine dumps' have been set up by neighbours; they owe their name to the fact that they are unauthorised. These dumps comply with none of the standards governing safety, hygiene or environmental protection.

13. See the city government's plan at http://www.sanmartin2010.gov.ar/, accessed 23 September 2011. The concerns of the residents of the shantytown, even those who might be lucky enough to get deeds to the houses built by the State, are many, and they merit a study of their own. Here, I will simply point out that the housing plans do not consider the size of the families or their basic needs due to their daily activities. For instance, trash rummagers need a place to keep their horses.

14. 'Fuerte Apache' is the name of a neighbourhood constructed as part of a plan to urbanise a shantytown. It consists of a complex of overcrowded buildings in extremely poor conditions that were never finished.

15. See, among others http://www.cels.org.ar/common/documentos/CELS_HRW.pdf, accessed 23 September 2011. In the case of the shantytown where this study was carried out, see http://argentina.indymedia.org/news/2011/02/771099.php, accessed 23 September 2011. This website speaks of an incident in February 2011 when the police killed three youths.

16. Although it is beyond the scope of this chapter, I would like to mention that one of the primary motivations for choosing to build shantytowns on these terrains is their proximity to trash dumps and landfills. When you are jobless, trash ceases to be waste and becomes a source of life: in the trash there is food, as well as paper, cardboard and metal that can be sold (see Grinberg 2009).

17. It was explained to me by the secretary in the school principal's office that, given the lack of official documentation, this suffices as verification of the age of students.

IV. Method, History, Potentiality

10

The Paradigm of Colonialism

Leland de la Durantaye

In July 1968 Giorgio Agamben took part in an international exchange programme at Harvard University. Its director was Henry Kissinger, not yet famous for a more and less ruthless policy of realpolitik, not yet known as a supporter of undemocratic colonial governments in Africa and elsewhere, not yet internationally known as a master political strategist. Though indeed he was not yet famous, the ideas that were to make Kissinger so were already in evidence. In response to a talk on the nature of global politics that summer the young Agamben stood up, surrounded by future leaders from around the world, and said, 'Professor Kissinger, I'm sorry to interrupt, but I don't think you understand anything about politics.'

Many years later, in a discussion with a political thinker of a very different sort, Agamben himself was interrupted, by Guy Debord, and told, 'Look, I'm not a philosopher – I'm a strategist' (Agamben 2006).[1] Agamben has crossed paths with political thinkers – and strategists – of the most varied sort. I mention these encounters, however, not for biographical, but for philosophical reasons: as an introduction to the topic of Agamben's conception of the relationship between politics and strategy, of what it means to understand politics and to recognise a strategist.

What is Politics?

Seventeen years before the publication of his most famous work of political philosophy, *Homo Sacer*, Agamben lamented the loss of continuity between 'poetry and politics' that earlier epochs had known and that was evident for him in such facts as that Aristotle's most ample treatment of music is found in his *Politics*, and that Plato dedicates an important part of his most quintessentially political dialogue, *The Republic*, to the arts (see Agamben 1993: 147 [148]). A still more condensed instance of what Agamben saw in the past and wished for the future is found in his *Idea of Prose*. This least obviously political of his books contains a passage in which Agamben invokes 'thought – that is, politics [*il pensiero – cioè la politica*]' (Agamben 1995: 98 [84]). Agamben equates thought with politics here not because the limits of the political are of no importance to him, but because his idea of politics is vaster than the one to which his readers are accustomed. Politics is concerned with nothing less than the lives we lead and the forms our society takes, and for this reason Agamben refers in a recent instalment of the *Homo Sacer* series to 'that indefinable dimension we are accustomed to calling politics' (Agamben 2007: 275).

Returning to the formula cited above – 'thought – that is, politics' – we might ask what it means. The equation seems strange, but for Agamben this is precisely the reason it needs to be stressed. What this remark highlights is that the realm delimited by politics is as complex and indeterminate as that of philosophy. This does not mean that politics is anything and everything one might choose to bring under its heading; but it does mean that, for Agamben, there are aspects of our lives that are informed by political conceptions and rich in political consequences we are inclined to neglect. For this reason Agamben will not simply ask, 'What is politics?' but instead, 'From where does our culture – both in mythic and in actual terms – derive its political criteria?' (Agamben 2007: 283). How, in other words, have we arrived at our ideas of what belongs to the realm of politics and what does not? Aristotle charged Plato with insufficiently distinguishing the things of the *polis* (city-state) from those of the *oikos* (home). Agamben does not wish to conflate the two, but he does want to understand by what means things, ideas and practices enter into what we call the political realm. Uncertainty concerning this question is precisely the reason he speaks in *Homo Sacer* of a neglected political vocation in urgent need of attention – and it is in the name of this urgency that he recognises a *strategic* element proper to thought – that is, politics.

What is Strategy?

What, then, does *strategy* mean in this context? One thing that Agamben is stressing is that his concerns have been intensely political, and that his conception of politics – like that of the two twentieth-century thinkers who have most influenced his political thought, Walter Benjamin and Michel Foucault – is not only intertwined with his idea of philosophy, but that it is at the same time a fundamentally *strategic* one. But no sooner is this said than an objection might be raised. Is strategic thinking not a very *un*philosophical form of thought? Strategy is a militant term. Viewed narrowly, it denotes the activity of a general. At its origins, it denoted the activity proper to a commander-in-chief or chief magistrate at Athens and in the Achaean League. Policy makers, priests and philosophers might discuss first and last things – but the general, the *strategus*, led armies, risked lives, won and lost battles. Debord did not further define his meaning, but Agamben does – and in a surprising manner. Agamben said that he had been struck by Debord's remark because he considered Debord – just as he considered himself – a philosopher and not a strategist. 'But what I think Guy meant', Agamben went on to say,

> was that every line of thinking, however pure, general or abstract it might endeavor to be, is always marked by its historical place, by the signs of its time, and thus always engaged in a strategy and motivated by a sense of urgency. (Agamben 2006)

Agamben's gloss of Debord's remark allows us to understand *strategy* in a more sweeping fashion. It would incline us to believe that the strategy in question is not limited to winning a certain debate or to marshalling certain spectacular forces for short-term gain. What Agamben suggests is that there is no line of thought which is not strategic. This is not to say that every discussion is about winning and losing, advancing or retreating, but, instead, that, simply stated, thinking and speaking are always bound to their time and place. We may invoke timeless issues but we know that such issues only arise at given times and in given places. There are terms, questions and problems common to fifth-century Greek culture and our own, but they are in every case inflected by their historical situation – even, and perhaps especially, the notion that ideas exist independently of their time and place, independent of their appearance in the mobile image of eternity which is our own.

In this light, one thing that Agamben is saying through his idea of strategy is something absolutely familiar – something which Hume called empiricism, Marx called materialism and Nietzsche, more trenchantly, called anti-Platonism. But Agamben is also saying something more specific and more timely than this. When Agamben suggests that he, like Debord, might be a political strategist, he is not giving voice to a deluded or self-aggrandising notion that he is like a general, that his ideas move masses of men. Nor is he simply taking up the cause of empiricism over and against rationalism; that facts matter as much as ideas. Instead, he is arguing for a corollary of this view: that philosophy always and everywhere has a political potential. I would argue that it is for this reason that Agamben recounts his conversation with Debord at the outset of his discussion of *metropolis* and *colonialism*. For Agamben, to be a philosopher implies being a strategist in the sense he gives it, of taking into account the time and place of ideas, their conditions of possibility, their genealogies, and the possibility, the potential for development they possess.

What is Colonialism?

With these ideas as a backdrop I would like to turn now to the question of colonialism. In over forty-five years of books and essays Agamben has had much to say on a variety of political questions. He has, however, had little to say about *colonialism* and *post-colonialism*. This need come as no surprise. No thinker is under any obligation to touch upon every topic and indeed no thinker *could* touch upon every topic. Something of the argument of this volume, however, is that Agamben's relative silence on the question of colonialism is a riddle to be solved, a lacuna to be filled. Something else of the argument of this volume is that Agamben's analyses of phenomena ancient and modern, his use of paradigms familiar and strange, speak to the problems raised by colonialism and post-colonialism. These are matters ably dealt with elsewhere. What I would like to discuss is that there *is* a point where Agamben discusses colonialism – albeit in both a surprising context and a surprising manner.

The argument Agamben makes in his brief lecture from 2006, 'Metropolis', is striking and strange. His discussion of colonialism begins with that from which the colony departs – the metropolis. And from this term he will develop a *paradigm* of colonialism. As with every one of his paradigms – from the *homo sacer* to the Muselmann, from the state of exception to the concentration camp – Agamben begins with a specific historical phenomenon. That initial historical phenomenon in this case is Western culture's early colony-formation, its early colonialism. In a certain sense colonialism is as old as mankind and its movements in and out of Africa. In the Western political tradition it begins in Greece. One of the key terms we use for the central spaces of our global politics – and of life in our increasingly urbanised world – is *metropolis*. As its etymology indicates, and as Agamben reminds his audience, this is an essentially colonial term. Taken literally, *metropolis* means 'mother city' and was the term used by Greek colonists to refer to that nurturing point of departure (and, frequently, return).

It is at this point, however, that Agamben's analysis moves in an unexpected direction. For clear geographical and cultural reasons, *metropolis*, in its initial Greek context, signified what Agamben calls a 'maximum dislocation', a 'political and spatial dishomogeneity', which 'defines the relationship between the state, or the city, and colonies'. Agamben is not concerned with noting this so that we might better understand the relation of Greek city-states to one another or their relationship to the colonies they formed around the Mediterranean. And this is not done so that we might better understand contemporary colonialism – European colonialism, for instance, in light of ancient Greek colonialism or American colonialism in light of Roman colonialism. Instead, what Agamben has in mind is something at once more sweeping and more strange. This is the 'dislocation and dishomogeneity' not between metropolis and colony, not between metropolitan subjugators and colonial subjects, but the 'dislocation and dishomogeneity' *within* every metropolis and every *polis* – and which Agamben claims is characteristic of all of today's cities and states.

As this makes clear, Agamben is taking a historical phenomenon – colonialism – and using it to illuminate a larger constellation of concerns (as is always his practice with paradigms). In other words, Agamben's interest in the paradigm of colonialism is *strategic*. As he makes clear in this talk, Agamben is not concerned with colonialism per se – that is, with the historical phenomenon of colonialism – but, instead, with the paradigm it provides for understanding life in all our cities, for its ability to illuminate a more vast and variegated space, its ability to articulate a set of more sweeping problems. *Metropolis* comes to mean, for Agamben, a dislocated and dishomogenous space – one that can be traced in every city of the Western world.

With this in mind Agamben turns from the paradigm of the metropolis to the 'apparatus [*dispositivo*]' of the city. The reason that the metropolis is a paradigm is that the city is an apparatus. The city is an apparatus that instantiates, that 'articulates' the dislocation and dishomogeneity characteristic of the modern modes of disciplining and punishing an increasingly supervised body politic. Foucault's central paradigms – opposing ones fused over time – concern the city beset by leprosy and the city infected with the plague. Lepers were expelled and excluded; plague victims were locked in, cordoned off, closely supervised and severely controlled. Above and beyond these individual public health measures Foucault famously saw paradigms for regimes of control, manners of subjecting a potentially unruly body politic. Saying that these were paradigms was another way of saying that they were strategies aimed at observing, charting, controlling and supervising the very bodies of its subjects. The threats posed by those diseases gone (or in comparative abeyance) the measures developed for controlling them remained – put to new, and far more generalised, uses. These uses are ones that Foucault so famously charted in the move from a sovereign model of spectacular power to a disciplinary one of maximum observation and control. And it is shades of these paradigms that Agamben feels are absolutely characteristic of our age, one where the dislocation and dishomogeneity which once extended across vast stretches of land and sea are now visible in the divisions within all of today's cities and all of our political life.

What is a Paradigm?

At this point we might pause and ask how Agamben balances an understanding of the historical specificity of a paradigm (in this case, that of colonialism) with its exemplary value (in this case, life in today's cities). An initial way of approaching this question is by means of disciplinary distinctions. 'I am not a historian', Agamben has stressed, 'and I do not use paradigms as a historian' (Agamben 2004a; see also 2004b: 16). Elsewhere he has written that his paradigms' 'goal is to render intelligible a series of phenomena whose relationship to one another has escaped, or might escape, the historian's gaze' (Agamben 2008: 33). If he does not then use paradigms as a historian, we might well wonder as what, and to what end, he does use them. 'I use a paradigm so as to circumscribe a larger group of phenomena', he has remarked, 'and so as to understand a historical structure [*eine historische Struktur*]'

(Agamben 2004b: 16). Although he stresses that he is not a historian and is not using paradigms as a historian would, he makes clear that his undertaking nevertheless has a historical component; the horizon of understanding is 'historical' and involves not only events but 'structures'. The reason Agamben stresses that although he employs historical materials and methods he does not do so as a historian is that his paradigms are aimed less at understanding the past than at understanding 'the present situation' (Agamben 2004a).

As the preceding suggests, to be genuinely illuminating Agamben's paradigms must strike an exceptionally delicate balance between respect for the uniqueness of historical phenomena and the use to be made of those phenomena for understanding other situations. 'For me', Agamben has remarked of the most controversial of his paradigms, 'the camp is a concrete historical fact [*ein konkretes historisches Faktum*] that at the same time serves as a paradigm, making it possible to understand the present situation [*unsere heutige Situation*]' (Agamben 2001: 19; see also Agamben 2004a). Expanding on this point he has then noted:

> The figures of the *homo sacer* and the camp serve as examples inasmuch as they are concrete historical phenomena. I do not reduce or cancel this historical aspect – on the contrary, I try first to contextualize them. And only then do I try to see them as paradigms through which to understand our present situation. This is simply another way of working historically, another methodological approach. (Agamben 2001: 19)

To this he has added the radical claim that 'every truly interesting book of history proceeds in this fashion' (Agamben 2001: 19). Agamben thus sees himself as 'working historically', but not as a historian. Although this offers some development of the question, it does not offer an answer to the question of how his readers are to balance the two elements of his paradigms.

The first part of *Signatura rerum*, entitled 'What is a Paradigm?', aspires to answer exactly this question and thereby to correct those who 'in more or less good faith believed that I intended to offer theses or reconstructions of a merely historiographical character' (Agamben 2008: 11). As he has on earlier occasions, Agamben begins by addressing the dual nature of his paradigms:

in my work I have had occasion to analyze figures such as the *homo sacer*, the Muselmann, the state of exception, and the concentration camp that are, of course, discrete historical phenomena, but that I have also treated as paradigms whose function was to constitute and render intelligible a vast historico-problematic context. (Agamben 2008: 11)

Agamben's next move also proves to be a familiar one in that he stresses that there is ultimately nothing new in his paradigmatic method; that it is simply a continuation of Foucault's work. Because Foucault never defined the term paradigm in his work, Agamben seeks to elucidate his own idea of paradigm by first answering the question for Foucault. The definition of a Foucauldian paradigm at which Agamben arrives proves to be virtually identical to the one he gave of his own paradigm in the opening lines of the essay: 'singular historical phenomena that [. . .] at once constitute and render intelligible a more ample problematic context' (Agamben 2008: 19). Although this definition clarifies Agamben's relation to Foucault, it complicates his idea of the paradigm. For Agamben, the paradigms of Foucault's work and his own do not function merely as lenses through which to see things that are already there; they not only render intelligible a given context, they 'constitute' it.

This allows us to understand better Agamben's idea of a paradigm, as well as what he has chosen to illustrate through his paradigm of colonialism. We might still ask, however, what all this has to say about colonialism. In what way does this analysis speak to the problem this volume was conceived of to address? In a certain sense the answer is simple: it has little to say. That is, it has little to say if what is at issue are historiographical questions about the formation of colonies and the process of colonisation, whether in the ancient or the modern world. If, however, the question is one of how we might view both the practical and theoretical questions of colonialism today, then it has much to say. The problems of colonialism and post-colonialism are far from confined to relations between colonies and their mother cities. These problems are of another order, and often manifest themselves in conflicts within given cities and states – the problems of African refugees in Paris, those of Turkish 'guest workers' in Berlin, of Indian émigrés in London, with the list extending on and on. The question Agamben raises is not how colonialism became a paradigm for certain states of exception – a question which his reader might more readily have expected, and which, of course, might be profitably raised and explored. It is, instead, how the idea of a division between a mother city and its colonies, how this disparity and disjunction ceased to be merely spatial and practical and has, instead, become intimately bound up with life in all our cities, how our cities have become sites of increasingly complex compartmentalisation, observation and subjectification. This is not an absolute evil, to be sure, but neither should it be seen as anodyne. If gone unchecked it would seem to betoken a dark future and it is in the name of the urgency or emergency such a situation presents that Agamben makes these '*strategic*' remarks. Here, as elsewhere, the strategy will be as complex as the situation – and it is by no means exhaustively mapped out in this brief talk. But that in the name of which such a strategy is to be formed *is* named therein: what Agamben calls 'ungovernability [*ingovernabilità*]'. Universalised ungovernability is, of course, anarchy. But the question does not lie there. Contemporary societies increasingly control and subject, discipline and punish their subjects – and the problems posed by colonialism and post-colonialism are intimately related to this phenomenon. This process is not mere progress, and should not be viewed with an indifferent eye. If thought is politics, then the freedom and potentiality which are the highest values of thought are also the highest ones of politics. For Agamben, it is thus in the name of this idea of politics that a strategy is to be formed whose aim is an 'ungovernability' which is our first home and true heritage.

References

Agamben, G. (1993), *Infancy and History: The Destruction of Experience*, trans. L. Heron. London and New York: Verso. [*Infanzia e storia: Distruzione dell'esperienza e origine della storia. Nuova edizione accresciuta*. Turin: Einaudi, 2001. First Italian edition published in 1978.]

—(1995), *Idea of Prose*, trans. M. Sullivan and S. Whitsitt. Albany: State University of New York Press. [*Idea della prosa: Nuova edizione illuminata e accresciuta*. Macerata, Italy: Quodlibet, 2002. First Italian edition published in 1985.]

—(2001), 'Das unheilige Leben: ein Gespräch mit dem italienischen Philosophen Giorgio Agamben', interview with Hannah Leitgeb and Cornelia Vismann, *Literaturen* (Berlin), 2(1): 16–21.

—(2004a), 'I luoghi della vita', radio Interview with Roberto Andreotti and Federico De Melis. RAI Radio Tre, 8 February.

—(2004b), 'Das Leben, ein Kunstwerk ohne Autor: ein Gespräch mit Giorgio Agamben', interview with Ulrich Raulff, *Süddeutsche Zeitung*, 6 April, 16.

—(2006), Lecture on 'Metropolis' given at Nomad University, trans. A. Bove, *Generation-Online*, available at http://www.generation-online.org/p/fpagamben4.htm, accessed 23 September 2011. Audio file available at http://www.globalproject.info/imG/mp3/giorgio_agamben.mp3, accessed 23 September 2011.

—(2007), *Il Regno e la Gloria: Per una genealogica teologica dell'economia e del governo. Homo Sacer, II, 2.* Milan: Neri Pozza.

—(2008), *Signatura rerum: Sul metodo.* Turin: Bollati Boringhieri.

Note

1. All translation from original languages is my own.

11

'The work of men is not durable': History, Haiti and the Rights of Man

Jessica Whyte

We have not brought half-a-million slaves from the coasts of Africa to make them into French citizens.

(President of the Colonial Assembly, St Marc, San Domingue)

If they had a thousand lives, they would sacrifice them all rather than be forced back into slavery again.

(Toussaint L'Ouverture)

'The separation between humanitarianism and politics that we are experiencing today', Agamben writes in foreboding tones in *Homo Sacer*, 'is the extreme phase of the separation of the rights of man from the rights of the citizen' (Agamben 1998: 133). In a critique that has been as controversial as it has been influential, he declares that, today, humanitarian organisations are able to grasp human life only in the figure of 'bare life' and therefore maintain a 'secret solidarity' with the powers they purport to oppose (133–4). Agamben's claim is twofold: first, he traces a *transformation* in human rights discourses and in the project of humanitarianism, in which the latter becomes increasingly complicit with state power, culminating in the management of survival of today's humanitarian biopolitics. Second, he suggests that the contemporary fate of human rights discourses was prepared at the origins of modernity when rights declarations enabled the passage from a divinely ordained sovereignty to a national one, thus enmeshing life in the order of the state. This chapter will interrogate Agamben's account of rights through the lens of Haiti – a nation that has been something of a crucible for the various stages of the development of human rights.

In the wake of the earthquake that devastated much of the capital in 2010, the US sent 20,000 troops to conduct what it termed a

239

'humanitarian mission' and what regional leaders Hugo Chavez and Evo Morales branded a 'military occupation' (AFP 2010). When asked by a reporter whether foreign troops were a threat to Haiti's sovereignty, President René Préval answered: 'We are talking about people suffering and you are talking about ideology' (Zengerle and Frank 2010). In a country in which human suffering has repeatedly formed the rationale for occupations and 'humanitarian interventions', including that following the coup against the popularly elected President Aristide in 2004, such a separation between politics and humanitarianism is difficult to maintain. Indeed, as Peter Hallward remarks in his extraordinary account of the fate of Aristide's Lavalas Party, 'in our age of responsible and humanitarian intervention what passes for the defense of human rights has long been one of the most openly ideological categories of political analysis' (Hallward 2007: 156). Precisely because Haiti presents us not with a humanitarianism separated from politics, but with a politics played out through the discourse of humanitarianism, it also offers a paradigmatic case of Agamben's critique of the complicity of humanitarian organisations with state power. Nowhere is it clearer than in this 'Republic of NGOs' that human rights discourses can be wielded not to empower but to reduce a population to the status of bare life that can be kept alive or killed with impunity (Kristoff and Panarelli 2010).

Yet, as US troops took control of the Toussaint L'Ouverture airport in the wake of the earthquake, the spectre of another politics of rights haunted the humanitarian re-colonisation of this ravaged nation. In what follows, I wish to examine the role played by the Haitian Revolution of 1791–1804 in the history of human rights, or the 'rights of man'. In his seminal study of the slave revolution, C. L. R. James draws attention not only to the impact the French Revolution was to have on those whose slavery was not simply metaphorical, but also to the importance of their struggle in realising its universal aspirations. News of the Revolution carried to San Domingue's plantations, James notes, and the slaves construed it in their own image: 'the white slaves in France had risen, and killed their masters, and were now enjoying the fruits of the earth' (James 1989: 81). Such an impression was, of course far from accurate. And yet, the slaves 'had caught the spirit of the thing. Liberty, Equality, Fraternity' (81). This spirit was to animate the first successful slave uprising, and lead to the eventual independence of the nation that would then rename itself Haiti. In the course of this uprising, the slaves, led at first by Toussaint L'Ouverture and then by Jean-Jacques Dessalines after L'Ouverture's arrest and kidnapping by Napoleon's troops, would push those ideas far beyond their original conception, for the first time opening the possibility of a genuine political universalism.

What are the consequences of this revolution for Agamben's account of the genesis and extension of human rights? For Agamben, the discourse of human rights is a biopolitical one, which erases the border between life and politics and enmeshes a life reduced to survival in the order of sovereign power. In tracing the development of biopolitics, he traces lines of continuity to reveal the hidden connections that link our present to the remote past. Responding to the 'bloody mystification of a new planetary order', he writes in *Homo Sacer*, requires the interrogation of an 'aporia that lies at the foundation of Western politics' (Agamben 1998: 11). From Aristotle onwards, he argues, the political realm has been predicated on a caesura that divides the human into a political and a natural life, and isolates what he terms 'bare life' (4). In this division of man's private life in the home (*oikos*) and his public life in the state – 'a division', Hannah Arendt suggests, 'upon which all ancient political thought rested as self-evident and axiomatic' (Arendt 1958: 28) – he locates the fundamental problem not only of ancient politics, but of contemporary politics also. A process that begins with the attempt to banish natural life from the *polis*, Agamben avers, culminates in the 'lasting eclipse' of politics today, and in 'the assumption of the burden – and the "total management" – of biological life, that is, of the very animality of man' (Agamben 2004: 77).

It is within this biopolitical narrative that Agamben places the 1789 Declaration of the Rights of Man and Citizen, which he argues marked the point at which natural life entered the *polis* as the very foundation of sovereign power. If the Declaration institutes a rupture with classical politics, in his view, it does not resolve the classical aporia of the separation of life and politics, but, instead, inscribes this separation in the very heart of the body politic. The various exclusions from the category of humanity that have typified modern politics, he argues, are simply the result of the politicisation of natural life, and thus of the category of humanity, inaugurated by the Declaration. Here, I want to trace a different historical possibility – a possibility, I suggest, that was brought into being by the slaves of San Domingue, yet violently suppressed by Napoleon's troops who were determined to restore slavery to their most profitable colony and return the former slaves, in Louis Narcisse Baudry Deslozière's words, to the 'political nothing-ness to which nature condemns' them (Sala-Molins 2006: 116). Examining the ruptures that punctuated the history of the rights of man allows us to look behind the triumphant mask of the present in order to reveal that which could have been otherwise. In doing so, we undermine both the attempt to glorify the politics of the present by recuperating the slave uprising into a self-flattering narrative of progress, and the reverse narrative that sees only the increasing incorporation of life into the order of sovereign power. To challenge such narratives requires that we do not presuppose that the ideals fought for the by ex-slaves of San Domingue are continuous with those that underpin today's politics of human rights, but seek to retrieve them from the history that has been built on their graves. This attempt to trace the imprint that their struggle left on the present is oriented to redeeming those hopes that had to be destroyed, not once but repeatedly, in order to bring this present into existence. It is to take seriously Walter Benjamin's observation that 'even the dead will not be safe from the enemy if he is victorious . . .' (Benjamin 2003: 388). In contrast to the argu-ment of *Homo Sacer*, according to which rights tends to develop according to a biopolitical logic, I suggest here that the question of rights can best be understood in terms of what Agamben elsewhere calls the 'messianic modality', exigency, which disrupts linear time and historical progress to enable a redemptive orientation to the past (Agamben 2005: 39).

On Rights and History

In her history of the invention of human rights, Lynn Hunt out-lines what she terms 'the bulldozer force of the revolutionary logic of rights' (Hunt 2007: 160). Once rights discourse is invented, she argues, it has a logic that tends towards its universalisation, as ever more groups take it up in order to contest their exclusion from civic status. Rights questions, she suggests, have a tendency to cascade uncontrollably. As James Sullivan wrote in a 1776 letter to John Adams, once rights are granted to some, 'there will be no end to it' (Hunt 2007: 147). Sullivan's letter epitomises the fear that accompanied the extension of rights to those who had for-merly been denied them. Attempting to alter the qualifications for voting, he wrote, was dangerous folly. Once some are granted the vote, new claims will arise: 'Women will demand a vote. Lads from 12 to 21 will think their rights not enough attended to, and every Man, who has not a Farthing, will demand an equal Voice with any other in all Acts of State' (Hunt 2007: 147).[1] Writing as the American revolution was beginning, Sullivan was clearly unable to conceive that one day slaves may also rise to demand rights of their own. Indeed, it would take until the thirteenth amendment in 1865 before the United States officially abolished slavery. Within twenty years of Sullivan's letter, the French Republic voted to abolish slavery, and, within another four, legislated to provide the former slaves with 'the same rights as those born on French territory' (Council of the Five Hundred 2006: 154). For Hunt, this suggests that rights come into being within a directional history: if the 'logic of the process did not necessarily move events in a straight line forward', she writes, '[. . .] in the long run it tended to do so' (Hunt 2007: 150). Even as political battles were fought, won and lost, the logic of rights continued to operate behind the backs, as it were, of their actors. Suggestive as Hunt's argument is, it minimises the contingency of the struggles that brought human rights into being and led to their victory over competing political visions with alternate conceptions of justice. Rights, as Samuel Moyn (2010) has stressed, only operate to the extent that people take them up and use them as the bases for their political claims, and not through any inherent logic.

At first sight, Agamben's account of rights would seem to diverge dramatically from Hunt's progressive narrative, and thus to avoid the pitfalls it entails. Between her argument that the human rights framework has succeeded in defining what is no longer acceptable and making violations 'all that more inadmissible', and his account of rights declarations as biopolitical instruments that enmesh life in the order of sovereign power, there would seem to be an unbridgeable divide (Hunt 2007: 214). Here, however, I would like to explore an alternate hypothesis: that is, that Agamben's critique of rights shares with Hunt's celebration of them the belief that rights operate according to an inner logic. Agamben's critique of rights, I suggest, can be viewed as a biopolitical 'dialectic of enlightenment', which reverses the trajectory of Hunt's progressive narrative, without challenging the premise that rights have a logic that moves, in the long run, in a straight line.[2] This teleological account of rights conflicts with the focus on potentiality, messianic redemption and the unfinished nature of the past that characterises other of his writings. Throughout this chapter, I suggest that the latter, Benjaminian, account of history is better suited to understanding the history of rights than the more Heideggerian account Agamben provides of their trajectory.

Agamben's discussion of rights crystallises around two key events, separated by more than a century: the 1679 writ of *habeas corpus*, which, he argues, placed the body, *corpus*, at the centre of political claims, and the 1789 Declaration of the Rights of Man and Citizen. Agamben tends to present his own critique of rights in relation to that of Hannah Arendt, who famously argued that civil rights are the presupposition for human rights and not vice versa. Like Arendt, Agamben focuses his attention on the relation between the rights of man and the nation-state, and on the ambiguous relation the French declaration establishes between the citizen and man. 'Rights', he argues, 'are attributed to man (or originate in him) solely to the extent that man is the immediately vanishing ground (who must never come to light as such) of the citizen' (Agamben 1998: 129). In the order of the nation-state, Agamben argues, man is subsumed into the figure of the citizen, disappearing even as his rights are supposedly safeguarded.

Despite the profundity of Arendt's work, Agamben suggests, her account of the tie that binds the rights of man to the fate of the nation-state has not been followed up, as the post-war period has seen both an instrumental recourse to rights and a proliferation of rights declarations, both of which have obscured the real historical significance of rights. It is time, he suggests, to stop regarding rights declarations as codifications of eternal ethical values, which bind legislators who would otherwise violate them, and to consider their 'real historical function in the modern nation-state' (Agamben 1998: 127). Here, it is already clear that Agamben is less interested in the role of rights in *constraining* state power, and more in their constitutive function in the modern nation-state. 'Declarations of rights', he insists, 'represent the originary figure of the inscription of natural life in the juridico-political order of the nation-state' (127). By affirming that man is *born* free and equal in rights, the 1789 Declaration politicises the fact of birth, turning natural life itself into the new foundation of sovereign power.

What is distinctive about Agamben's argument is not the suggestion that the French Revolution created a new basis for sovereign power, but his account of the political consequences of this novel conception of sovereignty. Hunt has argued that, in *declaring* rights, the French revolutionaries did more than simply signal a transformation in attitudes and expectations: they effected a transfer of sovereignty from the monarch to the nation and its representatives, and created a radically new form of political legitimacy, according to which rights flowed 'from the nature of human beings themselves' (Hunt 2007: 115). For Agamben, the location of sovereign power in the very *nature* of 'man' marks a fundamental shift in relation to pre-modern forms of political power, for which the question of life itself had been separated from that of politics. While ancient politics rested on the expulsion of natural life from the *polis*, modern power, in contrast, makes of this non-political life the very foundation of sovereign power. The consequences of this shift, in Agamben's view, will be far from benign:

> It is not possible to understand the 'national' and biopolitical development and vocation of the modern state in the nineteenth and twentieth centuries if one forgets that what lies at its basis is not man as a free and conscious political subject but, above all, man's bare life, the simple birth that as such is, in the passage from subject to citizen, invested with the principle of sovereignty. (Agamben 1998: 128)

Here we find the basis of what is perhaps the most controversial aspect of Agamben's critique of rights: that is, his argument that the development by which natural life appeared as the new political subject in modernity ultimately paves the way for the murderous racism of the Nazi state. When the mechanism that inscribes life in the nation-state began to break down in the wake of the First World War, he argues, what arose was Nazism and fascism, both of which made of natural life the locus of a decision and the key political concern. If, under National Socialism, the principle of birth would no longer be the hidden foundation of 'bloodless absolutes and spiritually empty delusions' – which was how the Nazi ideologue Alfred Rosenberg (1930: n.p.) conceived the idea of universal human rights – but would become the political task par excellence, this, for Agamben, was only possible because rights declarations had made this principle their 'hidden foundation' in the first place.

Here, we are reminded of Theodor Adorno's remark: 'No universal history leads from savagery to humanity, but one indeed from the slingshot to the H-bomb' (Adorno 1983: 315).

Agamben's thought, like that of Adorno, dramatically under-mines the progressive narrative of the Enlightenment. Reversing the direction of a progressivist 'universal history', however, is not sufficient to free us of the presuppositions underpinning it – most importantly, the conception of history as operating according to a logic that is largely impervious to human intervention. Agamben's vision of rights relies on viewing their referent as birth itself, or apolitical man – that is, a naturalised and passive figure. When we consider the role of the slaves of San Domingue in the history of the Universal Declaration, this picture is disrupted. Rather than a mechanism that inscribes the principle of birth as the founda-tion of sovereignty, we see a struggle that took seriously the dis-course of universal equality and used it to undercut the question of birth, ultimately leading to the extension of citizenship to all residents of the colonies including African-born former slaves. Further, Haiti reveals the way the Declaration was used by the slaves not to enmesh life in the realm of sovereign power, but as a tool with which to loosen the hold of a bloody power over bare life as brutal as any described anywhere in Agamben's *oeuvre*. As much as the former slaves were subjected to new forms of control, most notably that which tied their new rights to their continua-tion of productive labour, we cannot underestimate the brutality of colonial slavery or the significance of its abolition in enabling a form of freedom and equality that were previously unimaginable.[3] Attending to the role of the rights of man in the struggle against slavery, and in its reimposition under Napoleon, reveals only too clearly the contingency of both the victories and the defeats that made human rights what they are today.

The 'Rights Bulldozer' in Haiti

In 1789, a delegation from San Domingue arrived in 'a house still ringing with the famous declaration' to claim the rights of man (James 1989: 68). Despite the wealth of the free Mulatto petition-ers, many of whom were slave owners, the French bourgeoisie, afraid of losing order and ultimately the colony itself, 'went red in the face and put the Rights of Man in their pockets whenever the colonial question came up' (69). A year later, the Mulattoes petitioned again, relying on the argument that 'Protestants, comedians, Jews, the relations of criminals' had all been granted their rights (70). But where would it end? The question for the

Constituent Assembly was whether granting rights to free people of colour would ultimately lead to rights for the slaves, and thus Hunt depicts San Domingue as a key example of the logic of rights, even if she recognises that the revolt of the slaves left the French commissioners and the deputies in Paris little choice if they wanted to retain the colony (Hunt 2007: 165). Indeed, in 1794, the convention abolished slavery. 'Representatives of the French people', Danton declared immediately following the vote for abolition, 'until now our decrees of liberty have been selfish, and only for ourselves. But today we proclaim it to the universe, and generations to come will glory in this decree; we are proclaiming universal liberty' (National Convention 2006: 131). Danton's speech rings with a feverish Utopianism as he praises the actions of the Convention in 'hurling liberty into the free world' and expresses his confidence in 'the blessings of the universe and posterity' (132). There is no doubt that this was a momentous occasion, so much so that 'a female citizen of color' who regularly attended the Convention was so overcome by joy that she 'fainted dead away' (132). In abolishing slavery, the ideas of the Enlightenment met with the ideas and the resistance of the slaves of San Domingue, who saw in them more than had those who drafted the Universal Declaration without imagining that it would apply to those who were, after all, barely considered human.

How does the abolition of slavery and the extension of equal rights to all those who resided in the colony fit with Agamben's argument that the Declaration enshrined birth as the foundation of sovereign of power, thus establishing modern politics as a politics of bare life? In abolishing slavery, the Convention put an end to the condition of slavery, which was a quintessential example of what Agamben, following Jean-Luc Nancy, terms 'abandonment' – that is, the exposure through which life is at once excluded from the political community and captured in the realm of sovereign power (Nancy 1993: 36–47).[4] Stolen from the African continent and transported across the seas in the holds of slave ships, in spaces too small either to sit upright or to lie at full length, those who were bound for slavery were abandoned to the whims of their captors who exercised an absolute power over life and death (James 1989: 8). Once their journey was over, and they had been purchased like simple commodities at market, they were subjected by the colonists to a regime of 'calculated brutality and terrorism' that included the use of torture, mutilation and killings

(11).[5] The planters, James writes, exercised all the 'ingenuity' that 'fear or a depraved imagination could devise' in order to break the spirits of the slaves and satisfy their own lusts – by burning them alive, filling them with gunpowder and blowing them up, emptying boiling cane sugar over their heads, or burying them up to their necks and smearing their heads in sugar so the flies would devour them (12). Rather than the sadism of a few colonists, such brutality was explicitly sanctioned. 'Not only planters but officials made it quite clear', James writes, 'that whatever the penalties for the ill treatment of slaves, these could never be enforced' (22). A slave was a man's property, and the right of property was sacred. Reduced to pure working machines, slaves could literally be worked to death, and then replaced. 'The Ivory Coast is a good mother' went the colonial proverb . . . (22).

To point out that the slaves were, in Agamben's terms, 'bare life', absolutely subjected to the power of the slave owners and exposed to the permanent threat of death should not be controversial. My aim here, however, is not simply to add the slaves of San Domingue to Agamben's list of exemplary figures of bare life. Rather, it is to examine what the Haitian Revolution, in which the slaves overturned this condition, can tell us about the 'real historical function in the modern nation-state' of the Universal Declaration of Human Rights (Hunt 2007: 212). Before the slaves succeeded in having slavery abolished, the Declaration had been universal only in name. Through their struggles, they created, for the first time, the possibility of genuine political (if not yet economic) equality. The Haitian Revolution is a crucial moment in the history of human rights. Here, I do not simply want to reinsert Haiti into a great progressive history of human rights, according to which 'we must still continually improve on the eighteenth century version of human rights' (Hunt 2007: 212).[6] Such a narrative reduces this revolution to one moment in an ongoing process which can be claimed as a legacy that will glorify present power structures, even as these structures are sustained by the belief that we have continued to progress since the age of revolutions. In 1998, the 150th anniversary of the (second) abolition of slavery was commemorated in France, and a memorial was built in Paris. 'Names of slaves were carved in stones', writes Françoise Vergès. 'One night some people came to erase names that were theirs' (Vergès 1999). For Vergès this suggests that those whose names were carved in stone had no wish to be reminded of their shame, and of a history of which they were not proud.

Instead we could see their actions as a powerful objection to the teleological view of history that builds its monuments on the graves of the forgotten. There are various ways to forget. And as Agamben notes in *The Time That Remains*, 'the shapeless chaos of the forgotten is neither inert nor ineffective', but, on the contrary, is at work within us; it has a force that determines the status of both knowledge and understanding (Agamben 2005: 40). The Haitian Revolution, and its forgetting, continue to structure our present, which is built on the accumulated capital provided by the slave trade and out of the struggles of the slaves of San Domingue. The forgotten, Agamben suggests, exercises a demand upon us, but this demand is not simply to be remembered and inserted into a new tradition, nor to be frozen in commemoration, but 'to remain with us and be possible for us in some manner' (41). This demand can best be understood in relation to the 'messianic modality' – *exigency*, which, Agamben writes, 'consists in a relation between what is or has been and its possibility' (39). In examining the Haitian Revolution, my concern is with redeeming those other political possibilities that were briefly actualised, and whose *defeat* made human rights what they are today.

Man and Citizen

What other political possibilities did the Haitian Revolution bring into the world? Let us look again at the question of 'man and citizen'. In Agamben's view, the very politicisation of human life brought with it the attempt to redefine the borders of humanity. 'Once *zoē* is politicised by declarations of rights', he writes, 'the distinctions and thresholds that make it possible to isolate a sacred life must be newly defined' (Agamben 1998: 131). In *The Open*, he uses the term 'anthropological machine' to signify the process by which the human is created through the abandonment of an inhuman other. In modernity, he suggests, the anthropological machine works by excluding (not-yet) human beings from within the body of humanity. In contrast, 'the machine of earlier times', he writes – in a remark that seems to relegate slavery to a pre-modern condition – produces an inside through the inclusion of an outside, producing the human through the humanisation of the animal: 'the man-ape, the *enfant sauvage* or *Homo ferus*, but also above all the slave, the barbarian, and the foreigner, as figures of an animal in human form' (Agamben 2004: 37). While each of these attempts to constitute the human, in Agamben's view, must presuppose a zone of articulation between human and animal, in fact this zone is empty, a place of pure decision which produces a life separated and excluded from itself – a bare life.

The political importance of deciding on the human and the inhuman in the period of the French Revolution is starkly illustrated by a debate that took place in 1788, when the colonists of San Domingue successfully sought representation in the States General. When these slave owners claimed eighteen seats, in proportion to the total population of the colony, Mirabeau responded sharply:

> You claim representation proportionate to the number of inhabitants. The free blacks are proprietors and tax-payers, and yet they have not been allowed to vote. And as for the slaves, either they are men or they are not; if the colonists consider them to be men, let them free them and make them electors and eligible for seats; if the contrary is the case, have we, in apportioning deputies according to the population of France, taken into consideration the number of our horses and mules? (James 1989: 60)

While framed as a rebuke of the arrogance of the delegation, the power of decision nonetheless remained with the colonists. Indeed, the idea that the French had the power to bring human beings into existence *ex nihilo* pervades the discourse of this period, as the dark underside of the Enlightenment faith in human perfectibility (Sala-Molins 2006: 99). 'O' the sublime effect of true philosophy!' Etienne Laveaux wrote in 1789, in one of the clearest articulations of this idea:

> The Republic, on 16 *Pluviôse*, carried out a conquest of a kind unknown until then. It conquered for the *human race*, or rather, it created, through a single strong and precise idea, a million new beings and in doing so expanded the family of man. (Laveaux 2006: 156)[7]

While the colonists assured themselves of their capacity to create humans from thin air, the Haitian slaves seized the initiative, asserting their own humanity to challenge their status as bare life. By demanding they be considered amongst those 'men' that the Declaration pronounced, 'are born and remain free and equal in rights', the slaves, it could be argued, contributed to the politicisation of the category of humanity that Agamben sees as a key aspect of modern biopolitics. Nonetheless, it would be mistaken to reduce their struggle to merely a new articulation of the border between the human and the inhuman. Only with the Haitian Revolution was the very constitution of the human through the exclusion of an inhuman other explicitly challenged, and every justification for excluding certain groups as 'not-yet' human dramatically undermined. 'Only in Haiti', as Hallward writes, 'was the declaration of human freedom universally consistent' (Hallward 2007: 10). For Toussaint L'Ouverture, the fate of the slaves was that of humanity as a whole: 'Do not allow our brothers, our friends, to be sacrificed to men who wish to reign over the ruins of the human species', he pleaded, as Napoleon's troops prepared to restore slavery (Dubois and Garrigus 2006: 195).

If Haiti represents the possibility of humanity without remainder, what does it tell us about the citizen, or the possibility of political community? What does the extension of citizenship to all residents of the colonies, including a large population of African-born slaves, do to Agamben's argument that, in modernity, birth is simply the vanishing ground of nation? In the course of the French Revolution, he suggests, the principle of 'blood and soil' – which has become a condensation of Nazi ideology, but which can be traced to its more 'innocuous juridical origin' in Roman law, where it served to define the two criteria of citizenship: *ius soli* (birth in a certain territory) and *ius sanguinis* (birth from citizen parents) – gained a new importance, as it came to define that life that was now the bearer of sovereignty (Agamben 1998: 129). In fact, these principles had also determined membership of the state in pre-revolutionary France, where, as early as the sixteenth century, to be French was to be born in France of at least one French parent and to be domiciled in France. By the eighteenth century, to be born in France *or* born to a French parent was sufficient to allow for inheritance (the main restriction applied to foreigners), but the principles of blood and soil were still in place (Brubaker 1989). From Agamben's perspective, citizenship does not name a generic subjection to law or 'a new egalitarian principle', but the new status of life as the foundation of sovereign power (Agamben 1998: 129). He devotes only a sentence to dismissing the egalitarian interpretation of citizenship, which he attributes to Chalier,

who argued in 1792 that the title citizen should replace *monsieur*
and *sieur* in all public acts (129). Only by recognising that citizenship names the principle that makes of bare life the foundation of
sovereign power, he argues, can we understand 'the rapid growth
in the course of the French Revolution of regulatory provisions
specifying which *man* was a *citizen* and which one was not' (130).
    Agamben argues that, prior to the Revolution:

> the questions 'What is French?' 'What is German' had constituted
> not a political problem but only one theme among others discussed
> in philosophical anthropologies. Caught in a constant work of redefi-
> nition, these questions now begin to become essentially political, to
> the point that, with National Socialism, the answer to the question
> 'Who or what is German?' (and also, therefore, 'Who and what is
> not German?') coincides immediately with the highest political task.
> (Agamben 1998: 130)

It is true that in the course of the French Revolution, new repressive measures were introduced against foreigners, including reg-
istration and surveillance, expulsion and exclusion from civic
functions (Brubaker 1989: 43). The arrest of Thomas Paine, who
had been granted French citizenship as a friend of the Revolution,
is only one example of this. It is also true, however, that, prior to
the Revolution, anthropology had a distinctly political valence,
and the *Code Noir* or 'black code' served to politicise and to
minutely regulate the biology of the slave. From the Roman
juridical principle that the 'the fruit follows the womb', the *Code
Noir* drew the conclusion that a child born to a slave mother was
a slave, and one to a free mother was free (Sala-Molins 2006:
125) (a principle that expediently freed the male colonists of San
Domingue of responsibility for the children they 'fathered' with
their female slaves).
    Seen in this light, Agamben's argument that Nazism is the
extreme point of a process of regulating life that began in 1789
and whose 'rapid growth' has continued since that time, reveals
a lack of attention to both the intense regulation of biology to
which slaves were subjected in pre-revolutionary France, and the
dramatic contestation of the location of citizenship in biology that
followed the Haitian Revolution. For a short time, the French
Republic granted citizenship to those whose birth could never be
the vanishing ground of nation, to those who in pre-revolutionary

San Domingue had been subject to racial discriminations as 'matters of government policy, enforced by bullets and bayonets' (Brubaker 1989: 43). To propose a continuum linking the French Revolution with Nazism is to brush over the extent to which this other possibility had to be destroyed in order for such a horrific outcome to be actualised. For Agamben, Nazism is a response to the crisis of the nation-state brought about by mass migrations and the realignment of states in the wake of the First World War, which, he argues, severed the unity of birth nation and citizenship on which it was founded. But, in the early years of the French Republic, under the pressure of the slaves of San Domingue, there could be no unity of birth, nation and territory. In Agamben's terms, the modern nation-state was in crisis at its inception, split between the location of sovereignty in the nation and a principle of citizenship that implied a non-biological form of universality and equality.

As William Brubaker stresses, while we can see the French Revolution as giving rise to both nationalism and the frontier, in its early days, 'the Revolution was ostentatiously cosmopolitan' (Brubaker 1989: 41). Only the Haitian Revolution, however, would allow the concrete universalisation of the principle of equality. In their willingness to die rather than remain enslaved, the slaves of San Domingue invented a form of political community that resisted the biopolitical management of a life reduced to survival. In 1789, there were half a million slaves in San Domingue, two-thirds of whom were born in Africa (James 1989: 86). Never could their birth be the vanishing ground of nation. Rather, their citizenship could only be premised on a disregard for birth. Laurent Dubois is right to suggest that the 'pinnacle of republicanism during the era of the French Revolution was the decree abolishing slavery and granting citizenship to all peoples, of all colour' (Dubois 2006: 12). And, as he stresses, this decree was motivated not only by the ideas of the Enlightenment *philosophes*, many of whom combined universal claims with the belief that certain people were incapable of being granted natural rights. Rather, it was the political mobilisation of the slaves that forced the Republic to disregard birth by granting citizenship to all inhabitants of the colonies, thus pushing the universalistic aspirations of the Revolution to a conclusion not anticipated by many who espoused them. One of the clearest statements of this is also one of the most poignant, as it attests to the success with which the inhabitants of San Domingue were divided by the various colonial powers that coveted the colony: in 1799, the Mulatto leader Rigaud, who had broken with Toussaint, wrote a public proclamation to refute the latter's claims that he was unwilling to obey a Negro: 'From the beginning of the revolution I have braved all for the cause of liberty', he wrote, stressing that he had not betrayed his principles and would never do so. 'Besides', he continued, 'I am too much a believer in the Rights of Man to think that there is one colour in nature superior to another. I know a man only as a man' (James 1989: 230). C. L. R. James stresses that these words could not have been written before 1789. It was not simply the passing of the Declaration that made them possible, but the revolution of the slaves and the free men of colour of San Domingue which universalised the ideas of the Declaration in a way that its drafters seem not to have imagined (230).

It was this abstract equality that Napoleon would set out to defeat by sending General Leclerc to restore slavery in San Domingue, and to 'destroy all the *nègres* of the mountains, men and women, and keep only children under twelve years old' (Leclerc 2006: 179). 'The Republic of 1794 had been sincere in giving them liberty', James notes, 'but the Republic of 1796 might be equally sincere in taking it away' (James 1989: 179). It would not happen in 1796, but by 1802 the move to restore slavery was fully underway. The restoration began not in San Domingue but in Martinique, Île-de-Bourbon and the other colonies returned to France by Britain at the Treaty of Amiens. Eight years after the Convention had abolished slavery, refusing to subject the matter to the dishonour of a 'discussion', the Legislature voted to restore it to the islands by a vote of 211 to 60 (340). At this point, the so-called 'logic of rights' moved rapidly into reverse: the slave trade was officially restored, and all Africans arriving were to be slaves as before. Next, people of colour were prohibited from coming to France, mixed marriages were outlawed and Mulattoes subject to renewed discrimination. In June of 1802, L'Ouverture was arrested and transported to France, where he would die of starvation and maltreatment in prison. By July, slavery had been restored in Guadeloupe and Mulattoes stripped of their citizenship. 'Every ship', James notes, 'was bringing back émigré colonists to San Domingue thirsting for revenge, eager for the old days' (341). Those who returned were quick to return to their old sports – burning alive, hanging, drowning, torturing and 'burying blacks up to the neck near nests of insects' (360). This was what was necessary to reassert the coincidence of birth, nation and citizenship that Agamben sees as the trinity that defines the modern nation-state. Amongst those other possibilities that the Haitian Revolution brought into the world, and that lie forgotten in the past, is a form of political community that is indifferent to birth, utterly disregarding it as a criterion of citizenship. The modern nation-state with its unity of birth, nation and territory is the product of a defeat: the defeat of a different idea of non-biological political community held out by the Haitian Revolution.

Conclusion: 'The work of men is not durable'

Far from simply inaugurating a paradigm that led to Nazism, and that we still live within, the French Revolution, like the Haitian, was as much a failure as a success. Just as the former slaves of San Domingue were forced to fight, and in many cases to die, for their freedom, in France,

> [the] passionate desire to free all humanity which had called for Negro freedom in the great days of the revolution now huddled in the slums of Paris and Marseilles, exhausted by its great efforts and terrorised by Bonaparte's bayonets and Fouché's police. (James 1989: 270)

This is not to dismiss the achievements of the French Revolution, nor of the Haitian. What was revolutionary about these moments, however, as Hallward suggests, was not simply their affirmation of liberal freedom, but 'the direct mobilisation of the people to claim these universal rights and freedoms, in direct confrontation with the most powerful vested interests of the day' (Hallward 2009: 17). As L'Ouverture was only too aware, such a confrontation could not be determined by any logic. As he wrote, in a remark of great prescience: 'After my death, who knows if my brothers will not be driven back into slavery and will yet perish under the whip of the whites. The work of men is not durable' (James 1989: 260). Faced with the continued struggle of the former slaves, the French failed in restoring slavery in San Domingue. But, as Hallward notes of these two modern revolutions: the 'campaign to re-pacify the people has been running, in different ways, ever since' (Hallward 2009: 18). Nowhere is this truer than in Haiti, which has been punished, not once but again and again and again for the fact that its people dared to realise the ideals of liberty and freedom.[8]

The 1804 Haitian Declaration of Independence is a testament to both the powerful bravery and spirit that animated the Revolution and the bitter disappointment of the hope it invested in the French Republic. 'Victims of our [own] credulity and indulgence for fourteen years', it reads; 'defeated not by French armies but the pathetic eloquence of their agents' proclamations' (Haiti 2006: 189). While vowing to 'put to death anyone born French whose profane foot soils the land of liberty', the Declaration simultaneously warns against a 'missionary spirit' that would see the new nation attempt to give laws to its neighbours. 'Fortunate to have never known the ideals that have destroyed us', reads a devastating passage, 'they can only have good wishes for our prosperity' (190). Sadly, the same cannot be said of the rest of the world. Once more, the ideals of human rights are destroying Haiti, as they are mobilised to justify the political dispossession of the mass of the population (Hallward 2007). As the 'campaign to re-pacify the people' continues, the events of the Haitian Revolution continue to exert a claim on us, an exigency to which we should respond. To reinsert the Haitian Revolution into the narrative of the Enlightenment and the story of human rights cannot simply be to assign it a place in the history books. As Susan Buck-Morss notes, if we can salvage the historical facts about freedom from the narrative of the victors, then 'the project of universal freedom does not need to be discarded but, rather, redeemed and reconstituted on a different basis' (Buck-Morss 2000: 864). To focus on the other possibilities brought into the world by the slaves of San Domingue is thus to demand that they remain possible for us today.

References

Adorno, T. (1983), *Negative Dialectics*. London: Continuum.
AFP (2010) 'Chavez, Morales Claim US Using Relief Effort to Invade Haiti', *Terra Daily*, 21 January, available at http://www.terradaily.com/afp/100121032957.8nobh6hg.html, accessed 26 September 2011.
Agamben, G. (1998), *Homo Sacer: Sovereign Power and Bare Life*, trans. D. Heller-Roazen. Stanford: Stanford University Press.
—(2004), *The Open: Man and Animal*, trans. K. Attell. Stanford: Stanford University Press.

—(2005), *The Time That Remains: A Commentary on the Letter to the Romans*, trans. P. Dailey. Stanford: Stanford University Press.

Arendt, H. (1958), *The Human Condition*. Chicago: University of Chicago Press.

Benjamin, W. (2003), 'On the Concept of History', in H. Eiland and M. W. Jennings (eds), *Walter Benjamin: Selected Writings Vol. 4*. Cambridge, MA: Harvard University Press, 389–400.

Brubaker, W. R. (1989), 'The French Revolution and the Invention of Citizenship', *French Politics and Society*, 7(3): 30–49.

Buck-Morss, S. (2000), 'Hegel and Haiti', *Critical Inquiry*, 26(4): 821–65.

Clemens, J. (2011), 'The Slave, the Fable', in G. Reifart and P. Morrissey (eds), *Aesopic Voices*. Newcastle: Cambridge Scholars Press.

Council of the Five Hundred (2006), 'Law on the Colonies, 1798', in L. Dubois and J. D. Garrigus, *Slave Revolution in the Caribbean 1789–1804: A Brief History with Documents*. New York: Palgrave Macmillan, 153–5.

Dubois, L. (2006), 'An Enslaved Enlightenment', *Social History*, 31(1): 1–14.

— and J. D. Garrigus (eds) (2006), *Slave Revolution in the Caribbean 1789–1804: A Brief History with Documents*. New York: Palgrave Macmillan.

Haiti (2006), 'Declaration of Independence, 1794', in L. Dubois and J. D. Garrigus, *Slave Revolution in the Caribbean 1789–1804: A Brief History with Documents*. New York: Palgrave Macmillan, 188–90.

Hallward, P. (2007), *Damming the Flood: Haiti, Aristide, and the Politics of Containment*. London and New York: Verso.

—(2009), 'The Will of the People: Notes Toward a Dialectical Voluntarism', *Radical Philosophy*, 155: 17–29.

Heidegger, M. (1999), *Contributions to Philosophy (From Enowning)*, trans. P. Emad and K. Maley. Bloomington: Indiana University Press.

Hunt, L. (2007), *Inventing Human Rights: A History*. New York: W. W. Norton.

James, C. L. R. (1989), *The Black Jacobins: Toussaint L'Ouverture and the San Domingo Revolution*. New York: Vintage Books.

Kristoff, M. and L. Panarelli (2010), 'Haiti: A Republic of NGOs?', United States Institute of Peace, Peace Brief 23, 26 April, available at http://www.usip.org/publications/haiti-republic-ngos, accessed 26 September 2011.

Laveaux, E. (2006), 'A Celebration of the Anniversary of Abolition', in L. Dubois and J. D. Garrigus (eds), *Slave Revolution in the Caribbean*

1789–1804: A Brief History with Documents. New York: Palgrave Macmillan, 156–8.

Leclerc, P. (2006), 'Letter to Bonaparte, October 7, 1802', in L. Dubois and J. D. Garrigus (eds), *Slave Revolution in the Caribbean 1789–1804: A Brief History with Documents.* New York: Palgrave Macmillan, 179–80.

Marx, K. (1990), *Capital: A Critique of Political Economy, Vol.1,* trans. B. Fowkes. London: Penguin Classics.

Moyn, S. (2010), *The Last Utopia: Human Rights in History.* Cambridge, MA: Harvard University Press.

Nancy, J. L. (1993), 'Abandoned Being', in *The Birth to Presence,* trans. B. Holmes. Stanford: Stanford University Press, 36–47.

National Convention (2006) 'The Abolition of Slavery', 4 February 1794, in L. Dubois and J. D. Garrigus, *Slave Revolution in the Caribbean 1789–1804: A Brief History with Documents.* New York: Palgrave Macmillan, 129–32.

Rosenberg, A. (1930), 'Introduction' to *The Myth of the Twentieth Century An Evaluation of the Spiritual Intellectual Confrontations of Our Age,* available at http://www.gnosticliberationfront.com/myth_of_the_20th_century.htm#perface, accessed 26 September 2011.

Sala-Molins, L. (2006), *Dark Side of the Light: Slavery and the French Enlightenment.* Minneapolis: University of Minnesota Press.

Sonthonax, L. F. (2006), 'Decree of General Liberty, August 29, 1793', in L. Dubois and J. D. Garrigus, *Slave Revolution in the Caribbean 1789–1804: A Brief History with Documents.* New York: Palgrave Macmillan, 120–4.

Vergès, F. (1999), 'Colonizing Citizenship', *Radical Philosophy,* 95: 7.

Whyte, J. (2009), 'Particular Rights and Absolute Wrongs: Giorgio Agamben on Life and Politics', *Law and Critique,* 20: 147–61.

Zengerle, P. and J. Frank (2010), 'Haiti Pleads for Better Aid Effort', Reuters, 27 January, available at http://www.reuters.com/article/2010/01/27/idUSN27191132._CH_.2400, accessed 26 September 2011.

Notes

My thanks go to Justin Clemens and Adam Bartlett, who read and provided incisive feedback on an earlier draft of this chapter.

1. The logic of rights, Hunt (2007) argues, operates according to a 'conceivability scale', such that granting rights to one group creates

momentum for the rights of those who fall below them on the scale.

2. As I have argued elsewhere, while Agamben sees the Declaration of the Rights of Man and Citizen as enmeshing life in the realm of sovereign power, and sees this as a process that has intensified up to the present, unlike Adorno and Horkheimer he is not pessimistic about this development. Rather, in the biopolitical unification of life and politics, he sees the possibility of what he terms 'form-of-life', in which life could not be separated from its form (Whyte 2009).

3. The French Commissioners who initially declared the abolition of slavery on the island, prior to the vote of the Convention, stressed, in no uncertain terms, that the end of slavery must not be the end of labour, or even of forced labour. Léger Félicité Sonthonax's 'Decree of General Liberty', issued on 29 August 1793, warned in the starkest terms, 'do not think that the liberty that you will enjoy means laziness and inactivity. In France, everyone is free and everyone works; in Saint-Domingue under the same laws, you will follow the same model.' The Decree stipulated that 'nègres currently working on the plantations of their former masters are required to remain there', and introduced penalties, up to imprisonment and forced labour, for vagrants (Sonthonax 2006: 122–4). Here we are reminded of those 'bloody laws against the expropriated' detailed by Marx in *Capital*, which mobilised the utmost brutality in order to create the 'free' labour force required during the primitive accumulation of capital (Marx 1990: 896–911).

4. Martin Heidegger, an important influence on both Agamben and Nancy, uses the term abandonment (*Seinsverlassenheit*) to refer to the abandonment of beings (including human beings) by Being (Heidegger 1999).

5. In 'The Slave, the Fable', Justin Clemens (2011) provides a brilliant analysis of the way the 'irreducible "torturability" of slaves' conditions a form of discourse, the Aesopic, that must constantly dissimulate, pretending to speak of something else, in order to evade the constant threat of torture. In a similar vein, in *The Black Jacobins*, James (1989) suggests that the slaves of San Domingue accommodated themselves to the unceasing brutality of their lives by adopting a 'wooden stupidity before their masters' (15), and speaking as if they knew nothing. As an example, he writes of the slave, who denies stealing a pigeon, which is then found in his shirt, 'Well, well, look at that pigeon', he responded. 'It take my shirt for a nest' (15). While the Aesopic, as Clemens notes, speaks of animals, when really speaking of

people, James recounts a counter-example, which speaks volumes of
the way in which slaves were regarded in the colony. When a planter
asked a slave why he mistreated his mule, the slave responded, 'But
when I do not work, I am beaten, when he does not work, I beat him –
he is my Negro' (15). The 'stupidity' of the slaves before their masters,
James suggests, enabled the latter to assume that indeed these slaves
were, in the words of the Governor of Martinique, 'true beasts' (17).
It is therefore with real shock that those who chanced to see the slaves
apart from their masters responded to the 'dual personality' they
witnessed (18). James cites De Wimpffen, 'an exceptionally observant
and able traveller', who writes, 'One has to hear with what warmth
and what volubility, and at the same time with what precision of ideas
and accuracy of judgment, this creature, heavy and taciturn all day,
now squatting before his fire, tells stories, talks, gesticulates, argues,
passes opinions, approves or condemns both his master and everyone
who surrounds him' (16). In the course of the Revolution, it is notable
that the slaves no longer had recourse to this 'split personality', or
to the 'wooden stupidity' which had previously characterised their
interactions with their masters. Instead, they spoke openly of liberty
and equality, much to the chagrin of their former masters, and they
proclaimed their willingness to risk death in battle, rather than be
returned to slavery and the threat of torture to which it constantly
subjected them. Clemens notes that the Aesopic is a resource of the
weak. The slaves of San Domingue, they who defeated Napoleon's
army, were no longer weak.

6. Hunt suggests we must ensure that the human of human rights contains none of the ambiguities of the man of the rights of man.

7. As Louis Sala-Molins has stressed, a similar conjuring trick served to
justify French colonialism into the twentieth century: 'French colonization', wrote Sarraut in 1923, 'is essentially a creation of humanity,
a universal enrichment.' See Sala-Molins (2006: 99).

8. I owe this observation to David Ottina.

12

Potential Postcoloniality: Sacred Life, Profanation and the Coming Community

Simone Bignall

Australia comprises a settler society that has never undergone a formal process of decolonisation or treaty with its indigenous peoples. Nonetheless, the sovereign rule of the imposed power is far from confident and often appears anxious and fretful. The ongoing colonial dispossession of Australia's Aboriginal peoples destabilises the security of the settler consciousness and the cohesiveness of the national culture, challenging the self-evidential legitimacy and uniform authority of the transplanted sovereign power. Consequently, the nation-state of Australia must perpetually seek to (re-)establish itself as legitimate, undivided and unchallenged. One example of this ongoing effort to assert sovereign control and impose a measure of coherence over the 'forms of life' defining the Australian nation occurred in 2007, when the Federal Government declared a state of emergency, ostensibly with respect to the dire living conditions and issues of child abuse affecting Aboriginal communities in the Northern Territory. In the wake of the emergency suspension of universal legal and civil protections, the state imposed an extraordinary policy of intervention in the collectivist governing structures and cultures of these communities. This action aimed to 'protect' indigenous individuals by 'normalising' their collectivist forms of life, bringing them more closely in line with individualist principles of capitalist liberalism and in accordance with the dominant Australian *bios*. This event affirmed the self-preserving tendency of the colonial apparatus to (re-)establish itself through processes that reiterate the political structure and set of relations begun with the original event of the sovereign imposition. Accordingly, this latest effort to assert control over the lives and cultures of indigenous peoples reopened a space for critical public discussion about 'the time of the postcolonial' in Australia. This chapter engages with the neo-colonialism that has long troubled notions of 'postcolonial' temporality (for example, Hall 1996; Shohat 1992; McClintock 1992). The first part of the discussion employs Agamben's concepts of '*homo sacer*' and the 'sovereign exception' in order to explore some of the ways in which the expansive spatialising practices of sovereignty converge with disciplinary political technologies to produce contemporary colonial 'relations of ban'. The second section turns to Agamben's recent writings on method in order to discern the potential for a more positive, transformative and future-oriented political sensibility within his work. Finally, his writing on 'whatever being' and the 'coming community' is assessed with respect to its potential for enabling a new use of political concepts, which might assist in the task of theorising the postcolonial as a potential form of political community.

Little Children are Sacred

In Australia in 2006, the Northern Territory (NT) Government created a Board of Inquiry to investigate and report on allegations of sexual abuse of Aboriginal children living on remote communities within the Territory's jurisdiction. The Board was to recommend how the NT Government can effectively support communities in the tasks of tackling and preventing child sexual abuse. The resulting report was titled *Ampe Akelyernemane Meke Mekarle: 'Little Children are Sacred'* (Wild and Anderson 2007). Upon release, it immediately became the reference point for a national 'state of emergency', declared by the Commonwealth Government during the pre-election period in June 2007. The introduction of special measures of governmental intervention were applied to all people living in remote NT Aboriginal communities; the police and army were mobilised to help facilitate the implementation of the measures. The three bills containing the emergency response legislation were tabled in parliament with a haste that was remarkable, considering the long history of government neglect and lack of political response to the many previous calls for action to address the social issues at the heart of the *Little Children are Sacred* report (see Behrendt 2007). While Aboriginal communities living in the remote NT cautiously welcomed the prospect of new legislation targeting widespread social problems, with the tabling of the legislation it became apparent that there was a political intent in the measures that clearly exceeded the state's concern with the problem of child sexual abuse. The emergency measures included amendments to the Aboriginal Land Rights (NT) Act 1976, allowing the Commonwealth to take control of the communities through compulsory acquisition of town leases and the abolition of the permit system by which Aboriginal communities maintain control of access to their lands. A week before the intervention was announced, the Commonwealth Government had presented a proposal to the Central Land Council offering basic housing repairs in exchange for the lease back of Aboriginal land. The Council had rejected this offer, 'saying that the people concerned did not want to sacrifice their land, especially for basic infrastructure, which should not be bartered for by government' (Behrendt 2007: 16). These elements suggest that the government was using the *Little Children are Sacred* report as a pretext to 'act on its wider aspirations: in particular, to undermine the kin-based forms of ownership that characterise Aboriginal land title, and to substitute these with individual forms' (Hinkson 2007: 3).

Overall, the measures enabled the government to exert an extraordinary degree of control over Aboriginal life in the NT townships. They were applied indiscriminately to all residents: determining how welfare payments may be spent and making welfare payments contingent upon children's school attendance; controlling access to goods and services; conferring extra powers of police to enter private property without warrant when an Aboriginal person is believed to be affected by alcohol; requiring that detailed records be kept for three years of all users of computers purchased with government funds; and mandating compulsory participation in the 'Work for the Dole' scheme, which makes payment of unemployment pension benefits contingent upon recipients undertaking 'voluntary' labour. Beyond these measures of state intervention in the conventionally private sphere of habitation and individual choices concerning personal action, the legislation also conferred upon the Commonwealth significant powers to intervene in – or to suspend – existing structures of Aboriginal self-determination and community governance. These included the power of government to vary or terminate funding agreements; to specify how funding will be spent; to oversee local governing processes; to supervise and control community councils; to assess and appoint community store managers; and to exclude any person, including a traditional owner, from land compulsorily leased back to government (Hinkson 2007: 3–4). The legislation was thus drafted without due attention to the primary recommendations made by the Board of Inquiry in its report: that Aboriginal leaders in the affected communities be properly consulted with respect to the design of initiatives to address the problem of child sexual abuse; and that the major role of government should be to support community ownership of the suggested means for solving child abuse (Wild 2007: 116).

Agamben's works on *homo sacer* and the biopolitical management of 'bare life' (1998), the 'camp' as the exemplary space of exception (1998), and the sovereign decision that issues the state of exception (2005a), each are relevant in thinking about these recent events in Australian colonialism, reminding us that 'the colony represents the site where sovereignty consists fundamentally in the exercise of a power outside of the law' (Mbembe 2003: 23). However, the position of indigenous peoples within the settler-state presents a 'peculiar' situation of contested sovereignty, which calls for a revision – or an expanded interpretation – of Agamben's core concepts. Mark Rifkin claims that 'indigenising Agamben' enables analysis of the ways 'settler-states regulate not only proper kinds of embodiment ("bare life") but also legitimate modes of collectivity and occupancy [. . . as . . .] *bare habitance*' (Rifkin 2009: 90). That is, this form of colonisation not only brought indigenous *individuals* into a new (exceptional) relationship with a foreign ruling power and a nation of settler colonists; it also involved the radical transformation of indigenous *collectives* as distinct forms of life. This was brought about by the wilful displacement and dispersal of indigenous peoples from their ancestral countries, resulting in the destruction of forms of nomadic life as well as the erosion of kinship and governance systems. Colonisation further aimed to replace collectivist indigenous forms of life with naturalised Western modes of individualist political subjectivity. While these colonial strategies have always met with indigenous resistance, the imposed power has had some success in dismantling communities through policies of dispersal and displacement. However, state action directed towards the cultural replacement of collectivist forms of life through ideologies of individualisation has been much less triumphant. This is especially the case in the remote NT, where many indigenous communities retain their connection to ancestral territories and their collectivist modes of life.

As a result, in Australia as in other settler societies, the 'lingering presence of Aboriginal people[s] threatens the White imaginary of the nation' (Gulson and Parkes 2010: 308; see also Moran 2002); the settler state repeatedly must reiterate the original event of its sovereignty (itself an event marked by uncertainty) in order to assert its contemporary legitimacy. In 1992, in the benchmark case *Mabo v Queensland (no. 2)*, the Australian High Court for the first time recognised native title, thereby acknowledging the ongoing presence of indigenous Australians as 'peoples' within the nation and dispelling the colonial myth of *terra nullius*. In acknowledging the fact of original inhabitancy and associated indigenous entitlement to land deriving from indigenous polities, *Mabo* acknowledged the fact of political plurality at the original moment of the sovereign imposition. However, it immediately effaced the contemporary political implications of this recognition of original pluralism, by claiming its inability to rule on the historical legality of the sovereign act of state upon which its juridical power rests. In so doing, the Court placed itself (in respect of its power to judge the legality of its colonial origins) 'outside' law, in an exception that justified its refusal to treat Aboriginal law and community as evidence of the continuing existence of sovereign entities with distinct rights to self-determination. In fact, *Mabo* reinscribed a uniform conception of sovereignty and an absolute measure of inclusion in the national community, privileging individualistic notions of a proprietary relationship to land (Motha 2002). Furthermore, the power to decide upon indigenous identification as a basis for contemporary native title holdings was brought within the jurisdiction of the state, which therefore was reinvested with the power to decide on the existence and continuity of Aboriginal peoples and the relevance of this identification in matters of just entitlement. Instead of following through with the pluralist implications that the rejection of *terra nullius* implied with respect to the 'original *dis-position* of law, nation and community' (Motha 2002: 313), in its *Mabo* decision the High Court affirmed a conception of the political that retained but one sovereign source of community and law, and thus it repeated the original sovereign violence of colonisation even while inscribing the difference of native title. As Stewart Motha points out, 'in *Mabo*, the sovereign event [is] repeated with a difference that is projected back as having always already been in existence' (317), and thus is not permitted to challenge the sovereignty of the contemporary Australian state.

The state's effort to retain and reassert principles of sovereign indivisibility and national uniformity (thus reiterating the original basis of its legitimacy) is similarly exercised in a whole range of 'policy incursions', which impact upon indigenous Australians, reinscribing them as 'objects of state policy which attempts to erase collective identities and to constitute Aboriginal peoples, through reconfigured land relations, as "normalised" individualised subjects of the State' (Gulson and Parkes 2010: 311). The NT intervention can be seen as one such 'incursion'. Employing 'crisis rhetoric' to create a perception of urgency and a situation in which it appears acceptable to suspend citizen rights,[1] the intervention policy was notable not only in sanctioning extreme forms of biopolitical management bearing upon individual activities, but also in the way it constituted a series of 'hostile moves into Aboriginal symbolic and material territory' (310). This is particularly evident in the amendments made to the Aboriginal Land Rights (NT) Act 1976. The permit and lease system is important because it allows some measure of self-determination to Aboriginal communities, who can exercise a collective power to control access to traditional territories. The government's expressed rationale for changing the collective structure of the landholding was that 'normalisation' is necessary to protect children from harm. Here, the process of 'normalisation' apparently works by eroding existing measures protecting collective relationships to land and, in the process, destroying the collective territorial basis of indigenous structures of community governance. Accordingly, the state of exception not only was created in the NT to facilitate the state's biopolitical management of the lives of indigenous individuals, but also involved the policy management of 'bare habitance' in order to compel a change in collective 'forms of life'. The aim of the intervention was to 'normalise' Aboriginal *society* by 'individualising' it and instilling private ownership of property as a regulatory principle for indigenous Australians to aspire to, just as 'normal' Australians do. Accordingly, as Gulson and Parkes explain:

> These policy incursions, undertaken within a settler nation that has never negotiated treaties with Aboriginal peoples, underpinned by market logics, and drawing on the exploitation of a 'crisis', contribute towards the reinscription of white imaginaries in the histories and geographies [of neo-colonial Australia]. (Gulson and Parkes 2010: 310)

In fact, from the perspective of many of those affected, the government's avowed plan to 'stabilise, normalise and exit' remote NT communities by means of a state of exception betrayed a 'clear intent: to bring to an end the recognition of, and support for, Aboriginal people living in remote communities pursuing culturally distinctive ways of life' (Hinkson 2007: 5).

How might we understand the significance of the 'sacred child' as a frame of reference for the NT 'policy incursion'? It is important to note that the title of the *Little Children are Sacred* report is derived from evidence given to the Inquiry by a senior Yolngu law man: 'In our Law children are very sacred because they carry the two spring wells of water from our country within them.' This suggests that there are different kinds of cultural significance attached to sacred being, which may be employed variously in political manoeuvring around questions of sovereignty and communal identity. Agamben explains that, in Western traditions, the specificity of *homo sacer* lies in 'the unpunishability of his killing and the ban on his sacrifice'. Accordingly, he meditates on the question: 'What, then, is the life of *homo sacer*, if it is situated at the intersection of a capacity to be killed and yet not sacrificed, outside both human and divine law?' (Agamben 1998: 73). From the perspective of indigenous ontology, however, sacred being is situated *within divine Law, which is also at the same time the human Law* of Aboriginal society. Little children are sacred because they have a place in the natural order of things, as specified by ancestral Laws of creation that are intimately connected to country and which also structure the social realm of Aboriginal Law that regulates relationships between individuals, communities and territory.[2] The 'sacred being' that is the subject of Agamben's question is not easily identified with indigenous Australian concepts of law and religion, which do not separate the sacred from the profane.

Agamben repeatedly insists that his work concerns the expression of a particular, *Western* political framework in which 'life is sacred only insofar as it is taken into the sovereign exception' (Agamben 1998: 85). However, this qualification of his analytic perspective does little to obviate the continuing, insidious dominance of Western paradigms of analysis in globalised culture; nor does it prevent their spurious universalisation in colonial situations that require the imposed cultural power to exercise a strategic blindness to alternative epistemologies and ontological

traditions. In fact, the declaration of the state of exception in the
NT was predicated on the appropriation of an indigenous assertion that 'children are sacred', but the meaning of their sacred
nature was reductively interpreted with respect to the Western
notion of *sacratio* as described by Agamben:

> sacredness is [. . .] the originary form of the inclusion of bare life in
> the juridical order, and the syntagm *homo sacer* names something like
> the originary 'political' relation, which is to say, bare life insofar as it
> operates in an inclusive exclusion as the referent of the sovereign deci-
> sion. (Agamben 1998: 85)

Nonetheless, it is clear that the Australian Federal Government,
in deciding the state of exception in the NT, did not 'abandon'
the naked life of the 'sacred children' to sanction their abuse or
killing with impunity; the intervention was instead justified by
discourses of child protection and 'public mourning' over the
harm suffered by children (cf. Agamben 2005a: 65–73; also Butler
2004). What then, is the significance, for the Australian state, of
the sacred indigenous child, if sacred being is 'situated at the intersection of a capacity to be killed and yet not sacrificed, outside
both human and divine law'? If the life of this child may not be
taken with impunity, then what aspect of this sacred child may be
'killed'? In light of the 'normalising' legislation aimed at under-
mining indigenous structures of self-determination and culturally
distinct, collective ways of life based in legal and social traditions
intimately connected to country, it seems uncomfortably obvious
that the target of the state's action was the collective cultural existence of indigeneity per se. While the 'naked life' of indigenous
individuals was brought into an ambiguous relation of inclusive
exclusion with the state as an effect of the emergency legislation,
this biopolitical technique was mobilised in the service of a wider
cultural and political objective. In enforcing the state of exception, the implicit aim of the sovereign state was to abandon the
communal nature of Aboriginal life in the camps (and the threat
of indigenous self-determination or 'sovereignty' it hints at) to 'a
kind of violence that is all the more effective for being anonymous
and quotidian' (Agamben 2000: 112). Aboriginal 'sovereignty'
(and native title) may be 'extinguished' with impunity, when traditional structures of collective governance and the means to pursue
culturally distinct ways of life are abandoned without protection,

paving the way for their erosion and eradication at the imperial hand of settler-nationalist state violence. The colonisation of Aboriginal Australians thus continues in contemporary (yet hardly more subtle) forms of cultural and political annihilation, sanctioned here by the sovereign imposition of a state of exception and framed by spurious discourses of 'protection'.

It seems possible to concede that '[Western] *sacer esto* is [. . .] the originary political formulation of the imposition of the [Western] sovereign bond' (Agamben 1998: 85). It also perhaps is reasonable to say that, universally, 'sacred life is in some way tied to a political function' and that 'from the beginning sacred life has an eminently political character and exhibits an essential link with the terrain on which sovereign power is founded' (100). In fact, the case of the 'sacred children' at the heart of the NT intervention indicates that in situations of contested sovereignty, or in situations where the concept of the political as being fundamentally reliant upon a claim to sovereignty is challenged by alternative understandings of power (see Muldoon 2008), sacred life can become the figure around which assertions of sovereignty revolve. Here, the sacred child is not only a Western figure placed 'outside both divine and human law' in a state of exclusive inclusion that defines its relation to the sovereign power of the colonial state; it also figures at the heart of claims affirming that a form of indigenous sovereignty survives in the independent and culturally distinct legal traditions of Aboriginal nations. These traditions do not separate the sacred from the profane and continue to exist as forms of life that currently are not recognised or protected by the state; they are subsumed within the unitary and indivisible form of Australian sovereignty and the dominant national *bios*. 'Policy incursions' such as the NT intervention support the nation's reinvestment in single and indivisible concepts of sovereign power and, consequently, in the reiteration of colonialism in Australia. Indigenous conceptual and material geographies are devalued and violated by the intervention measures: collective structures of governance are disempowered, leaving little room for recognition of the forms of indigenous sovereignty exercised through pre-existing structures of self-determination, nor for the pursuit of indigeneity as a culturally distinct way of life that is valued within the social imaginary of the nation. Like previous colonial processes and policies of displacement and dispossession, the intervention utilises a restrictive form of social control, leading to the erosion or eradication of collective forms of life and, consequently, to indigenous 'placelessness' within the Australian nation (see Havemann 2005; Watson 2009).

However, the contested nature of colonial state sovereignty signals a potential for transformative resistance and the inauguration of the genuinely 'postcolonial' forms of justice and social existence that were gestured towards (yet immediately abandoned) by the Australian High Court in its *Mabo* decision. While we easily can recognise the force of Agamben's concepts in thinking about exemplary experiences and operations of modern power in general, and can situate this analysis within the context of historical and contemporary practices of colonialism in Australia and elsewhere, the ways in which we may mobilise Agamben's work in the service of a transformative and future-oriented politics are poorly understood unless we also attend to his writings on method and temporality. The following sections consider some of the less prominent aspects of Agamben's work, to assess whether these can assist contemporary efforts to think about postcolonial futures.

The Time of the Now

Taken together, Agamben's recently published essays on the 'apparatus' (2009a), the 'paradigm' (2009b) and the 'contemporary' (2009c) help to explain not only his analysis of Foucault's use of these concepts, but also his own philosophical and political points of departure and his long-term methodological orientation, evident from his earliest writings on language and ontology. In the first of these essays (on the 'apparatus' or '*dispositif*'), Agamben notes that in Foucault's early writings, the use of the term 'positivity' generally 'presages the notion of apparatus' (Agamben 2009a: 5). For Foucault, 'positivity' refers to 'the historical element' that is 'the set of institutions, of processes of subjectification and of rules in which power relations become concrete' (6). In other words, the 'positivity' of a society describes its current characteristic structures of meaningful practice, together with the political technologies that constrain individuals to act within these common-sense structures. The 'apparatus' is, then, the network of political technologies that operate upon bodies; it is the 'set of practices and mechanisms (both linguistic and non-linguistic, juridical, technical and military) that aim to face an urgent need and to obtain an effect that is more or less immediate' (8). This 'immediate effect'

is precisely the ordering of the positivity in any given moment
of time to produce a particular configuration of the present; it is
the organisation of unruly elements in the broadly universalis-
ing structures and classifications that render a society *temporally*
consistent. In Australia, the NT intervention constitutes a crucial
aspect of the apparatus that operates to render the nation consistent. The *dispositif* is thus an economy of spatio-temporal order: it
is a 'set of practices, bodies of knowledge, measures and institutions that aim to manage, govern, control and orient – in a way
that purports to be useful – the behaviours, gestures and thoughts
of human beings', rendering them immediately manageable in a
given social space at a particular moment in time (12).

Accordingly, the notion of 'positivity' or of 'apparatus' is connected to a notion of temporality, and more precisely, to a notion
of being in the time of the present, or to a present mode of being.
It is this temporality of the *dispositif* that Agamben interrogates
in his essay on 'the contemporary' (2009c). While Agamben's
other writings on 'the time of the now' draw particularly from
Heidegger, from Walter Benjamin's theses on history and from
the conceptualisation of messianic time expressed in Paul's *Letter
to the Romans* (see Agamben 1993a; 2005b), here he references
Nietzsche's comments on the 'untimely meditation' as a method
of taking a critical position with regard to the present (as the
material and temporal context that one inhabits and in which one
thinks). Accordingly, he defines contemporariness as 'a singular
relationship with one's own time, which adheres to it and, at the
same time, keeps a distance from it' (Agamben 2009c: 41). The
task of the contemporary thinker is to execute a disjunctive relationship with the present – to avoid coinciding too perfectly with
one's own time – in order to hold one's gaze firmly upon the epoch
and so to understand its foibles and its disabilities, its limitations
and its modes of constraint. To be contemporary is at once to
inhabit the present time in which one lives, and simultaneously to
'shatter' it; to attend to the possibility of developmental fracture
in the path that leads to the present era and that consequently
'displays its demented face' (43). In this way, the contemporary is
a person

> who firmly holds his gaze on his own time so as to perceive not its
> light, but its darkness. All eras, for those who experience contempo-
> rariness, are obscure. The contemporary is precisely the person who

knows how to see this obscurity, who is able to write by dipping his pen in the obscurity of the present. (Agamben 2009c: 44)

Perhaps more significantly, the contemporary is an individual who recognises in the darkness of the present era, those aspects of the present that remain virtual and potential: these constitute a 'light that strives to reach us but cannot' (Agamben 2009c: 46). The darkness of the present is 'nothing other than this unlived element in everything that is lived [. . .] to be contemporary means in this sense to return to a present where we have never been' (51–2).

In this respect, the method of the contemporary thinker is described by Agamben (following Foucault) as 'philosophical archaeology' (Agamben 2009d). Primarily addressed to the self-evidential traditions that constitute and characterise apparatuses, philosophical archaeology involves a critical 'destruction of tradition' (88). It is a science of extracting from the ruins of the present 'what could or ought to have been given and perhaps one day might be' (82). Philosophical archaeology thus seeks the 'prehistory' in history: it traces the emergence of a tradition and confronts the freezing of tradition in self-evidential forms, in order to enable 'the return to the past [. . .] which coincides with a renewed access to the sources' (88). A 'philosophical archaeology' of the NT intervention might thus reveal how the current mobilisation of this disciplinary apparatus relies upon old assumptions about the 'placelessness' of Aboriginal governance and sovereignty within the nation and upon archaic misconceptions concerning indigenous society that were imposed at colonisation. Despite their destabilisation at the time of the High Court's *Mabo* judgment, these assumptions continue to influence the present positivity that is Australian national life. 'Renewed access' to the constitutive colonial source of the discourses and understandings behind the NT intervention provides an opportunity to critically reject the continuing influence of the colonial order, and to constructively conceive of a new ordering of national life according to an alternative postcolonial principle of organisation.

However, the self-evident quality of the present that is lived entails that the philosophical archaeologist must struggle against the 'constitutive inaccessibility' of the origins of present tradition; he or she must strive to be contemporary in order to discern the repressed origins of the present, which persist in the obscure or dark forms of repressed 'unlived experience' that characterise any given socio-political arrangement. Philosophical archaeology therefore not only is concerned with historical memory, engaging a genealogical effort to 'remember' how the present has emerged through a series of constitutive events; it also is preoccupied with the willed forgetfulness that is crucial to the establishment of tradition, insofar as its self-evidential character 'determines the very status of the knowing subject' (87). In returning to the origins or source of the traditions that characterise a present arrangement, archaeology attends to the way in which the

> moment of uprising is objective and subjective at the same time and is indeed situated on a threshold of undecidability between object and subject. It is never the emergence of the fact without at the same time being the emergence of the knowing subject itself: the operation on the origin is at the same time an operation on the subject. (Agamben 2009d: 89)

In drawing attention to the *undecidability* at the source, the philosophical archaeologist destabilises the knowing subject by making visible the ways in which the *unexperienced* aspects of history

> give shape and consistency to the fabric of the psychic personality and historical tradition and ensures their continuity and consistency. And it does so in the form of the phantasms, desires and obscure drives that ceaselessly push at the threshold of consciousness. (Agamben 2009d: 101)

In this way, archaeology is a method of gaining access to a subject that never has been and a past that has not been lived through – and therefore is not actually or historically past, but rather remains virtually present, constituting the present like a kind of 'dark matter' (Agamben 2009d: 102). This renewed access to the ambivalence at the origin or source of a historical emergence, and to those constitutive aspects of the lived present that have been repressed by dominant tradition and so remain unlived or obscure, then provides new scope for a different act of subjective interpretation and an alternative reconstitution of the future-present. This, then, is the task of the contemporary, who is not only the one who, perceiving the darkness of the present, grasps a light that can never reach its destiny; he is also the one who, dividing and interpolating time, is capable of transforming it and putting it in relation with other times [. . .] It is as if this invisible light that is the darkness of the present cast its shadow on the past, so that the past, touched by this shadow, acquired the ability to respond to the darkness of the now. (Agamben 2009c: 53)

It is as a contemporary thinker or a philosophical archaeologist that Agamben seeks to 'situate apparatuses in a new context' (Agamben 2009a: 13), which explores new ways of confronting apparatuses rather than emphasising their operation in the production and management of docile bodies. As a way of bringing about this development, Agamben proposes 'nothing less than a general and massive partitioning of beings into two large groups or classes: on the one hand, living beings (or substances), and on the other, apparatuses in which living beings are incessantly captured' (13).[3] In-between these two opposing classes of 'ontological life' and 'power that captures' lies a third realm: that of the subject. In occupying the middle space that negotiates the processes of life and power, subjects are not simply opposed to the apparatuses that capture and constrain them. In fact, as much as the subject is a mode of desire or will that contests the limiting structures of the apparatus, equally it is constituted by the dispositional power of the apparatus, which captures and channels subjective desire in order to define distinct modes of human being as 'forms of life'. Accordingly, Agamben asserts: 'what we are dealing with here is the liberation of that which remains captured and separated by means of apparatuses, in order to bring it back to a possible common use' (17). In other words, Agamben seeks to 'make profane', to restore to common use, that human subjectivity which has been separated from the realm of human life and captured in the apparatuses of sovereign power and the modern disciplinary (and colonial) traditions they support (see Agamben 2007). It is this notion of the subject as a relentless movement of subjectivation and desubjectivation, taking place in the interstitial space between the bare life of bodies and the apparatuses that constrain and order them, that Agamben hopes will provide new possibilities for transforming 'the historical element' that is the present arrangement of social life. In the act of the profanation of the subject, Agamben sees a way of bringing about a shift in the exclusionary social structures (exemplified by the sovereign ban and the figure of *homo sacer*) in which modern life increasingly is captured. Arguably, his theorisation of 'whatever being' and the 'coming community' – those 'obscure' or 'dark' forms of existence, barely perceptible in our present modes of political thought – are proposed with this transformative ambition in mind. The following section offers a critical assessment of the postcolonial potential of these concepts, in the context of the recent interventionist action of the Australian State upon indigenous communities.

Postcoloniality and the Coming Community

The Australian government's exceptional policy decision to 'stabilise, normalise and exit' remote indigenous communities in the NT marked an exemplary exercise of colonial power as a 'process of ordering space and its inhabitants and temporality' (Rajaram 2006: 475). Colonisation has long been analysed as a political technology involving the mapping, fencing and dispersal of existing nations into ghettos, camps and reserves, thus producing a 'classificatory grid' that is temporally static and operates as a 'stable base against which identity, phenomena and experience in the colony could be understood' (476). As we have seen, the current Australian policy of intervention in NT Aboriginal societies aims at the disciplinary management of indigenous bodies and their collective modes of living. However, as Prem Rajaram points out, the political management of national space not only is a tangible demonstration of the sovereign power of a state in a *present* or currently existing capacity to order national space so as to reinforce uniform conceptualisations of national identity and modes of political belonging; it also operates as a way of orienting, directing and controlling social futures. When groups within the nation threaten to pursue culturally distinct trajectories and so to break away from the predictable path mapped out by a uniform and undivided sovereign control extending unbroken into the time of the future, the state strategically will employ dystopic images of social collapse: 'dystopia enables and vindicates the gridding of colonial space [and so] it is inherent in the identification of spaces of order that spaces of dystopia are presumed' (477).

In the Australian case, the widespread 'public mourning' over the child abuse occurring in the NT also carried an undercurrent of moral panic registering worry about the health of the national fabric. The feeling in the settler community was that if the 'nation' did not act immediately to control and limit the situation in the NT, then the entire 'Australian way of life' could be threatened, potentially sliding into a future where deviance and disorder triumph and the suffering of children is banal and systemic. On an alternative (more critical) reading of the politics of intervention, the imagined dystopia properly referred to a threatened loss of sovereign power: the intervention allowed the state to act in order to limit the independence and political efficacy of indigenous nations evidenced in alternative structures of collective life and self-determination, such as were being exercised in the remote NT Aboriginal townships. Intervening action was perceived to be necessary because the existence of these self-governing communities threatens the sovereign authority of the settler state, potentially moving Australia towards a 'chaotic' and 'divided' situation where it will need to acknowledge the existence of plural (sovereign) nations coexisting with (and within) the boundaries of the colonial nation-state. Through the aesthetic and affective device of imagined dystopia, indigenous spaces became subject to renewed 'relations of ban' resting on a sovereign politics of inclusion and exclusion, distinguishing 'those [identifications] that are deserving of protection and privileging and those that are not'; 'those that represent the desirable trajectories of history and those that are considered politically inconsequential to history' (Soguk 2007: 6).

Political identity is ascribed to an individual in terms of his or her belonging to a class by virtue of possession of a set of common features, which define the basis of inclusion to that class. For Agamben, the 'politics of ban' rests upon a power of representation, defining normative forms of politically qualified identity as 'being-called-X'. Accordingly, his political theory has an ontological dimension, in which he links law and language in a common operation: they are mechanisms 'of the division or caesura of being that generates political identities by representing forms of life' (McLoughlin 2009: 164). This division is twofold. At the level of actual political society, law and language operate to divide *bios* into distinct types of politically qualified existence, such as Jew or goy, settler or indigenous, masculine or feminine, and so forth. However, Agamben argues that the capacity of law to divide up different kinds of politically qualified life depends upon an *a priori* division of *bios* from *zoē*, of political life from bare life, and of actual or determinate being from indeterminate or potential being.

Thus, at a more profound ontological level, law and language are mechanisms for dividing politically qualified life, or *bios*, from life itself – purely potential bare life or *zoē* – thereby distinguishing a juridically determined order from an anomic political space (see McLoughlin 2009). However, Agamben argues this apolitical life is always already ambiguously implicated or included in political life, in the form of the latter's reliance upon a necessarily apolitical *a priori* state of existence, that is always also logically excluded with the act of the separation of the political. The sovereign power that issues the decision concerning political identity, as well the 'abandoned' or 'bare' life that is devoid of political identity and therefore also is stripped of power or political agency within the juridical system, accordingly sit within this 'zone of indistinction' *between* the juridical order and the anomic political space beyond legal jurisdiction.

For Agamben, law and language give representational form to being – to being in the world and to the experience of community – and the structure of determinate being emerges through the process of ontological division that law and language produce. While he is deeply critical of the effects of the ontological division between politics and life, which in modernity includes an unprecedented increase in biopolitical mechanisms of control and the expansion of sovereign powers of exception, Agamben's project does not seek to conceptualise a different structure for being, in which these political problems could not arise. Rather, he aims to identify a different way of thinking about this ontological structure of being, and in so doing, to identify a new use for it. He seeks to describe an alternative way of understanding the nature of 'being-called', a new way of experiencing existence, which is structurally oriented less towards the sovereign power of decision over political identities and normative forms of life, and more towards the potential associated with the radical indeterminacy of bare life conceptualised outside of its capture within the sovereign state of exception.

Thus, he seeks to introduce a change to present political circumstances, not by describing an alternative world to come, but by describing a different orientation to *this world*. In the alternative version of this world that Agamben invites us to access, then, 'everything will be as it is now, just a little different' (Agamben 1993b: 53). What marks this difference is a subject's capacity to cultivate an alternative relationship to the forces of life and of power, which hold him or her in permanent tension between a determined political identity and a radical potentiality or freedom to transform the significance of this identity. While the self is defined by relations of belonging to a class, which circumscribe political identification in the form of being-called-x, there always remains a potential to make use of this identity differently, or better, to employ a radically negative potentiality: to *not* be beholden to one's identity-x, to inhabit the self in such a way as if this identity-x had never developed from original indeterminacy to its lived actuality: 'In this manner, it revokes the factical condition and undermines it without altering its form' (Agamben 2005b: 24). The capacity to live one's identity 'as not' (*hōs mē*) returns to the free use of the self, the original potentiality of life and language before their capture in power and speech, thus opening up possibilities for experiencing new forms of subjectivity and community (see Agamben 2005b: 23–6).

If the (colonial) 'politics of ban' rests upon the classification and representation of an individual, a community or a cultural way of life as unworthy of protection, and so reinforces notions of exclusive belonging that privilege sovereign power of decision concerning normative forms of identification within the political community of a nation, then Agamben's theorisation of 'whatever being' and 'coming community' suggestively signal an 'outside' to this mode of politics and an alternative to normative 'forms of life'. Agamben explains that 'whatever being' is 'being such as it is; being such that it always matters' (Agamben 1993b: 1). Here, 'whatever being' first 'matters' in its singularity; it is 'being loved for its own sake, as such, not for its properties or its belonging in relation to a general category' (2). However, 'whatever being' also 'matters' in the sense that it 'takes place': '*taking-place, the communication of singularities in the attribute of extension, does not unite them in essence, but scatters them in existence*' (18, original emphasis). 'Whatever community' is then the 'being-together of existences' (68). Accordingly, Agamben considers that 'whatever' is 'exemplary': 'Neither particular nor universal, the example is a singular object that presents itself as such [. . .] not defined by any property, except by being-called [into existence]' (10). For Agamben, 'whatever' beings are pure singularities 'that communicate only in the empty space of the example, without being tied by any property, by any identity. They are expropriated of all identity, so as to appropriate belonging itself [. . .] they are the exemplars of the coming community' (11).

How, if at all, might Agamben's conceptualisations of 'whatever being' and the 'coming community' be germane to material experiences of postcolonialism? In the first instance, I would like to suggest that the characteristic feature of 'whatever' as being always loved for itself – for existing as such – is an essential starting point in postcolonial thinking. The colonial tendency to denigrate and annihilate alternative forms of life (perceived to be incommensurate with or deviant from the dominant or colonising authority) is unsettled by the notion of being valued *as such*, 'whatever' its material determination. Second, because it also 'matters' in the sense that it 'comes to be' or is 'called into being', rather than existing as essence, Agamben's conceptualisation of 'whatever' being is helpful for thinking the postcolonial because it aligns being with ethos, as '*a manner of rising forth*; not a being that is *in* this or that mode, but a being that *is* its mode of being' (Agamben 1993b: 28, original emphasis). As I have argued elsewhere, this emphasis on ethos is a crucial aspect of meaningful postcolonial transformation, which takes place only to the extent that it is materialised in practice, in an immediate mode of being and relating (Bignall 2010). Furthermore, the contingent and exemplary nature of 'whatever' being underscores a determined identity's permanent potential for transformation and its radical openness to alterity, attributes that may also be considered relevant in thinking the postcolonial as that which resists permanent capture by a dominant order of signification: '*Whatever is singularity plus empty space* [. . .] *Whatever, in this sense, is the event of an Outside*' (Agamben 1993b: 67, original emphasis). It is this '*ek-stasis*' that Agamben considers to be 'the gift that singularity gathers from the empty hands of humanity' (68). The 'experience of being-*within* an *outside*' (68, original emphasis) invests 'whatever' being with a structural undecidability at its origin, rendering it always open to reconfiguration and movements of becoming, according to performances of an alternative ethos or 'manner of rising-forth'. Inhabiting the 'empty space of the example', 'whatever' beings can be united in their permanent potential for being-called-postcolonial, rather than colonial.

However, there are also several worrying issues raised by these notions. The most obvious of these is that, for many indigenous individuals, their identification as such is only conceivable in terms of a collectivist ontology that defines their existence as 'peoples', which Agamben's emphasis on the radical singularity of being does not manifestly support. Furthermore, occupation of heterotopic spaces within the nation has been vital for supporting indigenous peoples' survival and their visions of radical futures following their experiences of colonisation; such spaces often are characterised by the assertion of a culturally distinct indigenous ontology and epistemology, in which a foundational (though often flexible) indigenous identification provides the basis for a contesting politics (for example, Soguk 2007). Another concern is that Agamben seeks to theorise a new form of political community in which the privileged content of dominant speech is subverted by a new emphasis on the common human capacity for language, which universally allows 'whatever' beings 'to experience [. . .] the fact itself of speaking' (Agamben 2000: 115). However, for many colonised peoples, the universal human potential associated with having language is sometimes politically inadequate, coercive and frustrating, especially when actual speech is forced, when a limited or false interpretation is imposed on actual speech, or when their human linguistic potential is materialised within colonial structures (such as courts of law) that are predicated upon the absence of indigenous structures and modes of expressing and knowing, which might, for example, privilege the use of silence as a valid form of political expression. There is a danger that the notion of 'full communicability' that Agamben associates as a condition of the coming community corresponds more easily to Western values of political transparency and equality than to indigenous conceptions. This is especially the case where privileged power of access to sacred knowledge is protected by principles of non-communication or secrecy that exist to resist profanation; for indigenous communities, the danger posed by 'full communicability' and desacralisation is especially well illustrated by the profanation and appropriation of sacred knowledge by colonising 'experts', who lack the appropriate frameworks for understanding (and respecting) such knowledge.[4]

These problems suggest that the potential postcoloniality of 'whatever' being and of the 'coming community' it augurs can only be celebrated with caution. Postcolonial modes of thinking will not seek to universally impose concepts of being – even radically indeterminate notions such as 'whatever' being – upon diverse peoples with ontological and epistemological traditions of their own. Nor will they naively assume that new forms of political community can emerge untainted by the colonial legacy; the colonial destruction of indigenous traditions arguably has limited our scope to (re)create the genuinely 'common' conditions needed for rendering a universal human *experience* of 'the fact itself of speaking'. I suggest that aspects of Agamben's thinking about 'whatever' existence and the 'coming community' offer positive scope for theorists attempting to envisage postcolonial futures by revising received and dominant Western understandings of being in the world with others. That is, I suspect that a postcolonial version of 'whatever' being and coming community can work best as a 'Western' complement to 'non-Western' ways of self-knowing and belonging, rather than as indeterminate concepts of the self and political existence that can be considered as universally applicable. But if 'whatever being' can really only be employed to reconceive 'Western' perspectives, we must again wonder about the nature of the relationship between 'Western' and indigenous frameworks of political transformation. How can the former (in which sociality is reconceived by moving beyond essence and identity) understand the latter (in which identity is the transformative basis of political community), without a certain tacit condescension towards forms of sociality 'still' mediated by particular conditions of belonging? And if we only can draw upon Agamben's notion of 'whatever' to rethink 'Western' traditions of philosophising being and community, then would only 'Western' beings be able to be united in their potential for being-called-postcolonial? What conditions would allow for both settler *and* indigenous 'forms of life' to join in being-called-postcolonial, and how could this be decided on mutually agreed terms? These questions can only be decided through effort of intercultural communication and understanding and by reconstructive practice, as culturally diverse peoples coexisting on single territories strive to engage each other in a shared manner of collective existence, conceived as such on mutually agreed terms of relationship.

References

Agamben, G. (1998), *Homo Sacer: Sovereign Power and Bare Life*, trans. D. Heller-Roazen. Stanford: Stanford University Press.
—(1993a), *Infancy and History: The Destruction of Experience*, trans. L. Heron. London and New York: Verso.
—(1993b), *The Coming Community*, trans. M. Hardt. Minneapolis and London: Minnesota University Press.

—(2000), *Means Without End: Notes on Politics*, trans. V. Binetti and C. Casarino. Minnesota: University of Minnesota Press.

—(2005a), *State of Exception*, trans. K. Attell. Chicago and London: University of Chicago Press.

—(2005b), *The Time That Remains: A Commentary on the Letter to the Romans*, trans. P. Dailey. Stanford: Stanford University Press.

—(2007), *Profanations*. New York: Zone Books.

—(2009a), 'What is an Apparatus?', in *What is an Apparatus? And Other Essays*, trans. D. Kishik and S. Pedatella. Stanford: Stanford University Press, 1–24.

—(2009b), 'What is a Paradigm?', in *The Signature of All Things: On Method*, trans. L. D'Isanto with K. Attell. New York: Zone Books, 9–32.

—(2009c), 'What is the Contemporary?', in *What is an Apparatus? And Other Essays*, trans. D. Kishik and S. Pedatella. Stanford: Stanford University Press, 39–54.

—(2009d), 'Philosophical Archaeology', in *The Signature of All Things: On Method*, trans. L. D'Isanto with K. Attell. New York: Zone Books, 81–111.

Behrendt, L. (2007), 'The Emergency We Had to Have', in J. Altman and M. Hinkson (eds), *Coercive Reconciliation: Stabilise, Normalise, Exit Aboriginal Australia*. Sydney: Arena, 15–21.

Bignall, S. (2010), *Postcolonial Agency: Critique and Constructivism*. Edinburgh: Edinburgh University Press.

Butler, J. (2004), *Precarious Life: Powers of Mourning and Violence*. London and New York: Verso.

Deleuze, G. (1988), *Foucault*, trans. Seán Hand. Minneapolis and London: Minnesota University Press.

Gulson, K. and Parkes, R. (2010), 'From the Barrel of the Gun: Policy Incursions, Land and Aboriginal Peoples in Australia', *Education and Planning*, 42: 300–13.

Hall, S. (1996), 'When was "The Post-Colonial"? Thinking at the Limit', in L. Chambers and L. Urti (eds), *The Postcolonial Question: Common Skies, Divided Horizons*. London and New York: Routledge, 242–60.

Havemann, P. (2005), 'Denial, Modernity and Exclusion: Indigenous Placelessness in Australia', *Macquarie Law Journal*, 5: 57–80.

Hinkson, M. (2007), 'In the Name of the Child', in J. Altman and M. Hinkson (eds), *Coercive Reconciliation: Stabilise, Normalise, Exit Aboriginal Australia*. Sydney: Arena, 1–14.

Kartinyeri v The Commonwealth, 195 CLR 337 (1998).

Mbembe, A. (2003), 'Necropolitics', trans. Libby Meintjes, *Public Culture*, 15(1): 11–40.

McClintock, A. (1992), 'The Angel of Progress: Pitfalls of the Term "Postcolonialism"', *Social Text*, 31(32): 84–98.

McLoughlin, D. (2009), 'The Politics of Caesura: Giorgio Agamben on Language and the Law', *Law Critique*, 20: 163–76.

Moran, A. (2002), 'As Australia Decolonizes: Indigenizing Settler Nationalism and the Challenges of Settler/Indigenous Relations', *Ethnic and Racial Studies*, 25(6): 1013–42.

Motha, S. (2002), 'The Sovereign Event in a Nation's Law', *Law and Critique*, 13: 311–38.

Muldoon, P. (2008), 'The Sovereign Exceptions: Colonization and the Foundation of Society', *Social and Legal Studies*, 17(1): 59–74.

Rajaram, P. (2006), 'Dystopic Geographies of Empire', *Alternatives*, 31: 475–506.

Rifkin, M. (2009), 'Indigenising Agamben: Rethinking Sovereignty in Light of the "Peculiar" Status of Native Peoples', *Cultural Critique*, 73(Fall): 88–124.

Shohat, E. (1992), 'Notes on the Post-Colonial', *Social Text*, 31(32): 99–113.

Soguk, N. (2007), 'Indigenous Peoples and Radical Futures in Global Politics', *New Political Science*, 29(1): 1–22.

Watson, I. (2009), 'Sovereign Space, Caring for Country and the Homeless Position of Aboriginal Peoples', *South Atlantic Quarterly*, 108(1): 27–51.

Wild, R. (2007), 'Unforeseen Circumstances', in J. Altman and M. Hinkson (eds), *Coercive Reconciliation: Stabilise, Normalise, Exit Aboriginal Australia*. Sydney: Arena, 111–20.

Wild, R. and Anderson, P. (2007), *Ampe Akelyernemane Meke Mekarle, 'Little Children are Sacred'*, Report of the Northern Territory Board of Inquiry into the Protection of Aboriginal Children from Sexual Abuse. Darwin: Northern Territory Government.

Notes

I am grateful to Daniel McLoughlin and Stewart Motha for their comments and advice, and I especially thank Sam Sellar for defining many of the critical questions raised in the concluding section.

1. This should not be taken to imply that the serial abuse of indigenous children is not a matter requiring urgent intervention, and nor is it

contested that children in the NT are subjected to abuse and neglect. However, this situation has been ongoing for decades, in spite of community-based efforts to address the underlying issues and despite the existence of numerous inquiries and reports to government. The problem is not new, and in this sense the 'urgency' of the situation was manufactured by the State.

2. Further discussion of indigenous ontology and religion is beyond the scope of my understanding and exceeds the limits of my access to such knowledge. Knowledge of indigenous Law is layered according differential access privileges; non-indigenous people must generally expect (and respect) that they will be allowed access to only the most superficial content and will at best develop only a limited understanding of such matters. Thus, my remarks here are qualified by the fact my non-indigeneity and my consequently piecemeal and superficial understanding. They are not intended to imply that I have an 'expert' knowledge of Aboriginal religion and Law; rather, I want to point out that the quote from the Yolngu Elder about the sacred nature of Aboriginal children illustrates how Western political concepts cannot be thought of as universal, and yet they continue to be applied as if they are.

3. A division of this sort has also been posited by Deleuze (1988) in his reading of Foucault; however, unlike Agamben (2009a: 13), Deleuze does not claim he is 'abandoning the context of Foucauldian philology', and nor does he claim to 'correct' and 'complete' Foucault's work (Agamben 1998: 9). As with many of Deleuze's interlocutions with his favourite philosophers, his text suggests that the distinction between 'ossified' structures of macropolitical power and fluid 'living' micropolitical relations is already evident in Foucault.

4. An example of this colonial profanation and misuse of indigenous sacred knowledge occurred during the Hindmarsh Island Bridge affair, which saw Ngarrindjeri accused of 'fabricating' their traditions in order to halt a commercial development on their Country. See *Kartinyeri v The Commonwealth* (1998).

Notes on Contributors

David Atkinson is a Reader in Cultural and Historical Geography in the Department of Geography at the University of Hull, UK. He has worked on the history and nature of geographical knowledge and, particularly, on Italian geopolitical theories and imaginaries. He also has interests in modern Italian urbanism and colonialism (especially under Fascism and totalitarianisms), and the geographies of monuments and memory. He co-edited *Geopolitical Traditions* (Routledge, 2000, with Klaus Dodds) and *Cultural Geography* (I.B. Tauris, 2005, with Peter Jackson, David Sibley and Neil Washbourne).

Ariella Azoulay teaches visual culture and political philosophy, and is an independent curator and film maker. Her recent books include: *From Palestine to Israel: A Photographic Record of Destruction and State Formation, 1947–1950* (Pluto Press, 2011), *Civil Imagination: A Political Ontology of Photography* (Verso, 2010) and *The Civil Contract of Photography* (Zone Books, 2008). She is Curator of *Untaken Photographs* (Moderna Galerija, Lubliana, Zochrot, Tel Aviv, 2010), *Architecture of Destruction* (Zochrot, Tel Aviv, 2008) and *Everything Could Be Seen* (Um Al Fahem Gallery, Um Al Fahem, 2004). Among her documentary films are *I Also Dwell Among Your Own People: Conversations with Azmi Bishara* (2004) and *The Food Chain* (2004), available at http://cargocollective.com/AriellaAzoulay.

Simone Bignall is a Vice-Chancellor's Postdoctoral Scholar in the School of History and Philosophy at the University of New South Wales in Sydney. She has published widely on issues concerning colonialism and postcolonialism. She is the author of *Postcolonial Agency* (2010) and the co-editor, with Paul Patton, of *Deleuze and* *the Postcolonial* (2010), both published by Edinburgh University Press.

Leland de la Durantaye is the Gardner Cowles Associate Professor of English at Harvard University. He is the author of *Giorgio Agamben: A Critical Introduction* (Stanford University Press, 2009) and of *Style is Matter: The Moral Art of Vladimir Nabokov* (Cornell University Press, 2007), which explores an ethics of style in Nabokov's literary thought and practice.

Silvia Grinberg is a researcher at the National Committee of Science and Technology in Argentina, Professor of Pedagogy and Sociology of Education, Director of the Centre for Contemporary Pedagogical Studies at the National University of San Martín and Coordinator of the socio-pedagogic division at the National University of the Patagonia. Silvia's work concerns governmentality, biopolitics and education, with a research focus in contexts of extreme urban poverty and hyperdegraded territories.

Stephen Morton is Senior Lecturer in English in the Faculty of Humanities at the University of Southampton. His publications include *Gayatri Spivak: Ethics, Subjectivity and the Critique of Postcolonial Reason* (Polity, 2007), *Salman Rushdie: Fictions of Postcolonial Modernity* (Palgrave Macmillan, 2008), *Gayatri Chakravorty Spivak* (Routledge, 2003), *Terror and the Postcolonial*, co-edited with Elleke Boehmer (Blackwell, 2009), *Foucault in an Age of Terror*, co-edited with Stephen Bygrave (Palgrave, 2008), and articles in *Textual Practice*, *Parallax*, *Interventions*, *Wasafiri*, *Public Culture* and *New Formations*.

Stewart Motha is Reader in Law, School of Law, Birkbeck, University of London, UK. Address for correspondence: stewart. motha@gmail.com. From 2008–10 he was Fellow of the Stellenbosch Institute of Advanced Study, South Africa. He has published widely on questions of sovereignty and political community. His articles have been published in a variety of international journals including *Journal of Law, Culture, and Humanities*, *Law and Critique*, *Journal of Law and Society* and the *Australian Feminist Law Journal*. In 2007 he edited a book titled *Democracy's Empire: Sovereignty, Law, Violence* (Blackwell). He has recently co-edited a volume of essays, *Reading*

Modern Law: Critical Methodologies and Sovereign Formations: Essays in Honour of Peter Fitzpatrick (Routledge, 2012, with Ruth Buchanan and Sundhya Pahuja).

Adi Ophir teaches philosophy and political theory at the Cohn Institute for the History and Philosophy of Science and Ideas at Tel Aviv University. He directs the Lexicon project at the Minerva Humanities Center and is the editor of *Mafte'akh: A Lexical Review for Political Theory*. Among his books are *The Order of Evils* (Zone Books, 2005) and *This Regime which is Not One: Occupation and Democracy between the Sea and the River* (Resling, 2008 [in Hebrew] and Stanford University Press, forthcoming, with Ariella Azoulay). His forthcoming book, *Divine Violence: Two Essays on God and Catastrophe*, will be published in 2012 by the Van Leer Jerusalem Institute.

Sergei Prozorov is Academy of Finland Research Fellow at the Department of Political and Economic Studies at the University of Helsinki. He is the author of four monographs, the most recent being *The Ethics of Postcommunism* (Palgrave, 2009). He has also published articles on political philosophy and international relations in *Philosophy and Social Criticism*, *Continental Philosophy Review*, *Political Geography*, *Journal of Theory, Culture and Society*, *Millennium*, *International Theory* and other international journals.

Mark Rifkin is an Associate Professor in the English Department at the University of North Carolina, Greensboro. He is the author of *Manifesting America: The Imperial Construction of U.S. National Space* (Oxford University Press, 2009), *When Did Indians Become Straight?: Kinship, the History of Sexuality, and Native Sovereignty* (Oxford University Press, 2010) and *The Erotics of Sovereignty: Queer Native Writing in the Era of Self-Determination* (University of Minnesota Press, 2012).

Yehouda Shenhav is a Professor of Sociology at Tel-Aviv University. Until recently he was head of Advanced Studies at the Van Leer Jerusalem Institute and editor of *Theory and Criticism* (2000–10). He is currently senior editor for *Organization Studies* and the series editor of *Theory and Criticism in Context*. His recent books include *The Arab Jews* (Stanford University Press, 2006),

Manufacturing Rationality (Oxford University Press, 2003) and *Entrapped by the Green Line* (Polity, 2011).

Marcelo Svirsky is a Lecturer and Marie-Curie Researcher at the Centre for Critical and Cultural Theory (School of English, Communication and Philosophy), Cardiff University. He researches on Deleuze's philosophy, Middle East politics and social movements. His recent publications include *Arab-Jewish Activism in Israel-Palestine* (Ashgate, 2011), *Deleuze and Political Activism* (Edinburgh University Press, 2010), 'Captives of Identity: The Betrayal of Intercultural Cooperation', in *Subjectivity* (2011) and 'The Empty Square of the Occupation', in *Deleuze Studies* (2010).

Jessica Whyte completed her doctorate on the political thought of Giorgio Agamben in the Centre for Comparative Literature and Cultural Studies, Monash University, in 2010. She has published widely on contemporary continental philosophy (Agamben, Foucault, Rancière), sovereignty and biopolitics, critical legal theory and critiques of human rights. She is a co-editor of the Theory and Event Symposium 'Form of Life: Giorgio Agamben, Ontology, Politics' (2010), of the *Australian Feminist Law Journal* special edition 'Law, Crisis, Revolution' (2010) and of the *Agamben Dictionary* (Edinburgh University Press, 2011). She is a Lecturer in Social and Cultural Analysis, University of Western Sydney.

Index